Bloodlines

THE IMPERIAL ROOTS OF TERRORISM IN SOUTH ASIA

BY
SUNIL DUTTA

AGILE PRESS
An imprint of Agile Research and Technology, Inc.

BLOODLINES: THE IMPERIAL ROOTS OF TERRORISM IN SOUTH ASIA

Copyright © 2015 by Sunil Dutta, Ph.D.
All rights reserved. No part of this book may be transmitted or reproduced in any form by any means without permission from the publisher.

Published in the United States by Agile Press,
an imprint of Agile Research and Technology, Inc. Salinas, CA

Printed in the United States of America
First printing, August 2015

ISBN 978-0-9830745-7-1

Cover design by Matthew Prichard

info@agilepress.com
www.agilepress.com

BLOODLINES: THE IMPERIAL ROOTS OF TERRORISM IN SOUTH ASIA

ACKNOWLEDGEMENT

Growing up in a refugee family made homeless in the Partition of India in 1947, I often heard from my elders stories of horrendous violence, loss, and longing for lost homes left behind an arbitrary border.

India and Pakistan have yet to come to terms with the sordid reality of their creation and the crisis it created for the two states. This book is dedicated to the victims of the Partition.

I am deeply in gratitude to all on whose intellectual and spiritual shoulders I have stood to see further; there are too many to list the names! There are numerous debts to be mentioned but Anders Strindberg's excellent editing and persistent focus on improvement of the manuscript was a tremendous help, special thanks to Jody Stecher for all his assistance as well. I alone am responsible for any and all the errors.

What we think is obvious is so far beyond our comprehension.
We are still dreaming even when we dream we are awake.
                                -Ghalib-

BLOODLINES: THE IMPERIAL ROOTS OF TERRORISM IN SOUTH ASIA

Table of Contents

Introduction — XI

Chapter 1

The History of the Indian Subcontinent — 1
- The British in India — 2
- The 1857 Rebellion — 8
- The Durand Line — 17
- The History of the Subcontinent's People — 26
- Institutionalizing Differences — 30
- The Indian National Congress and the Muslim League — 38
- Division of Bengal — 44
- World War II and Decolonization — 45

Chapter 2

Decolonization and Its Aftermath — 51
- The Partition of India and its Impact — 51
- Ideational Identities and the Origin of Conflict in South Asia — 62
- Kashmir and Partition — 65
- East Pakistan's Secession and the India-Pakistan War of 1971 — 78
- Conflict on the Western Front: Afghanistan — 85
- Zia, Afghanistan, United States, and the Gestation of Future Terrorism — 98
- After the Afghan War — 113

Chapter 3

The History of U.S.- Pakistan Relations — 131
- The United States as an Unreliable Partner — 146
- The United States and Pakistan Relations: A Study in Self-Defeat — 154

CHAPTER 4

Conclusions — 159
   Recommendations — 169

APPENDIX

Regional Maps — 179
   India in 350 A.D. — 180
   India in 1022. — 181
   India in 1795. — 182
   Kashmir Region — 183
   Before Partition — 184
   After Partition — 185

Bibliography — 187

Index — 213

About the Author — 223

BLOODLINES: THE IMPERIAL ROOTS OF TERRORISM IN SOUTH ASIA

INTRODUCTION

By April of 1988, the Soviet Union had failed to defeat Afghan resistance and was looking for a way out of what had become its own Vietnam. In response, the United States and the USSR guaranteed UN-sponsored Geneva Accords between Pakistan and Afghanistan, allowing the Soviet Army to extricate itself from an increasingly volatile situation. In *Killing the Cranes: A Reporter's Journey Through Three Decades of War in Afghanistan*, Edward Girardet offers the reason why the accords failed to bring peace to the region:

> Although the Geneva talks paved the way for the Soviet withdrawal, they completely failed to take into account on-the-ground realities. The Pakistanis, Americans, and Soviets were all making deals but neglected to include the Afghan resistance – which rejected the agreement… The talks also failed to involve Iran, China, India, and other key regional players.[1]

Consequently, Afghanistan went into a deep downward spiral. In the late 1980s, the United States and the USSR used their superpower muscle to block key South Asian players from involvement in the conflict's resolution. The superpowers' 1988 decision and their subsequent neglect of the region—which had been one of the hottest zones of the Cold War period—ultimately culminated in the flight paths of the planes that crashed into the World Trade Center and the Pentagon on September 11, 2001.

On May 21, 2012, NATO released their Chicago Summit Declaration on Afghanistan, proclaiming that the International Security Assistance Force (ISAF) would conclude their mission in Afghanistan by the end of 2014. The U.S.-led NATO coalition also discussed its plans to promote Afghanistan's state security leadership by mid-2013, transitioning foreign troops into support and training roles. As this transitional period approached, Taliban attacks increased in ferocity and deadliness.

The ostensible goal of the United States is to "responsibly wind down"[2] the Afghanistan War and to avoid the kind of civil war that had erupted after the Soviet exit two decades earlier. It is difficult to imagine a positive outcome, however, when the United States commits the same mistakes made by the Soviets in 1989 and afterwards. The chaos of early 1990s nourished the Taliban's emergence and

---

1 Edward Girardet, *Killing the Cranes: A Reporter's Journey through Three Decades of War in Afghanistan* (White River Junction, VT: Chelsea Green Publishing, 2011), 281.
2 Editorial, "Obama's Troubled Handling of Afghanistan" *Washington Post*, March 13, 2012.

the conditions under which al Qaeda found safe harbor in Afghanistan. As the United States and the NATO coalition sketch their new exit plan ending in 2014, the situation in Afghanistan does not look very promising.

The NATO gathering calls to mind Girardet's analysis: once again, Western powers made decisions about one of the most contested areas of the world without involving key regional players (for example, Iran, China, and India). These foreign decisions likely will prove unacceptable to the people upon whom they are imposed, and once again, the perceived "end" of a conflict will neither be the end of the conflict nor will it resolve the issues at its heart. Foreign powers need to take seriously the interests of regional powers when considering how to resolve a conflict that has displaced millions from their homes, killed and maimed hundreds of thousands of combatants and civilians, and radicalized many Muslims.

The current conditions in South Asia are similar to those of 1988: there is an ongoing internal conflict between the central government in Afghanistan and other regional power players within the country; additionally, there also is a multi-agent interstate conflict between Afghanistan and its national neighbors. Recent history indicates that Afghanistan may be on an even bloodier path if the United States walks away from its involvement before core conflicts are resolved. Pakistan will almost certainly be involved in this bloodletting, and the entities behind the 9/11 attacks will once again attempt to consolidate their power in the region.

This book provides an account for the historical roots of the conflict in South Asia, roots that have created an environment that has nurtured and continues to nurture insurgency along the Afghanistan-Pakistan border. Rather than characterizing the contemporary conflict there as somehow inherent to the region, it attempts to show that the current conflict can be traced back to decisions made by the British Empire during the 19th and 20th centuries—decisions that were meant to perpetuate British rule on the Indian subcontinent. The U.S. war in Afghanistan has been unnecessarily prolonged because policymakers have ignored the colonial history of South Asia and undervalued its impact on current events. A great deal of blood has been spilled and much capital has been squandered turning the region into a wasteland. Notwithstanding the rhetoric or actual intent of the U.S. intervention in South Asia, its return on investment has been a radicalized population, political and economic destabilization, and alarming violence. This book recommends policy actions that could lead toward the resolution of historical conflict in South Asia and, consequently, eliminate entrenched radical groups that engage in the rhetoric and practice of political and religious jihad.

Only a careful analysis of the region's history can provide insight into why it has lurched from one crisis to another in a seemingly never-ending war. One must look much further back into the past than 1994, when the Taliban rose and took power, or 1979, when the Soviet Army marched into Afghanistan, in order to understand the root causes of terrorism in South Asia. In fact, one must even look back to well before 1954, when the United States turned Pakistan into its pawn against the Soviet Union. Extant conditions arise from historical matrices: only by examining history can we understand the present and make better decisions for the future. The fact is, the roots of terrorism in Afghanistan and Pakistan go back to mid-19th century and they touch South Asia, America and the West today. These roots were nourished by colonial actions during the height of European (chiefly British) imperialism. While some of the damaging consequences of imperial actions were unintentional, others were more insidiously deliberate. The region's troubled history reflects a series of conflicts, bloodbaths, and radicalization, but current interventions by powerful nation states have the power to forge its future. A careful and dispassionate scrutiny of the region's history not only clarifies its current state; such scrutiny also shines a light on where these actions, if unchecked, will lead us in the future.

Reflecting on the law of unintended consequences in 2012, Ryan Crocker, the U.S. ambassador to Afghanistan, stated, "We're a superpower, we don't fight on our territory, but that means you are in somebody else's stadium, playing by somebody else's ground rules, and you have to understand the environment, the history, the politics of the country you wish to intervene in."³ Afghanistan remains a broken and fragmented state, rife with factionalism and overcome by the corruption of its rulers and warlords. Meanwhile, the Taliban waits in the wings, hoping and planning for a comeback. Afghanistan's neighbors continue to position themselves in ways that would ensure an agreeable regime in Kabul. Neighboring Pakistan—an ally of the United States in the war on terrorism, when convenient—is a state in turmoil, both a sponsor and victim of terrorism. India, semi-allied with the Soviet Union during the Cold War, is now a semi-ally of the United States. China, Iran, and Russia are also interested and involved in Afghanistan, and they forge their own regional policies accordingly. Clearly, while the Obama administration has been sketching out an exit strategy and a way to end its involvement in the war in South Asia, the outcome in Afghanistan will be dictated not by the United States alone but by a number of actors.

---

3   Alissa Rubin, "Retiring Envoy to Afghanistan Exhorts U.S. to Heed Its Past," *New York Times*, July 28, 2012.

XIV BLOODLINES: THE IMPERIAL ROOTS OF TERRORISM IN SOUTH ASIA

The history of South Asia demonstrates how imperial prerogatives have shaped the decision-making of powerful nations. Short-term benefits have trumped consideration of the long-term impacts of those expediencies, and some of these impacts have eventually proved disastrous. At the height of European colonial expansion in Asia and Africa, unchecked imperial power and beliefs about white racial superiority did not require colonizers to understand or care about the environment, history, or culture of their subjects. When efforts were made to understand their colonial subjects, they were often colored by an Orientalist perspective and shaped by the specific needs of the colonizer.[4] Artificial boundaries created in the Middle East in the aftermath of the two world wars are also stark reminders of expedient colonial decision-making and its dire consequences. And finally, the actions of the United States in South Asia in response to the Soviet invasion of Afghanistan, though successful in short-term, led to one of the longest wars that the United States has been involved in. The United States' choices in Afghanistan may have resulted in the defeat of Soviet Union, but its long-term impacts and costs to U.S. homeland security have been incalculable.

While the United States paid an enormous price for its proxy war against the Soviet Union, the suffering and human costs to inhabitants of South Asia have been exponentially higher. As the United States winds down its scale of involvement in Afghanistan, there are no guarantees that U.S. regional goals and interests will be met.[5] In fact, it is likely that unfolding events will work against American intentions and there is no doubt that, post-U.S. withdrawal, we will see a resurgence of violence in the region.

This book is a case study in the root causes of terrorism in South Asia. Its underlying philosophy is to clearly show that one can understand and predict terrorism only if one *knows and understands* history. Anyone who had been more than a casual observer of South Asia in the concluding quarter of the century could easily have predicted the evolution of conflict in Afghanistan, especially if one had adhered to Crocker's sage advice to "study[…] the environment, the history, the politics of the country you wish to intervene in.".

---

4   Edward W. Said, *Orientalism* (New York: Vintage Books, 1979). Said describes "Orientalism" as the comparative and dichotomous way of distinguishing the East (or the "Orient") from the West (or the "Occident"), where the West is constructed as civilized while the East constructed as exotic and uncivilized. The Orientalist mindset rationalized colonialism because it justified the superior West's civilizing mission in other "savage" parts of the world.

5   Christi Parsons and David Cloud, "U.S. to Reduce Troop Level in Afghanistan to 9,800 by Year's End," *Los Angeles Times*, May 28, 2014. The United States' declaration to end the war by the end of 2014 does not signify an end to U.S. involvement in Afghanistan. Washington has proposed keeping 9,800 troops in Afghanistan after December 2014 and reducing the troop strength to 5,000 by the end of 2015. The mission of the remaining U.S. troops will be to train Afghans, protect dignitaries, and participate in counter-terrorism efforts in Afghanistan and Pakistan.

INTRODUCTION

Contrary to conventional wisdom, terrorism is neither fogged by complexity nor colored by religious fanaticism.[6] Terrorism is a form of asymmetrical warfare: transparent, imbued with history, and aimed at changing power dynamics in specific locales. This book endeavors to provide a wider perspective of how historical factors have shaped South Asia, creating a matrix from which Islamic fundamentalism and terrorism have emerged. This project connects a series of decisions that have been made throughout South Asia's past in order to demonstrate that a profound understanding of a region's history, power players, and conflicts must inform the way that homeland security policies are shaped.

The United States' experience in Afghanistan has demonstrated that even the incredible military might and vast financial resources of superpowers do not give them the ability to ignore historical and regional conflicts in order to unilaterally impose their military and counterterrorism decisions. The historical context, culture, and environment of a locale should inform our understanding of present dilemmas, as well as aid in our policy-making. Furthermore, the United States' single-minded support of centralized authoritarian governments in Afghanistan and Pakistan has not returned a proper dividend in terms of regional stability. In their analysis of the events in Tunisia, Egypt, and Libya (the so-called "Arab Spring" of 2011), Nassim Nicholas Taleb and Marc Blyth have argued that artificially suppressing volatility in the name of stability is dangerous, as it masks the potential "Black Swan" events that can occur when highly constrained systems explode.[7] Their findings are directly relevant to events that have occurred in South Asia:

> Although the stated intention of political leaders and economic policymakers is to stabilize the system by inhibiting fluctuations, the result tends to be the opposite. These artificially constrained systems become prone to "Black Swans"—that is, they become extremely vulnerable to large-scale events that lie far from the statistical norm and were largely unpredictable to a given set of observers. Such environments eventually experience massive blowups, catching everyone off-guard and undoing years of stability or, in some cases, ending up far worse

---

6 I define terrorism as a media-oriented, deliberate use of violence on innocent civilians and non-combatants, with a political objective of coercing a stronger enemy into making concessions, forcibly changing enemy behavior, or causing sustained and significant economic damage to the enemy.
7 Nassim Nicholas Taleb, *The Black Swan: The Impact of the Highly Improbable*, 2nd ed. (New York: Random House, 2010), xxii. Taleb uses the metaphor of a "Black Swan" to describe a low-probability, high-impact event. A Black Swan is an unexpected rare event because there is a minute probability of it occurring; however, its consequences are enormous. As such, a Black Swan, compared to ordinary events, would have a major role in historical outcomes.

than they were in their initial volatile state. Indeed, the longer it takes for the blowup to occur, the worse the resulting harm in both economic and political systems.[8]

In South Asia, Britain's manipulative constraints on Indian nationalism during the late 19th and early 20th centuries led to the Black Swans of 1947 (the partition of India and its incredibly damaging aftermath), 1971 (when East Pakistan seceded to create Bangladesh, leading to Pakistan's ideological crisis and, consequently, its further radicalization), and of the early part of the 21st century (when numerous terrorist attacks were hatched in and exported from Pakistan). During the last five decades, U.S. policies have focused on manipulating "instability" in Pakistan; in reality, this was an excuse for perpetuating military dictatorships and relegating civilian governments to the background. Such policies have led to blowups, including the September 11 attacks on the United States, which, though not directly related to Pakistan, were contributed in large part by Pakistan's support of the Taliban.

This book begins with an examination of the colonial history of the Indian subcontinent, emphasizing the British decisions that eventually imposed expedient and contrived boundaries in the region. This includes the partition of Indian subcontinent into India and Pakistan, and the later formation of Bangladesh.[9] It then explores how colonial decisions culminated in the rivalry between India and Pakistan, and how this rivalry has resulted in the emergence of terrorism in the region. Historical analysis provides a broad canvas for understanding why the Taliban and al Qaeda found a safe haven in the Pakistan-Afghanistan hinterland.

After the September 11, 2001 attacks, the United States focused on al Qaeda and the Taliban insurgents, killing many insurgents through drone attacks and military strikes. Despite weakening al Qaeda and killing Osama bin Laden, depriving al Qaeda of its primary brand symbol, the United States has yet to resolve the regional conditions that allow Afghanistan and Pakistan to export terrorism.[10] The United States' disregard of the region's history has not only drained its economy, it has also unnecessarily prolonged its military efforts in Afghanistan. By fiscal year 2010, the U.S. government had expended approximately $444 billion

---

8   Nicholas Nassim Taleb and Mark Blyth, "The Black Swan of Cairo: How Suppressing Volatility Makes the World Less Predictable and More Dangerous," *Foreign Affairs* 90, no. 3 (2011): 33.
9   Throughout history, the boundaries of the Indian subcontinent have variously included areas now called Afghanistan, Bangladesh, India, and Pakistan. In contemporary terminology, this region is referred to as "South Asia," although other neighboring countries such as Bhutan, Nepal, and Sri Lanka are also considered part of South Asia.
10 Sunil Dutta, "Bin Laden, Pakistan and the End of Terrorism," *Daily News*, May 8, 2011, A12; Paul Staniland, "Caught in the Muddle: America's Pakistan Strategy," *Washington Quarterly* 34, no. 1 (2011): 133-148.

in Afghanistan on war and accessory operations.[11] Even after President Obama initiated an accelerated troop drawdown and successfully exited American "surge" troops, the approximate cost of operations in Afghanistan in fiscal year 2012 was still over $110 billion dollars. However, despite the excessive expenditure of American lives, capital, and other resources, the United States' efforts during the past twelve years have not eliminated the Taliban's foothold in Afghanistan or convinced Pakistan to stop its support of militant Islamists.

It is critical that the United States and its allies address the residual effects of colonialism that continue to destabilize South Asia. The primary issues they face are the bitter conflict between India and Pakistan over Kashmir, as well as the disputed borders between Afghanistan and Pakistan. In South Asia, contemporary jihadism and terrorism are directly connected to the way that religion is and has been used to create oppositional identities (between Hindus and Muslims, for example), and the fact that South Asian nations (and their colonial predecessors) have both sponsored and engineered fanaticism. These issues are prevalent to India-Pakistan relations as well as to the conflict between Afghanistan and Pakistan. Superpower rivalries during the Cold War further exacerbated these issues as the Soviet Union and the United States used regional proxies to battle each other. These issues continue to destabilize South Asia because global political superpowers seem to deliberately ignore the conflict between India and Pakistan.[12]

The Pakistan–Afghanistan border area has been described as the most dangerous frontier on earth, and it has proved to be the most challenging for U.S. national security interests.[13] Despite investing vast amounts of money in military and counter-terrorism efforts, diplomatic initiatives, and the American-supported Afghan government, the political situation in Afghanistan has yet to stabilize. The Afghanistan-Pakistan border continues to harbor actors who support al Qaeda, engage in attacks against the Afghanistan and Pakistan governments, support and

---

11 Amy Belasco, "The Cost of Iraq, Afghanistan, and Other Global War on Terror Operations Since 9/11," *Congressional Research Service*, March 29, 2011, 1; Linda Bilmes, "The Financial Legacy of Iraq and Afghanistan: How Wartime Spending Decisions Will Constrain Future National Security Budgets," *Harvard Kennedy School Faculty Research Working Paper Series* RWP13-006 (March 2013), 1. Harvard researcher Linda Bilmes concludes that the Iraq and Afghanistan conflicts will cost between $4 to $6 trillion, including long-term medical care, social, and economic costs.
12 For an overview of the India-Pakistan conflict and its impact, see Sumantra Bose, *Kashmir: Roots of Conflict, Paths to Peace* (Cambridge, MA: Harvard University Press, 2003); Sumit Ganguly, *Conflict Unending: India-Pakistan Tensions Since 1947* (New York: Columbia University Press, 2002); Sumit Ganguly and Nicholas Howenstein, "India Pakistan Rivalry in Afghanistan," *Journal of International Affairs* 63, no. 1 (2009): 127-140; Graham Usher, "The Afghan Triangle: Kashmir, India, Pakistan," *Middle East Report* 39, no. 2 (2009): 20-27.
13 Thomas H. Johnson and M. Chris Mason, "No Sign Until the Burst of Fire: Understanding the Pakistan-Afghanistan Frontier," *International Security* 32, no. 4 (2008): 73.

train the Taliban, and plot attacks against Western targets.[14] The coalition forces' inability to stabilize Afghanistan, despite injecting enormous resources for the last thirteen years into one of the poorest nations in the world, clearly suggests that U.S. policies and strategies have been fundamentally flawed and are in dire need of reassessment.

It is evident that U.S. homeland security depends upon a successful political resolution in Afghanistan. The border region between Afghanistan and Pakistan has been and continues to be a terrorist training factory for radicalized and disaffected Muslims from around the world. Homegrown terrorists in the United States have received spiritual guidance and practical training from al Qaeda remnants and other jihadist elements entrenched in Afghanistan-Pakistan border area. Furthermore, despite U.S. financial and military aid, Pakistan continues to work at cross-purposes with the United States. Pakistan is considered by many to be the most dangerous foreign policy problem facing the United States; it has been characterized as an unstable, radicalized, and nuclear-capable country.[15] In recent years, Pakistan has been the world's most active sponsor of terrorism while at the same time itself being a frequent victim of terrorist violence. Several high-profile terrorist incidents, including the September 11 attacks, the July 2005 subway bombings in London, and the November 2008 attack on Mumbai, had direct or indirect connections to individuals and groups operating from Pakistan.[16] According to a variety of experts, Pakistan continues to sponsor terrorism and advance its national security interests using proxies and jihadi elements.[17] Pakistan has historically utilized militants and terrorist groups to achieve its geopolitical objectives in both Afghanistan and Kashmir, supporting terrorist groups such as Harakat-ul-Mujahideen, Jaish-e-Mohammed, Lashkar-e-Taiba, and others, in

---

14   For an overview, see Melissa Chadbourne, "U.S. Policy Toward Afghanistan and Pakistan: Implications for the U.S. and Its Allies," *Johns Hopkins School of Advanced International Studies* (Spring 2009): 1-41; C. Christine Fair, "Pakistan's Partial War on Terror: The Deadly Results of Cooperation with Terrorists," *Wall Street Journal*, October 9, 2009; C. Christine Fair, "The Militant Challenge in Pakistan," *Asia Policy* 11 (2011): 105-137; Seth G. Jones, "Pakistan's Dangerous Game," *Survival* 49, no.1 (2007): 15-32; Seth G. Jones, "The Terrorist Threat from Pakistan," *Survival* 53, no. 4 (2011): 69-94.

15   For a discussion, see C. Christine Fair, "Time for Sober Realism Renegotiating U.S. Relations with Pakistan," *Washington Quarterly* 32, no. 2 (2009): 149-172; Jones, "Pakistan's Dangerous Game," 15-32.

16   Sumit Ganguly and S. Paul Kapur, "The Sorcerer's Apprentice: Islamist Militancy in South Asia," *Washington Quarterly* 33, no. 1 (2010): 47; Bruce O. Riedel, *Deadly Embrace: Pakistan, America, and the Future of the Global Jihad* (Washington, D.C.: Brookings Institution Press, 2012), 83, 87.

17   Husain Haqqānī, *Pakistan: Between Mosque and Military* (Washington, D.C.: Carnegie Endowment for International Peace, 2005); Ahmed Rashid, *Descent into Chaos: The U.S. and the Disaster in Pakistan, Afghanistan, and Central Asia* (New York: Penguin Books, 2009); Bruce O. Riedel, "Pakistan and Terror: The Eye of the Storm," *Annals of the American Academy of Political and Social Science* 618 (July 2008): 31-45; Varun Vira and Anthony H. Cordesman, "Pakistan: Violence vs. Stability: A National Net Assessment," *Center for Strategic and International Studies Burke Reports*, June 7, 2011.

their operations in India-controlled Kashmir. Elsewhere in the country, both the Haqqani Network and the "Afghan Taliban" find safe haven to launch attacks in Afghanistan. Pakistan's use of non-state actors allowed it to disclaim its connections to terrorism, denying that it uses proxies to achieve its political goals, and therefore enabling it to escape condemnation from the global community. Although in 2009 Pakistan's president Asif Ali Zardari alluded that the Pakistani government had supported terrorists to achieve tactical objectives in Kashmir, he claimed that after the 9/11 attacks, Pakistani establishment had stopped supporting Islamic militants. This coincides with a statement given by Pakistan's military ruler Pervez Musharraf, who also admitted in an interview that Pakistan had formed militant groups to fight India in Kashmir.[18] However, Pakistan has consistently denied supporting Islamic militant groups fighting the government in Afghanistan.

Peace and stability in South Asia are prerequisites for global powers hoping to strike at the root of terrorism in the Afghanistan-Pakistan border region. This book suggests that the United States' inability to gain control in the region has been due to a focus narrowed on short-term goals, as well as its disregard of South Asian history. India and Pakistan have been locked in a bitter adversarial relationship since the British departed in 1947. There are historical reasons that offer explanations as to why this is so, and why India and Pakistan have used Afghanistan as a pawn in their power play. Any policy to stabilize Afghanistan and eliminate terrorist threats emanating from the region can only hope for short-term success unless these historical factors are considered.[19]

It has been suggested that by constructing a system of communal representation and reinforcing this system through unequal treatment of different groups, the British reified oppositional Hindu and Muslim identities.[20] It is this artificially constructed opposition that has been at the core of ethnic conflicts in colonial and postcolonial India. In the case of India, the violence began before, but became worse after, independence.

---

[18] Dean Nelson, "Pakistani President Asif Zardari Admits Creating Terrorist Groups," *Daily Telegraph*, July 8, 2009; Susanne Koelbl, "Spiegel interview with Pervez Musharraf: 'Pakistan is Always Seen as the Rogue,'" *Der Spiegel*, October 4, 2010.

[19] For an overview, see Thomas Barfield, *The Durand Line: History, Consequences, and Future* (Istanbul: American Institute of Afghanistan Studies and the Hollings Center, 2007), 1-19; Peter Tomsen, *The Wars of Afghanistan: Messianic Terrorism, Tribal Conflicts, and the Failures of Great Powers* (New York: Public Affairs, 2011).

[20] For an analysis, see Zaheer Baber, "Race, Religion and Riots The Racialization of Communal Identity and Conflict in India," *Sociology* 38, no.4 (2004): 701-708; Paul R. Brass, "The Partition of India and Retributive Genocide in the Punjab, 1946-47: Means, Methods, and Purposes," *Journal of Genocide Research* 5, no. 1 (2003): 71-101; John Breuilly, *Nationalism and the State*, 2nd ed. (Chicago: University of Chicago Press, 1994); David Page, "Prelude to Partition: The Indian Muslims and the Imperial System of Control 1920-1932," in *The Partition Omnibus*, ed. Mushirul Hasan (New Delhi: Oxford University Press, 2005).

Eqbal Ahmad asserts that the British divided India along communal lines, especially between 1757 and 1920:

> When Muslims would resist British rule, as they did between 1757 and 1857, they were discriminated against in favor of bringing up Hindus. When Congress became organized (in the late nineteenth century), more Hindu nationalist figures were there than Muslim ones. Then they favored Muslims against the Congress. So there was a whole set of divide-and-rule policies that the British followed for two centuries.[21]

Lange and Dawson conducted a survey of 160 countries in an attempt to establish whether a history of colonialism was a predictor of inter-communal conflicts and civil war in countries around the world between the years 1960–1999. They did not find evidence that colonialism was a universal cause of civil violence, however, their findings supported the assertion that inter-communal violence was a common legacy of colonialism, especially in the case of British colonialism.[22] James Carroll similarly traces Hindu-Muslim hatred in the Indian subcontinent, Catholic-Protestant hatred in Ireland, and Arab-Jew hatred in Israel all to the British Empire's policy of "divide and rule,"[23] whereby British colonial powers would attempt to strengthen their control over a region by stirring up animosity between native populations.

Historical analysis indicates that decisions made by the British Empire in late 19th and early 20th centuries contributed to many intractable conflicts in South Asia. These conflicts would eventually lead to regional wars, an arms race (including a nuclear arms race), and Pakistan's use of Islamic militants and asymmetric warfare (terrorism) to achieve its primary irredentist objectives in Kashmir and secondary territorial objectives in Afghanistan. Britain's short-term interests were bolstered by expedient decisions that eventually led to the partition of colonial India in 1947 into the new nations of India and Pakistan. The partition was followed by a horrendous bloodbath and a massive forced population transfer, poisoning relations between the two nascent nations. India and Pakistan's unresolved conflicts have metastasized, turning Pakistan into a state that systemically and instrumentally used jihadi fighters and terrorism as state policy.

U.S. policymakers have consistently disregarded the history of South Asia, and this is the primary reason why, despite the full power of its military and treasury, it has been unable to effectively counter violent conflict and terrorism in South Asia.

---

21 Eqbal Ahmad and David Barsamian, *Eqbal Ahmad, Confronting Empire: Interviews with David Barsamian*; Foreword by Edward W. Said (Cambridge, MA: South End Press, 2000), 7.
22 Matthew Lange and Andrew Dawson, "Dividing and Ruling the World? A Statistical Test of the Effects of Colonialism on Postcolonial Civil Violence," *Social Forces* 88, no. 2 (2009): 785.
23 James Carroll, *Constantine's Sword: The Church and the Jews; A History* (Boston: Houghton Mifflin, 2001), 81-82.

INTRODUCTION

The colonial history of South Asia has shaped the current conflicts in Afghanistan, Pakistan, and India, and the United States has not yet recognized that it is also entangled in these historical forces. Instead, U.S. policymakers have refused to use historical lessons to formulate suitable policies in the region, allowing the conflict in South Asia to continue for more than a decade. The world's strongest nation has expended enormous resources, while earning the ire of people it claims to be helping. All of the U.S. military and counterterrorism efforts in the region, as well as its economic and military aid to Pakistan, have failed to persuade Pakistan to disengage from supporting and nurturing terrorism in Afghanistan and elsewhere. Consequently, the end result of United States' intervention in South Asia is at best a stalemate, as the United States has failed to completely disarm or eliminate the forces that have plotted attacks against the United States and the West.

The United States' efforts to eliminate agents responsible for terrorism on U.S. territory were not carefully thought-out. For example, in 2009 Obama administration released its "White Paper of the Interagency Policy Group's Report on U.S. Policy toward Afghanistan and Pakistan," reiterating the United States' goal to "disrupt, dismantle and defeat al Qaeda and its safe havens in Pakistan, and to prevent their return to Afghanistan."[24] The White Paper's proposed strategy emphasized five objectives that focus on security and governance in Afghanistan and Pakistan, as well as the role of the international community. These were (1) disrupting terrorist networks in Afghanistan and Pakistan; (2) promoting a more capable, accountable and effective government in Afghanistan; (3) developing increasingly self-reliant Afghan security forces; (4) enhancing civilian control and economic development in Pakistan; and (5) involving the international community to achieve these objectives, with the leadership of the United Nations.

The National Strategy for Counterterrorism identifies the "preeminent security threat to the United States" as stemming from *"al-Qa'ida and its affiliates and adherents."*[25] The Strategy also discusses the elimination of safe-havens for al Qaeda:

> Al-Qa'ida and its affiliates and adherents rely on the physical sanctuary of ungoverned or poorly governed territories, where the absence of state control permits terrorists to travel, train, and engage in plotting. In close coordination with foreign partners, the United States will continue to contest and diminish al-Qa'ida's operating space through mutually reinforcing efforts designed to prevent al-Qa'ida from taking advantage of these ungoverned spaces. We will also build the will and capacity of states whose weaknesses al-Qa'ida exploits. Persistent insecurity and chaos in some regions can undermine efforts to increase

---

24 The White House, White Paper of the Interagency Policy Group's Report on U.S. Policy Toward Afghanistan and Pakistan, Lanham: Federal Information & News Dispatch, Inc., 2009.
25 Ibid., "Fact Sheet: National Strategy for Counterterrorism," White House Press Releases, Fact Sheets and Briefings, June 28, 2011, 3.

political engagement and build capacity and provide assistance, thereby exacerbating chaos and insecurity. Our challenge is to break this cycle of state failure to constrict the space available to terrorist networks.[26]

Based on these two documents, U.S. strategy focuses solely on al Qaeda and its affiliates while doing little to eliminate the conditions that gave rise to radicalism and have allowed al Qaeda to find safe haven in the Afghanistan-Pakistan region. Additionally, in a speech at the National Defense University focused on U.S. counterterrorism policy, President Obama defended the use of drones to kill terrorist suspects, emphasizing the importance of achieving desirable end results, rather than on resolving the conditions that have given rise to increased terrorist activity:

> First, we must finish the work of defeating al Qaeda and its associated forces. In Afghanistan, we will complete our transition to Afghan responsibility for that country's security. Our troops will come home. Our combat mission will come to an end. And we will work with the Afghan government to train security forces, and sustain a counterterrorism force, which ensures that al Qaeda can never again establish a safe haven to launch attacks against us or our allies.[27]

President Obama's vision, the 2009 White Paper, and the National Strategy For Counterterrorism all fail to focus on two historical and interconnected key factors that continue to perpetuate pathological politics in South Asia: the conflict between India and Pakistan over the territory of Kashmir, and the conflict between Pakistan and Afghanistan over the status of the Durand Line.[28] Without accommodating India's and Pakistan's interests in Kashmir or adequately addressing the conflict facing Pashtun populations divided across the Afghanistan-Pakistan border, U.S. strategy cannot achieve its stated missions.[29] Focusing on counterterrorism, on drone attacks in the tribal areas of Pakistan, or relying on the Pakistan Army as an ally against the Taliban or al Qaeda cannot create lasting success. This policy oversight is also reflected in analytical research in the region, which is often weighted towards current issues and tends not to give sufficient attention to the impact of history on outstanding regional disputes.

---

26 Ibid., 9
27 Barack Obama "President Obama Speaks at the National Defense University," Washington, D.C.: White House Press Release May 23, 2013.
28 In 1893, Afghan despotic ruler Amir Abdur Rahman Khan and British Diplomat Mortimer Durand agreed upon the "Durand Line," the border between Afghanistan and British India. After Pakistan's creation, the Durand Line became the border between Afghanistan and Pakistan.
29 For a discussion, see Sunil Dutta, "Viewpoints: End to Afghan War Must Involve India, Pakistan," *Sacramento Bee*, August 1, 2010, E5; Husain Haqqānī, "The Role of Islam in Pakistan's Future," *Washington Quarterly* 28, no.1 (2004): 83-96; Thaza V. Paul, "Causes of the India-Pakistan Enduring Rivalry," in *The India-Pakistan Conflict: An Enduring Rivalry*, ed. Thaza V. Paul (New York: Cambridge University Press, 2005); Tomsen, *The Wars of Afghanistan*; Usher, "The Afghan Triangle," 20-27.

It is in the security interests of the United States and its allies to address the historical and political issues plaguing the region. Such a resolution is also imperative for the security and well-being of people of South Asia who have suffered horrendous violence and deprivations. For instance, between 1979-89, during the Soviet invasion, civilian casualties in Afghanistan ranged from 600,000 to 1.5 million, while approximately five million Afghans were made refugees.[30] The misery faced by South Asians has not stopped since 1989; indeed, its influence has begun to spread beyond the regional borders.

When South Asian conflicts are allowed to fester, U.S. homeland security is adversely impacted. The nuclear rivalry between India and Pakistan, as well as Pakistan's status as a nation troubled by profound internecine military, civil, ethnic, and cultural conflicts, pose a risk to regional stability. For more than one billion people in South Asia, their colonial inheritance is that of violence and suffering.

These are the issues that this book seeks to explore, and to which it offers practical solutions. Chapter 1 lays out the historical basis of the current political and social crisis in South Asia, showing how British imperial policies contributed to the contemporary situation. Colonial rulers required expedient strategies in order to most efficiently exploit their colony, to prevent emerging nationalism, and to consolidate and perpetuate their own empire. Decisions made over a century ago to perpetuate the British Empire in South Asia laid the foundation for current and future conflicts in the Indian subcontinent. Some of the British policies used to control resistance and subvert emerging nationalism directly contributed to exacerbation of the divisions between communities living in the Indian subcontinent, leading to later bloodbaths and radicalizing populations. The British Empire's need to expand, survive, and perpetuate created a cascading sequence of events in India, resulting in the rise of terrorism from the region in the latter half of the 20th century. The most critical consequence of the British rule was the partition of British India in 1947, which is tied directly to terrorism in the region. The Indian subcontinent's imperial history demonstrates that global dominance based on short-term expediencies lead to great harm, even if the harm may not be apparent for decades or even centuries after those decisions are made.

Chapter 2 focuses on relatively recent (post-decolonization) historical events that have been the proximate or peripheral causes for extant terrorism originating from South Asia, and connects them to earlier moments of the region's history.

---

30   Rodric Braithwaite, *Afgantsy: The Russians in Afghanistan, 1979-89* (London: Profile Books, 2011), 331.

Violent militant jihadism in Pakistan and Afghanistan are explored in the context of General Mohammad Zia ul Haq's regime, its relationship with the United States, and the United States' enabling of General Zia-ul-Haq.

Pakistan's current involvement in terrorism is connected to prior colonial decisions that made Pakistan consider terrorism a viable and attractive method of political action. The section analyzes the India-Pakistan conflict, its nexus to terrorism emanating from Pakistan, and its consequences to U.S. strategic goals in South Asia.

Chapter 3 focuses specifically on historical U.S.-Pakistan relations since the birth of Pakistan and their significance to the emergence of the Taliban, and al Qaeda's presence in South Asia.

Chapter 4 concludes the book and offers recommendations that may lead to stability in South Asia.

BLOODLINES: THE IMPERIAL ROOTS OF TERRORISM IN SOUTH ASIA

CHAPTER 1

THE HISTORY OF THE INDIAN SUBCONTINENT

As we must rule 150 million of people by a handful ... of Englishmen, let us do it in a manner best calculated to leave them divided (as in religion and national feeling they already are) and to inspire them with the greatest possible awe of our power and with the least possible suspicion of our motives.

Charles John Canning (1812-1862), Governor-General of India[1]

We have not been elected or placed in power by the people, but we are here through our moral superiority, by the force of circumstances, by the will of Providence. This alone constitutes our charter to govern India. In doing the best we can for the people, we are bound by OUR conscience, not theirs.

John Lawrence, Viceroy of India, 1864–9[2]

Starting in the sixteenth century when the Portuguese discovered a sea route to India, accessibility to the lucrative Asian trading markets brought traders from several European nations to the subcontinent. Portuguese, Dutch, French, and British mercantile forces battled with each other over the Asian trade monopoly, often aligning with rivaling regional Indian powers that recognized the authority of the Mughal Emperor. The British East India Company, chartered by the British Crown, ultimately defeated its rivals and established and expanded British rule in India, eventually replacing the Mughal Emperor. As Britain extended its power beyond trade monopoly, it acquired the right to collect revenue, began imposing British administration and law over the colonies, and created a mercenary army with which to control India as well as dominate its rivals elsewhere. The British employed a range of policies in order to check resistance to their rule, ranging from alliances with different local power blocs, accommodation, subversion, and military force. To defeat opposition to the imperial rule, the British employed several different Machiavellian techniques—from treachery to alliances to the exploitation of religious differences. To keep their empire's administrative costs low, Britain gradually dispensed limited local governance to the natives, intending to extend their imperial rule indefinitely. When British rule eventually ended, the Indian subcontinent had been carved into two new nation states and was wracked by horrendous religious violence.

---

1   Lionel Knight, *Britain in India, 1858-1947* (London: Anthem Press, 2012), 23.
2   Tariq Ali, *Can Pakistan Survive? The Death of a State* (London: Verso, 1983), 15.

Using the historical record, I will argue that the trajectory of the British Empire in the subcontinent that gave us the Taliban and provided al Qaeda with a haven in contemporary South Asia. As we analyze the progression of imperial policy in the Indian subcontinent through the past two centuries, it will become apparent that current events are closely associated with historical colonial decisions and the reactions to such decisions by the colonial subjects.

During the 18th century, Bengal was the wealthiest province in the Mughal Empire and, like most other parts of Mughal territory, it was ruled autonomously as a regional kingdom by a Mughal vassal, the Nawab,[3] who recognized the suzerainty of the emperor. When the British East India Company defeated Siraj-ud-Daula, the Nawab of Bengal, in the 1757 Battle of Plassey, it marked the beginning of British rule in India from its eastern front in Bengal. The British Raj continued its colonial rule using a judicious combination of military force and military and trading alliances with the regional kingdoms as well as with traders and bankers.[4] As the British Empire consolidated and expanded its empire on the subcontinent, the Mughal Empire, which had ruled for three centuries in India, quickly disintegrated. By 1858, the Raj had established either direct or indirect power over most of the Indian subcontinent.

THE BRITISH IN INDIA

The British Empire was not the first to colonize the region historically described as the Indian subcontinent. Over two millennia ago, even with primitive means of transportation and communication, the Maurya Empire controlled vast areas of the subcontinent, although it was a decentralized empire.[5] Other large empires, including the Gupta Empire (320 BCE-550 ACE), the Kushan Empire (circa first to third century ACE), the Delhi Sultanate (1206-1526), and the Mughal Empire (1526-1857), reflected the geographical unity of the subcontinent under a

---

3   "Nawab" was a title held by a provincial governor.
4   The word "Raj" comes from the root "to rule," from Sanskrit "rājā," or "king." The rule of the British East India Company in India is often referred to as the "Company Raj" and lasted until 1858 when rule was directly transferred to the British Crown. The period of direct British rule over the subcontinent (between 1858 and 1947) is also termed the "British Raj" in order to differentiate it from the British East India Company's rule. Sometimes the shorter term "the Raj" is used to describe the British dominion over India. The British India Company had its own military, which predominantly consisted of native mercenaries and their European officers. Eventually, the native British colonial army grew into a massive force. After Indian rule shifted directly to the British crown, the British Indian colonial army continued to rely on native soldiers to control and administer not only India but also the empire's other territories.
5   Robert D. Kaplan, "South Asia's Geography of Conflict," *Center for a New American Security Paper* (2010): 6.

suzerain. Various degrees of central power were exercised over client states, spread from north and south of the plains of Ganges all the way to Central Asia and present day Afghanistan.

Just prior to Britain's arrival on the subcontinent, much of India was under the effectively managed and administered political control of the Mughals. Mughal rule extended over vast areas of the subcontinent and reflected geographical unification; whether political unification of the subcontinent was ever accomplished or could have been accomplished remains an open question. When Mughal Emperor Aurangzeb (1658-1707) ruled the huge subcontinent, India had a population approaching 180 million people—almost twenty percent of the world's population. The region was an amalgam of tremendous heterogeneity, and the Mughal Empire ruled its vast spread through a system of allegiances. Some autonomous states considered themselves allies of the Mughal state, while other ruling units accepted Mughal suzerainty. Regional kings, especially at the distant periphery of the empire, managed to rule independently, while others challenged the emperor.

In the seventeenth century, the Mughal Empire's cities were said to be larger and more resplendent than either London or Paris. Besides material wealth, art, poetry, painting, and architecture flourished under Mughal rule. In 1700, India's share of the world's GDP stood at 24.4% while the United Kingdom's GDP was less than 3.0%.[6] India's lavish wealth invited merchants, but it also attracted notorious plunderers. The Persian Emperor Nadir Shah sacked Delhi in 1739, carrying away the legendary Peacock Throne and treasures worth a billion rupees.[7] Not twenty years later, the Afghan ruler Ahmad Shah Abdali led an army of Afghan plunderers to the city in 1756.

During the Mughal rule, the subcontinent had a strong, diverse industry. Its textile production was intricately organized, with weavers, dyers, bleachers, and painters producing an enormous range of cotton and silk cloth that was highly desired both in local as well as international markets. Similarly, commodities and labor markets were extensive and ingeniously organized. Overland and coastal trading routes connected local economies with the wider world, while skillful merchants and bankers traded in the coastal areas.

---

6   Aditya Mukherjee, "Empire: How Colonial India Made Modern Britain," *Economic and Political Weekly* 45, no. 50 (2010): 74.

7   Piers Brendon, *The Decline and Fall of the British Empire, 1781-1997* (New York: Alfred A. Knopf, 2008), 33.

Before British rule, the Indian subcontinent was an economic and mercantile powerhouse, possessing a large territory, rich resources, and a substantial population. The strength of its economy was so great that India generated a trade surplus, which paid for the only paucity in India's cash economy—precious metals.[8] Political governance and social control in India were comprised of complex dynamics of balance, accommodation, and conflict between several diverse agents, including the merchant class that controlled banking and money flow, a multi-hierarchical structure of petty chieftains and small kings, revenue collectors for the emperor, landlords, and regional power centers. These power players ultimately recognized the authority of the Mughal Emperor and paid tribute to him accordingly, while the emperors themselves exercised their control through means of force, mediation, accommodation, and the extension of privileges.

While India had a long history of trade with Arab and Asian traders, the Mughal Empire experienced increased attention from European mercantile agents. As they moved in on the Indian market, European disputes began directly manifesting in conflicts between European trading companies in India. In the 17th century, European traders from Portugal, France, Netherlands, and Britain were not only trading in India, they were competing for power and exercising influence in local wars and politics, especially in the coastal regions where maritime trading activities were concentrated. Of all the European powers present in the subcontinent, the French and the English were the most powerful. Britain and France exploited the fragmented governing structure of the Indian subcontinent by forming alliances with competing local rulers. Military means were used to secure mercantile power, creating a perpetual cycle: wealth generated from exploitative commerce and tax revenues was then used to win additional territories that could yield additional revenues to finance acquisition of more territories.

In the mid-1700s, as the French and English East India Companies interfered in regional Indian states, local princes also attempted to use the British and French power for their own ends. Generally the rulers asked for assistance against attacks by rival chieftains, succession disputes, and confrontations between smaller kingdoms.[9] In this competition, the British eventually defeated the French, securing their undisputed political and economic foothold in the region. As the Mughal Empire began to weaken and disintegrate in the late 18th century, its decline acted as a catalyst for various conflicts as regional power blocks reoriented

---

8   Christopher A. Bayly, *Indian Society and the Making of the British Empire*. The New Cambridge History of India, 2nd ed. (Cambridge, UK: Cambridge University Press, 1988), 45; Dharma Kumar and Meghnad Desai, *The Cambridge Economic History of India: Volume 1, c.1200-1750* (Cambridge: Cambridge University Press, 1983), 126-127.

9   Barbara N. Ramusack, *The Indian Princes and Their States*, The New Cambridge History of India. Vol. 3, pt. 6. (Cambridge, UK: Cambridge University Press, 2004), 59.

and built new strategic alliances. The British East India Company successfully played different opposing states against each other, allowing the states to create networks within which they could wield power, annex and expand territory, and employ monopolistic trade practices.

The Company used intrigue, military force, and alliances to begin its power grab, encroaching on local noblemen's authority and later expanding its scope to defeat the waning Mughal Empire entirely. The 1757 Battle of Plassey is an excellent example of this practice at work. While the British Royal Navy had established its preeminence in the oceans and external routes to India in the early eighteenth century, British traders sought to extend their hold from the seaports. In Bengal, they faced a complicated political landscape that involved both Indian and French powers.[10] The Indian polity was a competing balance between the Mughal emperor, the provincial governor the Nawab, prominent landlords, and powerful bankers. The British adopted a system of alliance in which they offered military services to Indian states in succession disputes or territorial rivalries in exchange for payments and trade monopolies. In Bengal, the British developed close relations with powerful bankers who financed the Nawab's military campaigns and controlled the economy of Bengal, including controlling the Bengal Mint. In 1757, the newly appointed Nawab, Siraj-ud-Daula, attempted to consolidate his power and in the process extracted more taxes from landlords and demanded more money from the merchants and bankers, alienating them.[11] The alienated factions then plotted with the British to overthrow of the Nawab. Using their alliance with the famous banking houses of Jagat Seth and Omichand, the British negotiated for the support of bankers, offering them payouts from the Bengal treasury.[12] At the same time, the British conspired with a disgruntled general, Mir Jafar, who was an uncle of the Nawab, offering him the nawabship. When the British went to war with the Nawab, the Nawab's army under conspirator Mir Jafar had been bribed to betray the Nawab by refusing to fight. The Nawab was captured and killed and the conspirator Mir Jafar took his place as the new Nawab.[13] It was a rewarding endeavor for the British: historian Nick Robins estimates that the British East India Company appropriated from the Bengal treasury a net sum of £232 million in current value as a consequence of the Battle of Plassey alone.[14]

---

10 Bayly, *Indian Society and the Making of the British Empire*, 45, 48-51; Peter James Marshall, *Bengal, The British Bridgehead: Eastern India, 1740-1828*, The New Cambridge History of India. Vol. 2, pt 2, 2nd ed. (Cambridge, UK: Cambridge University Press, 1988), 75-77.
11 Marshall, "Bengal," 75.
12 Marshall, "Bengal," 77.
13 Ibid.,78.
14 Nick Robins, *The Corporation That Changed the World: How the East India Company Shaped the Modern Multinational*, 2nd ed. (London: Pluto Press, 2012), 3.

The British East India Company's initial focus was not on military power but on monopolizing trade and control of commerce; later, land revenue rights and taxation were also brought under British control. To subdue its remaining rivals in India and to make the Company more profitable by acquiring more taxable territory, the Company employed a large standing army. Alexander Dow, a lieutenant colonel in the Company's private army, noted that in order to enhance revenue, "seven entire battalions were added to our military establishment to enforce collections."[15]

Meanwhile, Britain's imperial expansion and its subjugation of native peoples in the Americas, Africa, and Asia were rationalized based on the concept of Western civilizational superiority. The spread of the British Raj was similarly justified by painting India as a society beset by "oriental" despotism. Indian sovereignty was portrayed in negative terms, with local rulers and the emperor disparaged as unenlightened tyrants. This self-serving assertion facilitated Britain's claim to civilizational privilege over India, and Britain's control over the territory was characterized as accidental—it just "happened" while the country pursued its mercantile objectives.

The British faced no local opposition while establishing their commercial footprint in the subcontinent. Even their access to and manipulation of levels of regional power (for example, by annexing territories using strategies such as doctrine of lapse) faced little resistance.[16] Over the past millennia, the subcontinent had experienced, accommodated, assimilated, and subsumed a succession of foreign invaders, including the Persians, Greeks, Kushans, Arabs, Turks, and Turkic-Mongols; foreign conquerors were nothing new to the people of the subcontinent. The British were no more alien to the natives than the Mughal emperors who had conquered India in the sixteenth century. In the eighteenth century when the British began their expansion project, India could be described as fragmented or multi-layered: it hosted myriad ethnicities; various languages; complex religious, cultural, and social divisions; as well as different regional dynasties. The British won control over India by exploiting this diversity, using local powers or populations against one another. Perry Anderson quotes B. B. Misra's explanation of how this gradual takeover happened: "India's segmented society and denationalized governments did not constitute a serious challenge to the British."[17]

---

15 Quoted in Nicholas B. Dirks, *The Scandal of Empire India and the Creation of Imperial Britain* (Cambridge, MA: Belknap Press of Harvard University Press, 2006), 145.
16 The British policy of "the doctrine of lapse" allowed the British East India Company to annex states when a local ruler died without a natural male heir. Adopted sons were not accepted as heirs, creating great resentment in royal families.
17 Perry Anderson, "Gandhi Center Stage," *London Review of Books* 34, no.13 (2012), 3-11.

Opponents to British power—for example, native princes and others who resisted British expansion—were demonized, referred to as savages, and portrayed as oppressors. For example, Tipu Sultan, the ruler of Mysore who aligned himself with the French to fight the British, was characterized by the British as a dangerous radical, a sympathizer of French sans-culottes, a remorseless savage, an oppressor of Hindus, and a murderer of Christians.[18] Sir William Jones (1746–1794) proclaimed that the inhabitants of India were "incapable of civil liberty" and therefore justifiably "ruled by an absolute power".[19] The *noblesse oblige* rationale for British rule portrayed the Raj as a superior people looking after a backward and corrupt people.

This rhetoric elided Britain's careful and thorough appropriation of Indian treasures through the East India Company and British governmental forces. Lord Charles Cornwallis (1738–1805) claimed and perhaps even believed that the great object of Britain's presence in India was to serve the Indian public.[20] This high-minded lip service, however, concealed Britain's real actions as it extorted as much land revenue as possible and spread its commercial monopoly throughout the subcontinent. The outrageous nature of British land revenue control caused some Indian forces to rebel, but the profit inherent in such revenue extraction prevented any change in taxing policies. Imperial, authoritarian, and Orientalist justifications for Western intervention in foreign territories have remained remarkably unchanged since the centuries-old assertions of Jones and Cornwallis.

The financial benefit Britain gained from its conquest of the subcontinent drove the East India Company's expansion. For example, the conquest of the Punjab in the 1850s alone resulted in such a great revenue surplus that it not only covered the entirety of military spending required to control the region; after paying all the governance costs, a surplus of five million rupees per year, an extraordinary sum at the time, still remained.[21]

During its earlier trade with India, Britain had nothing to sell and thus had to pay for Indian exports in silver. The Indian surplus thus was paid for in bullion, causing an economically undesired outflow of the precious metal from Britain. After the Battle of Plassey, the British import of silver into India ceased and Britain began paying for Indian imports using revenues raised the taxation of conquered Indian populations. This effectively meant that India was now forced to pay for its own exports.[22] The surplus of trade thereafter was transferred to Britain as tribute,

18 Brendon, *The Decline and Fall*, 107.
19 Quoted in Brendon, *The Decline and Fall*, 98.
20 Ibid.
21 Wolpert, Stanley A., *A New History of India*, 6th ed. (New York: Oxford University Press, 2000), 226.
22 Mukherjee, "Empire," 76; Robins, *The Corporation That Changed the World*, 3.

which financed the British economy. Later, the British economy further benefited from the export of Indian opium in exchange for silk and tea exports from China. As Britain, again, had nothing to sell to China, exports had to be paid in bullion; this time, that role was filled by opium. In effect, the British silk and tea trade was financed by India's "tribute" of opium, which again enriched the British economy. Britain's gain was not insignificant; in the span between 1871 and 1916, scholars have estimated that surpluses transferred from India to Britain exceeded 3.2 billion pounds.[23]

While these initial imperial motives have focused on the monetary benefits Britain reaped from its Indian colonial possession, one of Britain's most overlooked but significant benefits was a native Indian army financed by revenues extracted from India; in effect, this was a free band of mercenaries fighting for British interests and global dominance.

THE 1857 REBELLION

> *"India and Burma have no natural association with the Empire, from which they are alien by race, history and religion, and for which neither of them has any natural affection, and both are in the Empire because they are conquered countries which have been brought there by force, kept there by our control, and which hitherto it has suited to remain under our protection."*
>
> Victor Hope (1887-1952), 2nd Marquess of Linlithgow, Viceroy of India[24]

In order to understand the evolution of political violence and terrorism in South Asia, it is critical to focus on how the British Empire attempted to establish itself and perpetuate its rule on the subcontinent. Certain salient historical events reflect how British imperialism demanded alliance formation with the native groups. The Empire's needs remained at the forefront; any alliances it made were expedient, to be broken or modified as necessary. One of the first major shifts in-group alliances was seen after the mutiny of the Bengal Army in 1857, to which the secession of East Pakistan, the creation of Bangladesh, and the radicalization of Pakistan can be traced.

---

23 Ibid., Amiya K. Bagchi, "The Other Side of Foreign Investment by Imperial Powers: Transfer of Surplus from Colonies," *Economic and Political Weekly* 37, no. 23 (2002): 2232; See also Amiya Kumar Bagchi, *Perilous Passage: Mankind and the Global Ascendancy of Capital* (Lanham: Rowman, Littlefield Publishers, 2008); Irfan Habib, "Colonization of the Indian Economy, 1757-1900," *Social Scientist* 3, no. 8 (1975): 23-53.
24 Lawrence James, *The Rise and Fall of the British Empire* (New York: St. Martin's Press, 1994), 425.

To rule over distant lands, European rulers were forced to collaborate with local allies, using these partners to buttress the structure of their colonial rule. It was essential that colonial powers identify these allies and incorporate them within the colonial apparatus; this not only consolidated the imperial force's power but also reduced material and human costs, as a great deal of resources were required in order to control vast, distant areas and large populations. As such, European powers sought and obtained collaboration from various groups, including the ruling classes, large landholders, petty chieftains, and merchants.[25] The most important of the collaborating groups, without whose help the imperial control could not be sustained, were the natives who joined as mercenaries in the imperial army. Without this critical foreign-native military alliance, colonial empires could not expand, control, and perpetuate their rule: the geographic distance between the mother country and its colonies prohibited it from being able to swiftly mobilize European soldiers to squelch native uprisings. The British military recruiting strategies, used for identifying and absorbing local military allies into the imperial military, were crucially important for the empire's success.

The British also engaged in important alliance-formation with indigenous Indian rulers in order to extract resources such as military personnel and tribute payments, and to purchase goods at favorable prices. Later, these alliances would enable Britain to annex territories, increasing their imperial foothold. Shifting alliances consolidated and perpetuated British imperial rule; however, as will be evident in later chapters, it also created communal schisms that eventually culminated in a blood-soaked, religious-based division of the subcontinent.[26]

Direct interventions in distant foreign lands require more than just strong militaries. Conquering weaker nation states is relatively easy for imperial powers. As the 2003 U.S. invasion of Iraq and its experience in Afghanistan demonstrate, a powerful army may deliver a quick military victory, but maintaining control over distant foreign lands requires more than military might. To pacify native populations and prevent insurgencies, the imperial presence needs the consent of the elite from at least some factions of the local population. The British efficiently and adeptly used factions to their benefit as they laid the foundation of their empire in South Asia. The Imperial British Indian Army played a crucial role in Britain's conquest of India and the establishment of its empire there. The British

---

25 Tai Yong Tan, *The Garrison State: Military, Government and Society in Colonial Punjab, 1849-1947*, SAGE Series in Modern Indian History (New Delhi: SAGE Publications, 2005), 31.
26 The origin of the partition was based more upon the interests of the Muslim and Hindu elite than a real Hindu-Muslim religious divide.

domination was brought about by a colonial military composed mostly of native Indian soldiers led by British officers.[27] The Empire remained a garrison state until its end, with the army as its last line of defense for internal security.

The British East India Company had initially established its presence in three areas in India: Bengal, Madras, and Bombay, each called a Presidency town. Each of the three Presidencies had its own army and collectively the three formed the British Indian Army. These armies consisted of British and Indian regiments commanded by British officers. The Bengal Army was the largest of the three. The British Indian Army, consisting of more than 200,000 sepoys (from the Persian *sipahi*, "soldier"), was the largest employer in the British Raj and absorbed a significant amount of imperial revenue.[28] In 1856, there were 235,221 native soldiers—comprising 84% of the Indian Army—compared to 45,104 Royal and Company troops.[29] Lord Salisbury (1830-1903) voiced British views when he called the imperial army "an English barrack in the Oriental Seas from which we may draw any number of troops without paying for them."[30] In effect, the British Indian Army was raised from the natives, paid for by the native's own revenues, and helped to keep the empire in control, therefore serving as a free mercenary army for its imperial masters.

The recruitment process for British Indian Army soldiers took into account their castes and religion. As early as 1770s, Warren Hastings, the first governor-general of British India, favored the military's consideration of caste as a means of forestalling the growth of a national identity that might oppose the British. Accordingly, Hastings encouraged high-caste predominance in the Bengal Army.[31] Recruitment initially took place in the coastal regions where the British had established their foothold; later it expanded inland, seeking manpower from across the Indian territory. This was another reason why the large military force was divided into the three separate components centered in Madras, Bombay, and Bengal: to control vast swaths of land. The Madras Army found its recruits among diverse ethnic groups in South India. By the early 19th century, the Bombay Army was overwhelmingly composed of Hindustanis and Konkanis from the Gangetic plains. The Bengal Army was more restrictive in its recruitment, picking "handsome and clean" looking men from high-caste Brahmins and Rajputs from Rohilkhand, Oudh, and Bihar.[32]

---

27   Yong, *The Garrison State*; G. J. Bryant, "Indigenous Mercenaries in the Service of European Imperialists: The Case of the Sepoys in the Early British Indian Army, 1750-1800," *War in History* 7 (2000): 23.
28   Anderson, "Gandhi Center Stage."
29   Ibid.
30   Ibid.
31   Bryant, "Indigenous Mercenaries in the Service of European Imperialists," 122.
32   Yong, *The Garrison State*, 32.

The native soldiers in the employ of the British defended the Empire within India and abroad. The soldiers were sent to fight in places as far away as Sumatra, Moluccas, Egypt, Macao, Mauritius, and Java. The sepoys bolstered British military power, creating the impression that India, as a garrison state, was a vital source of Britain's strength in addition to being a source of revenue and profit.

The inevitable struggle between the colonizer and the colonized created a series of revolts and disturbances against colonial rule.[33] Britain was extracting India's natural resources, imposing exploitative taxes on its citizens, monopolizing trade at native traders' expense, expropriating native rulers' power and authority, and perpetuating incipient racism; all of these factors resulted in Indian resistance, which manifested on many different levels. Princes and landlords resisted British attempts to impose its allies as nominees to the thrones of princely states. Such interference in local politics naturally caused opposition from the followers of the claimants to the thrones who were pushed away in favor of colonial proxies. The British encountered additional resistance when they attempted to expand and control territories to increase their tax revenue. During the earlier colonial period, Indian demonstrations and disturbances were generally directed against British taxation.[34]

The most serious threat to British authority in India evolved from a military mutiny, transforming into a widespread rebellion in 1857, when several regiments of the British Indian Army revolted. The Rebellion (alternatively known as the Indian Mutiny, the First War of Independence, the Muslim Conspiracy, or the Sepoy Mutiny) was a watershed event in the history of British India. It was the largest and most widespread threat to British rule in India in the 19th century, and as a consequence of the rebellion, the East India Company was removed and control of India was transferred directly to the British Crown.

The Bengal Army's uprising was a complex affair. Many reasons have been postulated for the rebellion: exploitation, discriminatory treatment, racism, and, most significantly, the belief that Christian British officers deliberately engaged in acts to defile the religious sentiments of Hindu and Muslim soldiers.[35] The British ignored several earnest grievances of the sepoys, who were upset by their service conditions. The General Service Act of 1856 had decreed that all sepoys, irrespective of their caste, would have to work overseas when needed. This single

---

33 Christopher A. Bayly, *Indian Society and the Making of the British Empire*, 2nd ed. (Cambridge, UK: Cambridge University Press, 1988), 170.
34 Ibid., 170-180
35 Ibid., 8; See also Irfan Habib, "The Coming of 1857," *Social Scientist* 26, vol. 1/4 (1998): 6-15; Ramesh Rawat, "Perception of 1857," *Social Scientist* 35, no. 11/12 (2007): 15-28; Heather Streets, "The Rebellion of 1857: Origins, Consequences, and Themes," *Teaching South Asia: An Internet Journal of Pedagogy* I, no. 1 (2001), 87-89.

step alone alienated the high-caste Hindus in the Bengal Army, as crossing the ocean (dubbed as "black waters") signified a loss of caste. The disconnect between the imperial officers and their native soldiers was compounded by a reduction in pay. Another major contributor to the mutiny was the concern that the British were undermining the natives' religion by trying to convert them to Christianity, as the most proximate catalyst for the revolt touched on the religious sensitivities of the native soldiers: the introduction of a new greased cartridge for the Lee Enfield rifles used by the sepoys. Rumors spread that the cartridges were greased with the fat of cows and pigs, and in order to use the cartridges, they had to be prepared with the mouth. The sepoys were outraged: Hindus believe that cows are sacred while Muslims consider pigs unclean. The rumors aided the fear that the British were trying to pollute the native soldiers and convert them to Christianity.[36]

Some soldiers refused to use the greased cartridges; these acts of insubordination were severely punished. Resentment broke out explosively, quickly turning into a mutiny. The rebellion began on May 10, 1857, in Meerut (where the Bengal Army was headquartered), when rebel soldiers killed their British officers and released the imprisoned sepoys who were punished for insubordination. From Meerut, the rebellion moved to Delhi, the seat of the Mughal Empire. The mutiny caught the British by surprise, exposing the vulnerability created by the empire's dependence on its local mercenary army. The European troops, who were outnumbered by natives, saw their control over north-central India disappearing. On May 11, the mutineers reached Delhi and began massacring its British residents. The Mughal King of India, Bahadur Shah II, who was an impotent figurehead with only nominal power (the real power was wielded by the British Resident at Delhi) was designated the leader of the rebellion by the motley group of rebels.[37] It is notable that the mostly Hindu rebel soldiers chose a Muslim king as the leader of their revolt, as it reveals a close alliance between Muslim and Hindu soldiers against foreign rule.

As the rebel forces amassed in Delhi, other revolts broke out across north and central India, transforming the rebellion into a popular uprising in which peasants, local notables, and urban groups joined together to fight against British rule. In June and July, mutinies and urban revolts followed in other garrison towns north and west of Delhi.[38] The rebellion posed a serious threat to the British but lost its steam due to poor planning, lack of coordination between various groups, and

---

36 Heather Streets, "The Rebellion of 1857: Origins, Consequences, and Themes," *Teaching South Asia: An Internet Journal of Pedagogy* I, no. 1 (2001), 87-89; See also Bayly, *Indian Society and the Making of the British Empire*. Vol. 2, pt. 1. 179-182.
37 William Dalrymple, *The Last Mughal: The Fall of a Dynasty, Delhi, 1857* (New York: Knopf, 2007), 7, 38.
38 Bayly, *Indian Society and the Making of the British Empire*, 179-183.

THE INDIAN MUTINY 1857-1859 - © IWM
Image reprinted with permission from Imperial War Museum, Lambeth Road, London, SE1 6HZ

weak leadership. The bulk of the European regiments at the time were stationed in the Punjab and were mobilized, in conjunction with the loyal Punjab Frontier Force soldiers, to defeat the rebels. British authority was re-established with ruthless force, and by the end of 1858 the British had overwhelmed the resistance in all parts of north and central India. British colonial rule in India was finally consolidated over the subcontinent after the rebellion.

After their successful suppression of the mutiny, the British undertook a devastating purge, including indiscriminate mass slaughter and the burning of villages. Tens of thousands of soldiers and village fighters were hanged, shot, or tied to the barrels of canons and blown to bits.[39] The last Mughal Emperor was humiliated, imprisoned, and exiled to Burma. Thousands were hanged and vast areas of Delhi, the primary cultural center of the subcontinent, were obliterated. Delhi's fall signaled the end of the once-grand Mughal Empire, and Muslim

---

39 Thomas R. Metcalf, *Ideologies of the Raj*. The New Cambridge History of India. Vol. 3, pt. 4, 2nd ed. (Cambridge: Cambridge University Press, 1997), 43; Streets, "The Rebellion of 1857."

political and cultural domain was destroyed on the subcontinent.[40] British rule in India would now be unchallenged and governance was formally taken over by the British Crown.

The British military and the Indian soldiers in their employ were forced to implement many structural changes after the rebellion. Racial antagonism dramatically increased between Britons and Indians. On the British side, the rebellion was portrayed as savage attacks on British women and children, who were allegedly being raped and murdered by fanatic soldiers. There was great public outrage over the violation of the "innocent" British by subhuman Indians.[41] On the Indian side, the widespread slaughter, mass hangings, and other atrocities perpetrated by the vengeful British on both native soldiers and innocent Indian civilians left little doubt that British notions of justice and due process did not apply to their colonial subjects. This was also evident in Britain's wanton destruction and leveling of Delhi.[42] The 1857 Rebellion had exposed the barbarous violence of colonial rule in India.

The short-term impacts of the rebellion were the humiliating defeat of the rebel forces, the Mughal Empire's demise in India, and Britain's dominance over the subcontinent. The Crown formally took over Indian administration, and Queen Victoria fashioned herself as the Empress of India. British reprisals in Delhi purged the Muslim aristocracy and forced the majority of Delhi's Muslim residents to flee the city. The rebellion made the British suspicious of the natives, further entrenching the racial divide between Europeans and Indians.

However, there were wider, deeper and longer-lasting impacts as well. It was obvious that military force alone would be insufficient for controlling the subcontinent: British colonial domination required a readjustment of its alliances. Native associates had to be selected more carefully and potentially rebellious natives needed to be rendered harmless. A consequential ramification was that Muslim and Hindu identities in the subcontinent were further defined, not only against the British, but also against each other. These developments had a major impact on decolonization nine decades later and still continue to impact South Asian politics. As a result of the rebellion's defeat, the syncretic, tolerant, and sophisticated culture and composite Hindu-Muslim Indo-Islamic civilization that the Mughal court under the last emperor had fostered were damaged. The Indian

---

40 Dalrymple, *The Last Mughal*, 355-358, 361-362, 369-373, 376-78.
41 Streets, "The Rebellion of 1857," 85; For an overview, see Jenny Sharpe, "The Unspeakable Limits of Rape: Colonial Violence and Counter-Insurgency," *Genders* 10 (1991): 25-46.
42 See George Wagentrieber's description in Dalrymple, *The Last Mughal*, 387-388.

Muslim became a pariah in British eyes. In the period following the rebellion, the British openly expressed profoundly contemptuous attitudes against Muslims and Mughal culture; these attitudes were absorbed by the now ascendant Hindus.[43]

Britain's most significant strategy during the 1857 Rebellion was to take advantage of regional differences, interests, and internal rivalries amongst the Indians. The British realized that Punjabi Sikh and Muslim soldiers did not sympathize with the easterner Hindus and high caste-soldiers. This culminated in a major move to augment the Punjab Force that was used to crush the rebellion in Delhi. The bulk of the British mercenary forces that re-conquered the rebellious region were composed of Sikhs, Punjabi Muslims, Pathans, and Nepalese. The mercenaries were not motivated to help the British preserve their empire, but rather to plunder the now-crumbling Mughal Empire. Besides looting, the Sikhs also desired to avenge the humiliation they had suffered at the hands of Mughal rulers.[44] The successful exploitation of such rivalries paid dividends to the British Empire and would perpetuate their rule in India for another 90 years.

After the British Indian Army put the rebellion down, Britain focused on preventing future rebellions. One of the most consequential of their measures was to change patterns of recruitment for the Indian Army. This change is in turn connected to the horrendous violence associated with the partition of India in 1947, the eventual breakup of Pakistan in 1971 and the subsequent hardening of Pakistan's Islamic identity, as well as the way political Islam is currently used to mobilize populations in South Asia. The Peel Commission, appointed in July 1858 to review the Mutiny and provide recommendations for the Indian Army's future security, quickly learned that it was unfeasible to deploy only European or British troops to the subcontinent. In the first place, it was not possible to raise a sufficient number of European soldiers due to manpower scarcity. Secondly, the cost of creating an all-British army to control India was prohibitively expensive; native mercenaries cost less and were dispensable. The British considered replacing untrustworthy native Indian soldiers with cheaper mercenaries from Asia and Africa, but this was also found to be impractical. The Commission ultimately concluded that native troops were essential for controlling and policing the empire in India. Its recommendations thus were directed at preventing any group from within the army from mutiny. The Punjab Committee, formed to advise the Peel Commission, recommended that the British reorganize the Bengal Army by exploiting ethnic, provincial, and religious differences:

---

43 Dalrymple, *The Last Mughal*, 440.
44 Prem Mahadevan, "The Paradoxes of Ethnographic Intelligence: A Case Study of British India," *Faultlines* 20 (2011).

> To preserve the distinctiveness which is so valuable, and which while it lasts makes the Muhomedan of one country despise, fear, or dislike the Muhomedan of another, corps should in future be provincial, and adhere to geographical limits within which differences and rivalries are strongly marked. Let all races, Hindu and Muhomedan, of one province be enlisted in one regiment, and no others, and having thus created distinctive regiments, let us keep them so against the hour of need by confining the circle of their ordinary service to the limits of their own province, and only marching them on emergency into other parts of the Empire, with which they will then be found to have little sympathy. By the system thus indicated, two great evils are avoided; firstly, that community of feeling throughout the native army, and that mischievous political activity and intrigue which results from association with other races and travel in other Indian provinces, and secondly, that thorough discontent and alienation from the service which has undoubtedly sprung up since extended conquest has carried our Hindustani soldiers so far from their homes in India proper.[45]

The proposed reorganization policy was transparently divisive, suggesting that the Indian Army should remain segregated and organized in a manner that would allow one part to check the other. The Army had to change both its modes of recruitment and the composition of its regiments. Distance and separation between different castes, as well as regional, religious, ethnic, and linguistic differences, were exploited in order to preserve separatism between the native components of the British Indian Army and prevent the army regiments from unifying against their imperial masters. For example, Sikhs could be used to counterbalance Muslims in a regiment (whom they considered adversaries) and Pashtuns could be used to counterbalance both the Sikhs and the Punjabis. This would create a regional regiment composed of four different religio-ethnic and geographical groups of Sikhs, Muslims, Pashtuns, and Hindu Jats (who were historically cultivators and herders and considered a non-elite caste). It was thus recommended that each company of a regiment should consist of a different caste or race.

Prior to the mutiny, Britain's recruitment for the Bengal Army had focused on high-caste Hindus mainly from central and eastern India. Afterward, the British began to seek recruits from Punjab and the northwestern regions of India (in present-day Pakistan) at the expense of other regions, especially Bengal. The Punjab region provided a large bank of illiterate poverty-stricken villagers desperate for jobs and unlikely to agitate for independence, unlike the high-caste Hindu soldiers of the Bengal Army, now considered traitorous. This era also heralded the

---

45 As quoted in Yong, *The Garrison State*, 52-53.

Orientalist notion of the so-called "martial races," when British officers suggested that Punjabis were racially superior to their Bengali counterparts and therefore made better warriors.[46]

The shift in recruitment was so radical that by 1929, 62% of the entire British Indian Army was Punjabi, even though Punjab constituted only 10% of the British Indian population. Despite its population of 45 million, Bengal was allowed only 7,117 recruits into the Indian Army whereas Punjab, with a population of 20 million, provided 349,689 soldiers. Even within Punjab, only a select group comprised of Muslims and Sikhs was favored, while the rest of the population were discouraged. During the Second World War, Punjab alone provided over 800,000 soldiers for the British war efforts.[47]

The Punjabi soldiers internalized the British attitude toward the Bengalis, who were described as untrustworthy, disloyal, and effeminate. Britain's tactics were incredibly powerful, as the ethnic group it had put in a privileged position began displaying the same prejudiced attitudes toward another ethnic group from the same country. Its methods for preventing future rebellions, which included selective recruitment based on ethnicity and religion, were profound and long lasting. Their full ramifications will be discussed later in this book's sections on the partition of India and Bangladesh War.

THE DURAND LINE

In the context of international security, the Durand Line—the border between Afghanistan and Pakistan—has been one of the most important regions in the world since 9/11. The boundaries of this border have been a source of conflict between the Afghan and Pakistan governments ever since the birth of Pakistan in 1947; however, the source of conflict has much farther-reaching roots. The bilaterally contested nature of this border became an international issue when the U.S. military removed the Taliban government from power in Afghanistan in 2001. As the United States launched its attack, insurgents fled across the eastern border to Pakistan to seek safe haven, regroup, and to launch cross-border attacks against the United States and allied forces. Parts of the boundary region, especially the FATA (Federally Administered Tribal Areas), have served as a haven for al Qaeda leaders and as a base for the Taliban.[48] During Afghanistan's war against

---

46   Syed H. S. Soherwordi, "'Punjabisation' in the British Indian Army 1857–1947 and the Advent of Military Rule in Pakistan," *Edinburgh Papers in South Asian Studies* 24, (2010): 7.
47   Soherwordi, "Punjabisation," 12.
48   Barfield, *The Durand Line: History, Consequences, and Future*, ii; For an overview, see also Thomas Barfield, *Afghanistan: A Cultural and Political History*, Princeton Studies in Muslim Politics (Princeton: Princeton University Press, 2012); Nasreen Ghufran, "Pashtun Ethnonationalism and the Taliban Insurgency in the North West Frontier Province of Pakistan," *Asian Survey*

the Soviet invaders, insurgents mastered the art of crossing the border without detection. Taliban and al Qaeda members later learned this art as they battled the U.S. forces, post-9/11.

While a cursory look at Afghanistan might suggest that its spiraling descent began in 1978 with the communist coup and the consequent Soviet invasion, Afghanistan's problems really began more than a century ago. Here too, expedient British imperial decisions were at the root of these problems. A review of the border's history reveals how British colonial decisions shaped the frontier between British India and Afghanistan. This disputed region—the product of imperial needs and convenience—would not only turn into a national security issue for the United States, but also serve as a source of terrorism, destabilization, and competition in the relationships between India, Pakistan, and Afghanistan.

The border between Afghanistan and Pakistan is about 1,640 miles long. Prior to 1947, this was the loosely defined border between British India and Afghanistan. Policing this area was and remains difficult, as large parts of the frontier cover exceptionally forbidding terrain: narrow valleys, desert plains, inaccessible mountains, and difficult rocky regions, all scattered with villages inhabited by subsistence farmers. The Pashtuns, the largest tribal group in the world, constitute the overwhelming majority of this region. The Durand Line is far more apparent on printed maps than it is on the ground since local populations have never paid much attention to it, crossing the border at will and neglecting to treat it as a boundary.[49] This is hardly surprising as it is poorly demarcated in most places and completely unmarked in others. Because state authority has always been weak or non-existent in the area around the line, no one has ever policed its border. Both Afghanistan and British India instead used indirect forms of rule, relying on tribal elders to settle problems and ensuring security through the use of armed local militias.[50]

Any discussion of the strategic importance and history of Afghanistan requires a discussion of the "Great Game" played between Russia and England for supremacy over Central Asia. The strategic importance of the region now called Afghanistan rose in the mid-19th century as the British Empire extended and consolidated its power on the Indian subcontinent and Russia was looking to

---

49, no. 6 (2009): 1092-1114; Jones, "The Terrorist Threat from Pakistan," 69-94; Rashid, *Descent into Chaos*; Shibil Siddiqi, "Afghanistan-Pakistan Relations: History and Geopolitics in a Regional and International Context: Implication for Canadian Foreign Policy." *Walter and Duncan Foundation* (2009), 1-55.
49 Barfield, *The Durand Line*, 3.
50 Barfield, *The Durand Line*, 3.

expand eastward.⁵¹ Since the British imperialists viewed India as the "crown jewel" of its colonial possessions, they took an aggressive stance toward any threat they perceived toward their control of India. Britain considered the possession of India as the key to its wealth, and fear of Russian encroachment from the north made the tribal areas between Afghanistan and India important territory. During the mid-to-late-19th century, the British and Russian Empires competed for influence in Afghanistan by backing rival tribal groups. Ultimately, the British goal to exercise direct military control of Afghanistan failed due to tough native resistance and a lack of financial and military resources; consequently, it was abandoned and was followed by a policy of indirect influence that would create an Afghan buffer state between British India and Russia. Afghanistan was treated by the British as a dependency and, until the 1919 border war in which Afghanistan won its complete sovereignty, Afghan foreign relations were directed by British India.⁵²

In 1893, the British imposed an administrative boundary line between their Empire in India and the subcontinent's western flank. Although to the British the so-called Durand Line was a demarcation of their sphere of influence on India's western border, its immediate effect on the ground was to divide Pashtun tribes as well as the Baloch population that lived between Afghanistan and British India, separating communities and creating resentment.⁵³

During the height of its power in India, Britain was haunted by fears that Czarist Russia would march into India through Afghanistan. As a result, the British made several attempts to directly control Afghanistan. In 1836, London annexed Peshawar from Afghanistan. In 1838, they invaded Afghanistan and placed their nominee on the throne in Kandahar, but the Afghans forced them to retreat from Kabul in June 1842. The British Indian Army had marched in more than 4,500 troops and 12,000 Indian servants, and every last one was slaughtered.⁵⁴ The British then undertook a second invasion in 1878, in which they were able to gain control over Afghan foreign policy, but were still unable to establish direct colonial rule over the Afghans. The British thus began to resort to more practical and less expensive means of indirectly ruling in Afghanistan: bribery and intrigue.

---

51 Samuel S. Lieberman, "Afghanistan: Population and Development in the Land of Insolence," *Population and Development Review* 6, no. 2 (1980): 272.
52 For an overview, see Barfield, *Afghanistan: A Cultural and Political History*; Amin Saikal, *Modern Afghanistan: A History of Struggle and Survival* (London: IB Tauris, 2004), Nasreen Ghufran, "Pashtun Ethnonationalism and the Taliban Insurgency in the North West Frontier Province of Pakistan," 1092-1114; David Isby, *Afghanistan: Graveyard of Empires* (New Tork: Pegasus, 2010).
53 Barfield, *Afghanistan: A Cultural and Political History*, 153-156; Hafizullah Emadi, "Durand Line and Afghan-Pak Relations," *Economic and Political Weekly* 25, no. 28 (1990): 1515; Johnson and Mason, "No Sign Until the Burst of Fire," 67-68.
54 Angelo Rasanayagam, *Afghanistan: A Modern History; Monarchy, Despotism or Democracy? The Problem of Governance in the Muslim Tradition*, rev. ed. (London: I.B. Tauris, 2005), xvii.

In 1893, Sir Mortimer Durand, the Foreign Secretary of British India, persuaded Amir Abdur Rahman of Afghanistan to accept what was a de facto line of influence between the British Empire and Afghanistan in return for money and armaments. This was a great strategic victory for British imperial interests on the Indian subcontinent. Abdur Rahman had opposed the boundary because it might force him to relinquish his nominal sovereignty over the Pashtun tribes in the region, but he needed British subsidies to maintain his campaign against the Hazara tribes.[55] The Durand Line formally annexed Britain's Afghan territory; this included Peshawar, Afghanistan's old winter capital that had been taken over by the Sikhs in 1834, as well as the North West Frontier Province (NWFP) region that is now called Khyber Pakhtunkhwa (KPK).[56] The Durand Agreement afforded the British strategic control of border passes and established an international boundary for Afghanistan. The British mapped out their administrative territories based on their governability: moving westward from Peshawar, the British paid less attention to more distant territories, and as a consequence, those areas had proportionately less colonial control. This state of affairs would continue even after decolonization. The British assumed control of the easier-to-manage zones, while the neighboring tribal zones that were more difficult to rule were kept under British sovereignty but left to govern themselves. The Durand Line indicated the outermost limit of British control on its India-Afghanistan border.[57]

Colonial prerogatives allowed the frontier region to remain ungoverned, creating an autonomous area where the tribes refused to accept any federal authority. The British kept the tribal areas under their jurisdiction in check with oppressive and abusive regulations, alienating the frontier population from the colonial government. This alienation and distrust of government persisted even after the British departed, especially as Britain's successor, Pakistan, adopted its colonial practices in the area.

In 1947, the areas surrounding the line went from being the borderland between British India and Afghanistan to being the borderland between Afghanistan and the newly created state of Pakistan. Pakistan declared that the Durand Line, though an artificial creation of the British Raj, was its international border with Afghanistan, a claim that all subsequent Afghan governments have contested. Additionally, since the Pakistani government refused to take responsibility for

---

55 Barfield, *Afghanistan: A Cultural and Political History*, 153-154; Rasanayagam, *Afghanistan: A Modern History*, 11.
56 After the division of British India in 1947, Peshawar became a part of Pakistan.
57 Barfield, *The Durand Line*, 4.

governing some of the territory adjacent to the Afghanistan-Pakistan border (the FATA), it resulted in a lack of effective governance and the perpetuation of political alienation in the region.

The Durand Line was an imperial necessity rather than a topographic reality. Perceiving Russian interest in the Indian subcontinent, the British feared that their monopoly in India might be challenged. The British also believed that Russia had designs on Afghanistan as a conduit to warm water port access in the Indian subcontinent, which would enhance Russia's economic power and present a strong challenge to British hegemony. Afghanistan thus became a buffer state between the two imperial powers.

In effect, the Durand Line provided two benefits to the British: the Raj could take over areas that were easy to administer by excluding troublesome tribal areas, and it could create a buffer zone against a perceived Russian incursion into the Indian subcontinent.[58] David Isby has argued that Britain created the frontiers of Afghanistan without any intention of making it a cohesive or self-supporting country. The creation of Afghanistan began its legacy as a pawn in the conflicts of other nations, including Britain, Russia, India, Iran, Pakistan, and the United States.[59]

Unlike Afghanistan's international boundaries with Russia in the north or Iran in the west, which were recognized by all involved parties at the time of their creation, the natives on the British India-Afghanistan border refused to recognize the legitimacy of Britain's political demarcation. In 1947, the Afghans described the 1893 British negotiations with the Amir for Durand Line creation as an internal colonial issue rather than an international one.[60] The Durand Line was imposed on the region without regard for ground realities; as such, the status of the Durand Line remains controversial.

For all practical purposes, the border does not exist for the majority of Pashtun tribes inhabiting the frontier in eastern and southern Afghanistan.[61] Pashtuns, the largest tribal group in the world, constitute the overwhelming majority in this region, which has been a haven to the al Qaeda network, the Taliban, and other militants who engaged in violence against U.S. forces in Afghanistan and Indian forces in Kashmir. Additionally, the Taliban operating on both sides of the Afghanistan-Pakistan border are predominantly Pashtuns.[62]

---

58 Barfield, *Afghanistan: A Cultural and Political History*, 139
59 Isby, *Afghanistan: Graveyard of Empires*.
60 Johnson and Mason, "No Sign Until the Burst of Fire," 69; Siddiqi, "Afghanistan-Pakistan Relations," 11.
61 Johnson and Mason, "No Sign Until the Burst of Fire," 68.
62 Barfield, *The Durand Line*, 1-19.

When Afghanistan became fully independent in 1919, it accepted the Durand Line as its de facto border with British India. Before the British left the Indian subcontinent in 1947, a referendum was held in the North-West Frontier Province in British India regarding the possibility of its populace joining Pakistan.[63] The Afghan government protested that the referendum must include two additional choices: the union of the North-West Frontier Province with Afghanistan, or the establishment of separate Pashtun nation. The British ignored Afghan demands.

The people of NWFP voted to join Pakistan; as a result, Afghanistan challenged the proposal, questioning the continuing validity of the Durand Line as a legitimate international boundary. When Pakistan became an independent state, Kabul revived its earlier objections to the Line's legitimacy; since then, the contentious border has been used as a bargaining tool by successive Afghan governments. Though Pakistan has declared the Durand Line its international border with Afghanistan, Afghanistan has claimed since 1947 that the border created by the departing colonialists was invalid, as the treaty was signed under duress.[64]

After a loya jirga in 1949 in Afghanistan declared the Durand Line invalid,[65] subsequent Afghan governments have proposed the creation of Pashtunistan, an independent state for Pashtun people. The Pashtun dominated Awami National Party (ANP) of Afghanistan also agitated for the creation of a new Pashtun province in Afghanistan, which would incorporate majority Pashtun areas from the Pakistan side of the border. Afghanistan proposed that during the partition of British India, the adjoining Pashtun regions of British India should have been offered the additional option of either becoming an independent state or joining with Afghanistan. Furthermore, Afghans argued that the various agreements between British India and Afghanistan, including the Durand Line, lapsed when the British left South Asia. Imperial agreements could not be transferable to the new state of Pakistan, a successor state to British India. The Durand Line remained illegitimate because the British had coerced Afghanistan into accepting its proposal. The antagonism between the Afghan and Pakistan governments was so fierce that Afghanistan was the only nation that opposed entry of Pakistan in United Nations in 1947, and most Afghan maps still show the territory across the border as Pashtunistan, beginning the Pakistan boundary at Punjab.[66]

---

63 Referenda concerning whether the people wished to join Pakistan or India were held in the Punjab and Bengal provinces.
64 For a discussion, see Emadi, "Durand Line and Afghan-Pak Relations," 1515-1516; Khurshid Hasan, "Pakistan-Afghanistan Relations," *Asian Survey* 2, no. 7 (1962): 41-77; Johnson and Mason, "No Sign Until the Burst of Fire," 41-77; Nazif M. Shahrani, "War, Factionalism, and the State in Afghanistan," *American Anthropologist New Series* 104, no. 3 (2002): 715-722.
65 A jirga is a gathering to make communal decisions and to settle local problems. A loya jirga is equivalent to a grand council convened to make major decisions.
66 Barfield, *The Durand Line*, 7.

Relations between Afghanistan and Pakistan further deteriorated in 1973 when Mohammed Daoud Khan, the Prime Minister of Afghanistan (1953-1963), deposed his first cousin and the king of Afghanistan, Mohammad Zahir Shah. Daoud provided sanctuary, arms, and ammunition to Pashtun and Baloch nationalist groups in order to support the creation of Pashtunistan. Zulfikar Ali Bhutto, who served as President of Pakistan from 1971-73 and as Pakistan's Prime Minister from 1973-77, responded to Daoud by supporting radical Islamist factions inside Afghanistan. Zulfikar Ali Bhutto's government also supported Afghan radicals in order to counterbalance what Pakistan saw as the pro-India and pro-Soviet policies of Daoud. This will be elaborated on further in chapters related to Soviet-Afghan War, but it is sufficient to state here that Pakistan's support for radical Islamists[67] began long before the Pakistani dictator General Mohammad

---

67 Since there will be a discussion of radicalization, Islamism, and militant Islam, a clarification about the terminology is in order.

The diversity of the Muslim world makes it difficult to use standardized and monolithic terms. Islamism is one such term that has been used loosely in contemporary discourse. While Islamism is variously described as instrumental use of Islam for political purposes on one end of the spectrum all the way to "a religious ideology with a holistic interpretation of Islam whose final aim is the conquest of the world by all means," both of these definitions presuppose that there is an agreement or understanding over goals of Islam.

As Anders Strindberg and Mats Warn note in *Islamism: Religion, Radicalization, and Resistance* (Cambridge: Polity, 2011), defining Islamism is fraught with difficulty because the key concepts within Islam differ widely, and local and regional agendas can vary greatly based on the needs of local constituencies. I define Islamism as instrumental use of Islam for political purposes within the context of the movement we are analyzing. Thus, in case of the Taliban, Islamism would be within the context of Afghanistan's colonial history, its weak governance, the communist-influenced regime of President Daoud and others, the Soviet invasion, and the inter-ethnic rivalries between the Pashtun, Hazara, Tajik, and other tribes. It also exists within the schema of Afghanistan's geo-political manipulation by India, Pakistan, United States, Iran, and Soviet Union/Russia. Needless to say, Afghan Islamism cannot really be compared to that of the Muslim Brotherhood of Egypt or of Hamas in Palestine.

The term *Islamist* need not be seen as threatening or pejorative. There is nothing radical or militant about Islamists, individuals who advocate that their states adopt Islam. Despite seeking a separate state for South Asia's Muslims, Pakistan's founder, Mohammad Ali Jinnah, was a secular and moderate individual who envisioned Hindus, Sikhs, and other minorities living peacefully in Pakistan with its Muslim majority. In Jinnah's conception of an Islamic nation, religion was personal and unrelated to the affairs of state. However, carrying the political ideology of Islam to the next step, with the focus on Islam as the centerpiece of the state, does not necessarily guarantee intolerance. Malaysia, for example, has claimed Islam as its official religion; nevertheless, though 80% of its population is Muslim, the state still guarantees other religious minorities their religious freedom.

In this book, I eschew the term Islamist and instead use the terms "radical Islamists" or "militant jihadis" when I am speaking within the context of asymmetric warfare and terrorism. As such, I would describe the ideology of the Taliban, al Qaeda, and other militant groups that use violence and coercion to dominate over others and stifle political disagreements (including those who follow Islam) as radical Islamists.

Zia ul Haq attempted to introduce orthodoxy and extremism in what had been a nominally Islamic nation. (Previously, Pakistan had been run by a secular elite with a history of exploiting Islam but eschewing religious orthodoxy in state affairs.)

The Durand Line created boundary disputes in South Asia and directly contributed to radical South Asian politics, including the utilization of extremists Islamists by Pakistan. President Daoud, who refused to recognize the Durand Line, consistently demanded that an independent, Afghan-linked Pashtunistan should be established in the Pashtun areas that had belonged to Afghanistan before British annexation. Prime Minister Bhutto retaliated against Daoud by sending and supporting anti-Daoud fighters in Afghanistan's ethnic minority areas. In a statement to journalist Selig Harrison, Bhutto said,

> Two can play at the same game. We know where their weak points are, just as they know ours. The non-Pashtuns there hate Pashtun domination. So we have our ways of persuading Daoud not to aggravate our problems.[68]

Pakistan has also been concerned with Afghanistan's exploitation of separatists in Baluchistan and the NWFP. Disaffected Balochis and Pashtuns in those regions have, since Pakistan's creation, argued that Baluchistan and the NWFP effectively have been the colonies of Pakistan, as they were of British India. The British-created border thus became a source of internecine warfare between the native successor regimes in the subcontinent, and unfortunately they have been unable to see past their immediate conflicts to identify the colonial roots of their disputes over boundaries and identities.

Although the people on the eastern side of the Line were absorbed into British Indian Empire, they retained an unusual stateless status. The British indirectly exercised control in those areas by appointing dictatorial proxies, "Political Agents" who worked through local clan leaders and employed the draconian punishments afforded by the Frontier Crimes Regulations (FCR) of 1901, which included house-burning and group punishments without the right of appeal. Even though it is a part of Pakistan now, the FATA was ruled for over six decades by colonial-era FCR regulations.

When I use the term "radicalization" or "radicalism" as related to Islam, I refer to the particular form of Islam that is not only political, but also prepared to impose itself on others both through state power as well as using violent non-state actors. In radical Islam, modernity, syncretism, and prevailing ancient practices are rejected from the discourse, and, instead, the actors seek a glorified past and a puritanical form of Islam subject to their interpretation. For a further discussion, see Mehdi Mozaffari, "What is Islamism? History and Definition of a Concept," *Totalitarian Movements and Political Religions* 8, no. 1 (2007): 17-33.

68 Diego Cordovez and Selig S. Harrison, *Out of Afghanistan: The Inside Story of the Soviet Withdrawal* (New York Oxford: Oxford University Press, 1995), 61.

For those six decades, no serious attempts were made to assimilate the FATA region into Pakistan. Instead, Pakistan continued Britain's colonial policy, keeping the area ungoverned, marginalizing its population, and exploiting the Pashtuns, including aiding various Pashtun factions during the Afghan civil war as it suited the state's needs. National Pakistani law did not apply in these territories and the central government had only indirect control over its people, creating a paradoxical situation for the border region across the Durand Line, where an international boundary exists but where the state claiming the territory does not or cannot exercise authority over the people who live there.[69] And it is only as recently as 2011 that Pakistan's government has allowed political parties to operate in the FATA.[70]

After Britain's departure, the Pakistani government kept the FATA as a region in which the laws of Pakistan existed but were not enforced. Beginning in 1948, Pakistan recruited an armed Pashtun group from the region across the Durand Line to fight the Indians in Kashmir. Furthermore, during the Soviet invasion of Afghanistan, the Directorate for Inter-Service Intelligence (ISI), Pakistan's spy agency, created a network of camps on both sides of the Durand Line to manufacture and support insurgency against the Soviets.[71] In the 1980s, the ISI brought into the area militants engaged in terrorist actions in Kashmir. The ISI used both sides of the Line to support terrorist and insurgent networks, providing safe houses, logistics, communications, transportation, and a supportive population. This network was expanded in the 1990s with Pakistan's support of the Taliban and other militant organizations such as Harkat-ul-Mujahedin (HM), Jamaat-e-Islami (JI), Lashkar-e-Taiba (LeT), Jaish-e-Mohammad (JeM), Hizb-ul-Mujahideen (HuM), to name only a few.[72]

In these circumstances, the Taliban's ideology, which supported the belief that the Durand Line should not be a barrier to the Pashtuns it divided, made the region across the Durand Line a hotbed of insurgency and terrorism. When the

---

69 Shabana Fayyaz, "Towards a Durable Peace in Waziristan," *Pakistan Security Research Unit Brief* Number 10 (2007): 4-5. See also Barfield, *The Durand Line*.
70 "Frontier Crimes Regulation Amended: Political Activities Allowed in FATA," *Daily Times*, August 13, 2011.
71 For a detailed overview, see Steve Coll, *Ghost Wars: The Secret History of the CIA, Afghanistan, and Bin Laden, from the Soviet Invasion to September 10, 2001* (New York: Penguin Books, 2004); Haqqānī, *Pakistan: Between Mosque And Military*; Rashid, *Descent into Chaos*.
72 For additional information and analysis, see Ryan Clarke, "Lashkar-I-Taiba: The Fallacy of Subservient Proxies and the Future of Islamist Terrorism in India," *The Letort Papers* (Carlisle, PA: Strategic Studies Institute, U.S. Army War College, 2010); Fair, "The Militant Challenge in Pakistan," 105-137; C. Christine Fair, "Lashkar-e-Tayiba and the Pakistani State," Survival 53, no. 4 (2011): 29-52; Nicholas Howenstein, "The Jihadi Terrain in Pakistan: An Introduction to the Sunni Jihadi Groups in Pakistan and Kashmir," *Pakistan Security Research Unit Research Report* 1 (2008): 28-31; Jones, "Pakistan's Dangerous Game," 15-49; Jones, "The Terrorist Threat from Pakistan," 1-25; Rashid, *Descent into Chaos*.

Soviets arrived in Afghanistan, the United States tacitly supported the insurgent networks that Pakistan had created across the Durand Line, ignoring the terrorist networks and camps being used to train insurgents to wage war in Kashmir. This situation changed dramatically in 2001 when the United States military removed the Taliban government in Afghanistan. As the Islamists fled into Pakistan, the United States pressed upon Pakistan the need to end FATA and Baluchistan's role as safe havens for the Taliban and other Islamic radicals. With American troops based in Afghanistan's border areas, the question of where the border was, along with the question of Pakistan's responsibilities for maintaining order in its own territories, acquired international significance. The porous nature of the Durand Line and the quasi-autonomous status of the region on both sides of the Line had a serious impact on U.S.-led operations against the Taliban and al Qaeda in Afghanistan because insurgents could launch attacks in Afghanistan and regroup in safe havens on the Pakistani side. In this way, the vestiges of colonial-era expediencies that left the frontier region ungoverned by Pakistan's national government facilitated the emergence of violent Islamists and establishment of their safe havens in the region proximate to the Durand Line.[73]

Conflicts surrounding the Durand Line are the legacy of colonial decisions made more than a century ago in British India. The Line is not merely the locus of a border dispute between Afghanistan and Pakistan; it is an illustration of the unresolved social, economic, and historical relationships that still impact Afghanistan and Pakistan as nations, South Asia as a region, and ultimately, the rest of the world.

THE HISTORY OF THE SUBCONTINENT'S PEOPLE

The country we now call India has had an extremely diverse population for millennia, but two conflicting forces have been apparent from the time Britain established its colonial rule in the region and through its departure from the subcontinent: one was the emergence of a unitary nationalism, which evolved from myriad diverse populations in opposition to the British rule; the second was the deteriorating relations between the two main social groups—Hindus and Muslims—which eventually became adversarial.[74] It was this schism between the Hindu and Muslim communities, aggravated by the divergent interests and attitudes of the

---

73 For a discussion of the context and dynamics of Taliban insurgency in Pakistan-Afghanistan, see Ghufran, "Pashtun Ethnonationalism and the Taliban Insurgency in the North West Frontier Province of Pakistan," 1092-1114; Barnett R. Rubin and Abubakar Siddique, "Resolving the Pakistan-Afghanistan Stalemate," *United States Institute of Peace Special Report* (2006), 1-7; Siddiqi, "Afghanistan-Pakistan Relations," 1-55.

74 This is stated while keeping in mind that these two social groupings are in no way homogeneous or monolithic.

Hindu elite in the Indian National Congress and the Muslim elite of the Indian Muslim League, that provided the grounds for subcontinent's partition in 1947. Emerging Hindu and Muslim nationalisms, economic competition, and each group's perception of its cultural and religious "domination" at the hands of the other group created deep anxieties within both communities. These anxieties did not go unnoticed: especially within the context of political competition between the Congress and the League, the British used, manipulated, and exacerbated their political and social differences in order to subvert emerging Indian nationalism and perpetuate their own colonial rule. This competition between Hindus and Muslims, with Britain as its arbiter, culminated in the partition of India.

It will be argued in subsequent chapters that the partition of British India is responsible for creating boundary disputes and conditions for radical and violent political Islam in the region. In order to understand the emergence, localization, and persistence of violent jihadi groups in this region, it is essential to understand the history, nature, interactions and collisions of the subcontinent's social groupings before and during the colonial era. Additionally, the concept of "India" as a unified entity must be addressed. Since the thesis of this book suggests that the division of India was based on engineered abstractions that consequently destabilized South Asia and contributed to extant terrorism, it is prudent to explore whether a unified India—whether a predominantly unified "Hindu" or a predominantly unified "Muslim" India—ever existed before colonial rule in the region.

Richard Eaton's study of ancient texts suggests that during the past millennium, language evolved as the identifying feature of the peoples of the Indian subcontinent. In the south, the language of Andhra—Telugu—was used to identify people as far back as 1053.[75] Similarly, in Marathi religious texts from the thirteenth and fourteenth centuries, geographical divisions were defined with reference to linguistic characteristics. Nation state formation in these regions thus could be connected to geographical as well as linguistic similarities and boundaries. Eaton's work has shown that ruling chiefs in Deccan's interior regions patronized local vernacular languages, as opposed to Sanskrit or other regional languages in twelfth and thirteenth centuries. Furthermore, Eaton suggests that during this period, birth-ascribed caste rankings are absent in the inscriptional records. Instead of caste (jati), or caste-rank (varna), occupational status appeared to be the main feature of an individual's identity. This suggests that social status was

---

75 Richard M. Eaton, *A Social History of the Deccan, 1300-1761: Eight Indian Lives*, New Cambridge History of India. Vol. 1, pt. 8, 1st ed. (Cambridge: Cambridge University Press, 2005), 13.

not necessarily inherited, which meant that identity could be more or less fluid.[76] Eaton's findings provide a compelling argument against the claim that there was a monolithic Hindu religion that enforced a rigid, hierarchical caste system.

In the series of empires in the Indian subcontinent dating from the Kushan Empire in early first century ACE, rulers often belonged to a religious minority and were themselves migrants to the region. India had been subject to waves of invasions from western raiders for over two millennia. By the 13th century, the Muslim conquest had reached Delhi, expanding into southern India during the next century. The Muslim warriors who settled in India included, among others, Turks, Persians, and Afghans. The Delhi Sultanates, whose rulers comprised of Sunni Muslims, ruled from 1206 ACE until their defeat at the hands of the Mughals during the 16th century. When the Mughals took power, the people of India had already acclimated to their Muslim conquerors.

The governance of a diverse population with distinctive religious, ethnic, linguistic, cultural, and historical differences required the assent of the ruled. The alternative—to "rule by the sword"—would be enormously expensive and involve unceasing military campaigns. The foreign rulers who had adopted India as their native state had instead learned to rule by assimilation and accommodation, using force only when those tactics failed. Muslim regimes prior to the Mughals had used local Hindu warriors and aristocrats to maintain order and help extract taxes in the countryside. Similarly, under the Mughal rule, local Hindu kings and chieftains became a part of the Muslim political order. The warrior Hindu castes, including the famed Rajputs and Marathas, were allowed to dominate in their regions provided that they accept Mughal suzerainty. To administer their vast empire, Muslim Mughals relied heavily on Hindu generals, moneylenders, and administrators.

The founder of the Mughals, Emperor Babar, was born in central Asia and was thus a migrant to India, which meant that the Mughal Empire ruled over a predominantly alien culture and religion. However, over the years, the Mughal dynasty became indisputably Indian, as their political focus was on India and not their ancestral lands.[77]

In order to adjust to the new political order that had supplanted the Hindu kings, the Hindu castes specializing in trade and secretarial tasks learned Persian, the language of the court, as well as the administrative procedures required by the Indo-Muslim state. In respect to the rest of the native population, several

---

76 Eaton, *A Social History of the Deccan*, 15-16.
77 John F. Richards, *The Mughal Empire*, New Cambridge History of India. Vol. 1, pt. 5, 3rd ed. (Cambridge University Press, 1996), 2.

accommodations had to be made in order to satisfy both communities. For example, in around 1720, in the Mughal successor states of Hyderabad, the ruler—the Nizam—was an Urdu-speaking Muslim ruling over an overwhelming 90% Hindu population. The Nizam used Persian as an official language, despite the fact that the population itself mostly spoke native languages, including Telugu (46%), Marathi (26%), and Kannada (14%). Additionally, only ten percent of Hyderabad's people were Muslim.[78] Despite this vast difference, the Nizam and his people were able to accommodate one another relatively peacefully, and this was a pattern that was common throughout the subcontinent. The rulers and the ruled of the Indian subcontinent managed to exist within an inclusive framework of difference throughout centuries of foreign rulers. This mode of governance and assimilation underwent a violent and destructive change upon the arrival of the British, who emphasized the differences between themselves and the people they were ruling and refused to assimilate into a larger Indian culture.

Imperial rulers in any colony must seek out supporters from among their native subjects. The British did this by engaging in a sophisticated process of defining and labeling their peoples on the Indian subcontinent, identifying groups that might be shaped to serve the Raj.[79] Once the 1857 Rebellion challenged their control on the subcontinent, Britain's need to identify and mobilize supporters became even more critical. Consequently, British actions promoted the boundaries between and within populations. As nationalism and resistance against the British Raj began to evolve, the Raj mobilized its supporters with by manipulating the divisions they had created between different populations. As a result, these group differences became reified, resulting in conflict and violence among the native populations.

Evidence suggests that the geographical, cultural, ethnic, and religious diversity of the subcontinent had prevailed for millennia. Different empires had periodically unified India but had generally ruled by accommodating group differences rather than exploiting them. Kings and chieftains could be of a different religious community than those they ruled. In fact, there is nothing in pre-colonial history to suggest that there would be a bloody conflagration between the Hindus and Muslims in the 20th century that would result in India's division along religious fault lines. It was not until the last three decades of British rule that Hindu-Muslim relations significantly deteriorated, and this happened as Indian nationalism against the Raj grew stronger. Even then, the notion that Hindus and Muslims would be unable to share a state was not pronounced until the last seven years of the imperial rule. Several imperial decisions facilitated this schism.

---

78 Ramusack, *The Indian Princes and Their States*, 210.
79 For a detailed analysis, see Thomas R. Metcalf, *Ideologies of the Raj*, The New Cambridge History of India. Vol. 3, pt. 4, 2nd ed. (Cambridge: Cambridge University Press, 1997).

Institutionalizing Differences

The vast Indian Empire was managed by a relatively small number of British civil servants. At the end of the nineteenth century, approximately 6,000 British officials governed about 300 million subjects. Forced to rely on such a small number of British personnel, the Indian Army consisted mostly of native soldiers, so the British required innovative and efficient means to govern their distant colonial territory. While their ultimate tool of governance was iron-fisted repression, Britain's preferred strategy was to seek collaborators among the native populations.

As mentioned in the previous chapter, due to the Bengal Army's primary role in the 1857 Rebellion, the British Indian Army's recruitment practices were made overtly discriminatory against Bengali Hindus and other upper caste groups. Employing the racist rhetoric of the "martial races," Britain divided the natives in order to prevent them from unifying in resistance to their colonial government. In 1871, the introduction a new administrative tool—the decennial census—further divided native communities. In Ian Talbot's words, "the new institution of the census was the crowning glory of the colonial rational bureaucratic state."[80]

The British used the information that their census provided both to gain knowledge of their colonial subjects and to extract revenue from them. The Indian population was classified into mutually exclusive groups, even though in reality the boundaries between the diverse socio-religious groups were fluid and dynamic. The Mughal Empire had previously mapped and measured the land under its control for revenue estimation and extraction, but unlike the British, the Mughal state did not conduct a census of persons. As Arjun Appadurai notes, "Enumeration of various things was certainly part of the Mughal state *imaginaire* as was the acknowledgment of group identities, *but not the enumeration of group identities.*"[81] Pre-colonial non-Mughal states in the subcontinent used enumeration for taxation, accounting, and land revenue collection, but they did not seem to be concerned with enumerating group identities or the population at large.

In Britain's Indian census, people were forced to identify themselves according to religious, caste, and tribal categories. Those who could not define their religion or described it as other than a recognized religion were classified as a "Hindu."[82] Interestingly, the "religious" category was not a part of Britain's own domestic census at the time; the fact that it was a central component of the Indian census reveals the Orientalist bias behind the "objective" fact gathering the British were

---

80 Ian Talbot, *India and Pakistan: Inventing the Nation* (London: Arnold, 2000), 13.
81 Arjun Appadurai, "Number in the Colonial Imagination," in *Orientalism and the Postcolonial Predicament: Perspectives on South Asia*, ed. C. A. Breckenridge and P. V. D. Veer (Philadelphia: University of Pennsylvania Press, 1993), 329.
82 Ibid., 314-339; Metcalf, *Ideologies of the Raj*.

conducting. These kinds of distinctions would go on to have a significant impact on identity and self-perception within subcontinent's communities. The categories of a colonial tool that would comprise a significant part of Britain's emerging political understanding of India was eventually internalized by the native Indians, shaping their conceptions of themselves and each other.

The introduction of census to India, with its emphasis on clearly demarcated religious, caste, and ethnic categories, created new communities and restructured those that already existed. For example, the census category of "depressed classes" aggregated different untouchable groups with no real commonalities.[83] Leather workers, street sweepers, and village servants from different regions and communities were lumped into a single classification, regardless of the fact that neither these groups nor other Indian groups would classify them as a uniform community. In many ways, these "imagined" communities in the Indian subcontinent owe their clear delineation to British rule. The census' rigid system of pre-defined categories could not reflect the subcontinent's diverse population. It was conducted and controlled by imperial administrators whose Orientalist preconceptions about Indian society were supplemented chiefly by informants selected from the native elite and it reflected their biases as well. Eventually, the census would construct political groups and shape ethnic and social identities. It has been suggested that census enumeration initiated during the British rule contributed significantly to modern politicized communities in India, changing the dynamics of interaction and accommodation in the political arena and later resulting in large-scale violence.[84]

As colonial subjects learned that their census information was being used in state affairs, including the recruitment of specific groups for specific jobs, they began to manipulate this new imperial classification system. For example, when the British decided which communities were "manly" enough to provide recruits for the Indian Army, Indians found it beneficial to misrepresent their caste or grouping if they wanted to join. This indicates that the colonial subjects were able to manipulate imperial requirements when it suited them, but that it also had a lasting effect on them and their self-identities. Toward the end of the nineteenth century, census reports led to the development of an imperial framework that listed and assigned people of particular titles and backgrounds to certain orders or statuses. People were divided into honorable sounding "ruling" or "military"

---

83 The lowest rank in the caste system in India, which was considered below the four main castes. A higher caste individual would consider him- or herself polluted if touched by an "untouchable" (hence, the moniker).
84 For additional analysis, see Appadurai, "Number in the Colonial Imagination," 314-339; Bernard S. Cohn, "Census, Social Structure and Objectification in South Asia," in *The Bernard Cohn Omnibus* (Delhi: Oxford University Press, 2004), 224-254.

castes, or in contrast, "scavenger" and "lower village menial" groups. Britain's census and its declarations about caste, religion, race, blood and nationality, which were really products of the way the state operated, imposed upon Indians identities from above and influenced their ideologies of faith and nationhood.[85]

In pre-colonial times, Indian people and their rulers had a different kind of relationship, a relationship that was never defined solely by religion. During two thousand years of invasions, assimilation, and rule by diverse sovereigns who did not necessarily share the religions, cultures, and the languages of their subjects, the subcontinent had developed dynamic, interdependent cultural, economic, and social linkages. Perhaps its most remarkable feature was the way that multiple layers of sovereignty developed: each social group was allowed to have multiple identities. The British-Indian census, on the other hand, created rigid monolithic categories and shaped and consolidated diverse identities into mutually exclusive ones.

The British actually aided the emergence of Indian nationalism by identifying subjects under religious categories—Hindu, Sikh, Christian, or Muslim—while ignoring cultural, ethnic, linguistic, regional, caste, occupational, and class differences. Often, the differences that separated co-religionists had been stronger than the singular commonality offered by religious affiliation. The groupings thus provided a sense of connectedness in heretofore fragmented, cross-cultural, and diffusible identities. British administrative classification bundled together high and low castes of linguistically, culturally, socially, economically, and geographically diverse groups by creating a new, monolithic "Hinduism"; similarly, elite Muslims and poor native converts to Islam, each from different geographical cultural, linguistic, historic, social and economic groups, were pigeonholed together to create a monolithic "Islam." The natives were not passive participants in this enterprise. In response to the census and its method of classifying castes and communities, as well as the way it ranked them in accordance with their ritual "purity" and standing in local society, people began petitioning the administration for placement in a "higher" order of caste precedence. One census commissioner's observations are quite revealing:

> Muslim Rajputs in large numbers suddenly, between 1901 and 1911, took to calling themselves Pathans, the title Singh yielding place to Khan. Practically all... [Muslims] of low degree – weavers, oil-pressers,

---

85 Susan Bayly, Caste, *Society and Politics in India from the Eighteenth Century to the Modern Age*, New Cambridge History of India. Vol. 4, pt. 3. (Cambridge: Cambridge University Press, 1999), 126.

barbers and so on – aspired to the status of Sheikh, though the better class Mussalmans would not recognize them, nor would they recognize each other as such.[86]

The colonial administration constructed institutions and shaped native Indian society; meanwhile, the natives attempted to use colonial institutions for their own betterment. This challenge-and-response dynamic between the Raj and its subjects evolved throughout imperial rule. As Van der Veer concludes:

> The "establishment" of both the Hindu majority and the Muslim minority as social and political categories… was largely the result of the manner of classification, not of preexisting facts. To some extent one may say that the project of the colonial state created these facts. Again, this is not to say that there was no division of Hindu and Muslim communities in the precolonial period. There was: the division was not a colonial invention. But to count these communities and to have leaders represent them was a colonial novelty, and it was fundamental to emergence of religious nationalism.[87]

The colonial bureaucracy's expedient creation of administrative groupings, combined with its exploitation of group differences in order to perpetuate the Raj, led to serious communal problems as it promoted a severe new split in India based on religious differences.[88] This split was Britain's key means of perpetuating its colonial rule, especially during the inter-war years, and British policy has been blamed for much of the subsequent communal violence in India as well as the strained relations between the Hindus, Sikhs, and the Muslims in the region. These conditions continue to destabilize the region even decades after the British departed from the subcontinent.[89]

Indeed, historians have suggested that British colonialism on the Indian subcontinent contributed to postcolonial violence precisely because it constructed oppositional identities (specifically between the majority Hindus and the minority Muslims, but also class-based distinctions), exacerbated communal differences,

---

86 Gyanendra Pandey, *The Construction of Communalism in Colonial North India*, (New Delhi: Oxford University Press, 1990), 83-84.
87 Peter V. D. Veer, *Religious Nationalism: Hindus and Muslims in India* (Berkeley: University of California Press, 1994), 19.
88 "Communal," a pejorative term, is widely used across South Asia to describe the systematic misuse of religion, including manufacturing prejudice, tension, violence, and conflict between communities, for political purposes.
89 Cf. Ishtiaq Ahmed, "The 1947 Partition of India: A Paradigm for Pathological Politics in India and Pakistan," *Asian Ethnicity* 3, no. 1 (2002): 9-28; William A. Green and John P. Deasy, "Unifying Themes in the History of British India, 1757-1857: An Historiographical Analysis," *Albion: A Quarterly Journal Concerned with British Studies* 17, no. 1 (1985): 15-45; Mushirul Hasan, *India Partitioned: The Other Face of Freedom* (New Delhi: Roli Books, 1997); Page, *Prelude to Partition*; Gyanendra Pandey, *Remembering Partition: Violence, Nationalism and History in India* (Cambridge: Cambridge University Press, 2001); Pandey, *The Construction of Communalism in Colonial North India*; Narendra Singh Sarila, *The Shadow of the Great Game: The Untold Story of India's Partition* (New York: Carroll, Graff Publishers, 2005).

and imposed arbitrary political borders (by dividing the subcontinent into India and Pakistan, for instance).[90] Furthermore, historians have also suggested that the changing the abstract concept of Hinduism into objective reality was largely in response to the dynamic patron-client relationships between Hindus, Muslims, the British, and other groups due to the shifting patron-client relationships as the rulers changed into the ruled with a change in empire.

Conflict between Hindus and Muslims or Muslims and Sikhs predated Britain's arrival in India. Group conflicts and differences typically manifested as riots between the subcontinent's communities. In some cases, these communities had existed in proximity with one another for centuries. For example, violent conflicts between the "left hand" and "right hand" castes were documented in the 17th century.[91] From around the eleventh century until the nineteenth century, several caste factions in South India, under the category of *Idangai* (left hand) and *Valangai* (right hand), were involved in a rivalry that often manifested in violence. The disputes between the communities were related to symbols, rites and precedents; to groups' social, economic and political life; and to local power grabs. Thus violent inter-group conflicts existed in the Indian subcontinent in neighboring communities though these conflicts were not necessarily the result of a unified religious identity or affiliation. What the British imagined as implacable and irreconcilable religious conflict between the Hindus and the Muslims was not a monolithic religious conflict, but had other socio-economic reasons that were given a convenient color of religion by the colonialists.

Using colonial records of significant "riots" from 1809 onwards, Gyanendra Pandey has provided evidence that several riots between Hindus and Muslims might have been influenced by the way in which rich Hindus (who were considered exploitative) lent money to the poor Muslim weaver class (its own separate class within the social underclass).[92] In this case, the conflict between the Hindu moneylenders and the Muslim weavers was not really about religion, or at least, religion played a secondary role. At its heart, the conflict was truly about economic grievances. However, due to colonial preconceptions and stereotypes that have foregrounded the importance of religious classifications, class-based conflicts due to economic grievances have been described and erroneously documented as

---

90 See also Samar Hasan, "India and Pakistan: Common Identity and Conflict," *Refugee Survey Quarterly* 24, no. 4 (2005): 74-80; Ashis Nandy, *Intimate Enemy: Loss and Recovery of Self Under Colonialism* (Delhi: Oxford University Press, 1983); Brian Pennington, *Was Hinduism Invented? Britons, Indians, and the Colonial Construction of Religion* (New York: Oxford University Press, 2005); Page, *Prelude to Partition*.
91 Gijs Kruijtzer, *Xenophobia in Seventeenth-Century India*. (Leiden: Leiden University Press, 2009), 105-152.
92 For a detailed analysis, see Pandey, *The Construction of Communalism in Colonial North India*.

religious riots. Pandey's research on the Muzaffarabad weaver community and the accounts of riots in the village demonstrate that so-called "Hindu" and "Muslim" politics were actually expressions of several distinctive subdivisions.

Christopher Bayly has also indicated that group differences based on religion existed before and during the colonial period.[93] However, he questions whether any broader or homogeneous Hindu or Muslim or Sikh "consciousness" existed during colonization. If it did exist, it is unknown the extent to which such a consciousness provided an impetus for intergroup conflict. For example, as Francis Robinson argues:

> That Muslim identity would become a prime theatre of activity did not seem likely in the eighteenth century. Amongst Muslims who were descended from, or who liked to claim that they were descended from, those who had migrated to India to seek service at its many Muslim courts–Turks, Persians, Arabs, Afghans–their Muslim identity was not a matter of overriding concern. At the courts of the Mughals they divided not into Hindu and Muslim factions but into Turkish and Persian ones. They shared their Persian high culture with Hindus, including their poetry which rejected Indian life and landscape as fit subjects for poetic response and found its imaginative horizons in Iran and Central Asia.[94]

Muslim identity was variously constructed based on a number of factors, including regional culture, language, the place of one's settlement, and whether a given individual was Shia or Sunni. The vast majority of Indian Muslims were descended from converts to Islam and expressed themselves through the regional cultures and languages of India: Bengali, Tamil, Malayalam, Gujarati, Sindhi, Punjabi, and so on. The syncretic traditions of converted Muslims made it difficult to classify them within a monolithic and static "Muslim" identity. In fact, such syncretism could be described as an "Indian religion" as expressed through different localized religious idioms.[95] Within some local Sufi cults, religious participation was not exclusive and people of all faiths participated in expressions classically understood to be Muslim.

When the British arrived, Muslims had ruled over a predominantly Hindu population for seven centuries.[96] First, note that the conventional chronological tendency of historians has been to divide Indian history into periods of religious

---

[93] Christopher A. Bayly, "The Pre-history of 'Communalism'? Religious Conflict in India," *Modern Asian Studies* 9, no. 2 (1985): 177-203.
[94] Francis Robinson, "The British Empire and Muslim Identity in South Asia," *Transactions of the Royal Historical Society (Sixth Series)* 8 (1998), 271.
[95] Ibid., 272
[96] It should be kept in mind that unless the concept of religious affiliation was absolutely static in the subcontinent (which would be difficult to establish), religious identity alone may not tell us much about group affiliations, interactions, or hostility, across the span of seven centuries. As Talbot says, "Communities of the past were not identical to those of the present." Ian Talbot, *India and Pakistan (Inventing the Nation)*, 2st ed. (London: Arnold, 2000)

rule, moving from ancient "Hindu" India to pre-colonial and medieval "Muslim" India. These divisions are based on Orientalist assumptions, and are thus oversimplified and inaccurate, as well as damaging to our understanding of the complexity of Indian identity in a given period. As Jalal notes, "naming entire periods of history by the religious affiliation of rulers makes no allowance for the multiple social identities of the ruled."[97] Indeed, a substantial body of research shows that the categories "Hindu" and "Muslim" were institutionalized only after the establishment of British colonial rule.[98] While one might reasonably conclude that differences between the various diverse communities of India have existed for millennia, social identities within populations were much more flexible and variable before British colonial administrators imposed on them a system of fixed identity.

Ironically, it was when Indian communities opposed colonial rule that communal differences became reified and intensified to the point of xenophobia. In Religions in Conflict, Antony Copley quotes Susan Bayly's conclusion that "[a]t no time in the immediate pre-colonial period was there a clear and unambiguous process at work by which the boundaries between different south Indian groups or communities were being irrevocably hardened."[99] Bayly claims that the British East India Company's rule severed the ritual relationships and schemes of honor and incorporation that had integrated earlier kingdoms, resulting in the emergence of more rapid and exclusive "communal boundaries."[100]

There are several examples from the pre-colonial and colonial periods in India that show widespread Hindu-Muslim symbiosis within a predominantly syncretic culture.[101] While their status as foreign invaders and part of a religious minority did not hinder the Mughals' superior forces from overcoming native armies, administering vast territories and diverse subjects required their accommodation. Thus it was necessary for Muslim emperors to employ Hindu generals and administrators. Hindu kings themselves hired Muslim mercenaries. Antony Copley described Indian Islam as "chameleon-like" as it took on many of the features of Indian religions, becoming significantly different from its Arab ancestral form. Because Islam could not completely absorb Indian society, and Indian society

---

[97] Ayesha Jalal, "South Asia" in *Encyclopaedia of Nationalism*, ed. A. Motyl (San Diego: Academic Press, 2000), 740.
[98] See also Robinson, *The British Empire and Muslim*; Romila Thapar, "Imagined Religious Communities? Ancient History and the Modern Search for a Hindu Identity," *Modern Asian Studies* 23, no. 2 (1989): 209-231; Romila Thapar, "Tyranny of Labels," *Social Scientist* 24, no. 9/10 (1996): 3-23.
[99] Antony Copley, *Religions in Conflict. Ideology, Cultural Contact and Conversion in Late Colonial India* (New Delhi: Oxford University Press, 2011), 4.
[100] Ibid., 5.
[101] Dalrymple, *The Last Mughal*, 4-5, 74, 77.

could not completely absorb Islam, the result was substantial syncretism between the two cultures.[102] It was common for Hindus and Muslims to share festivals as well as religious sites; this was practiced in the Hindu kingdoms that predated the Moghul Empire and also during the reign of Muslim rulers since the time of the great Mughal Emperor Akbar (1542-1605). Unlike the British, who governed India as a distant dependency, disregarding its culture, earlier Muslim invaders had settled in the subcontinent, married Hindu women, and adopted the customs of the country.

In the Islam of the Indian subcontinent, although the notion of brotherhood was stressed conceptually, there was no unifying strand between the many followers of Islam. Muslims made up between 20 to 25 percent of the British Indian population. Their demographics ranged from almost one hundred percent of the population in the North West regions to less than five percent in the central provinces. They were peasants, artisans, merchants, and landowners. They belonged to different castes and were the descendants of Muslim royalty, of "converts" (identified as a lower status), or of the elites (the Saiyids, Shaiks, Mughals, Pathans). They were mostly Sunnis, though some were Shia. Nevertheless, in one administrative sweep, the British reduced this diversity into a single religious category. Muslim immigration to the subcontinent had necessitated accommodation as well as assimilation. As Peter Gottschalk states, "…they started to develop shared identities that complemented identities they did not and could not share… Imperial efforts to define, maintain, and manage South Asian social and political formation, as well as the later introduction of representational politics, worked to alter religious identities."[103]

Throughout its history, India has been invaded and occupied by successive forces from the west: Arabs, Turks, Afghans, and the Mughals, and so forth. Muslim rulers generally held local converts to Islam—most of them of low caste—in low esteem. It was only after the British replaced Muslim rule and fully established themselves as the predominant power in the subcontinent that elite Muslims began to stress "Islamic brotherhood." The Muslim elite needed local Muslim support to assert their political strength in the new world of British domination. Thus, the new principle of Islamic brotherhood was not emphasized for religious reasons, but rather primarily due to socio-political needs.

---

102 Copley, *Religions in Conflict*, 47
103 Peter Gottschalk, *Beyond Hindu and Muslim: Multiple Identity in Narratives From Village India* (New York: Oxford University Press, 2000), 175.

During the latter part of the eighteenth century, as the British began to establish and expand on the subcontinent, the logistics of controlling a large territory and population in an alien land became increasingly challenging. However, as Cohn notes, "Vast ignorance about the actual nature of Indian society, indigenous law, economics and political structure characterized most of those in London and in India who made the decisions which shaped the ultimate nature of British rule in India."[104]

Scholars have conducted substantial analysis of how British policies raised Muslim communal identity in order to counter-weigh emerging Indian nationalism, but there remains a need to fully assess the impact of the reification, creation, and hardening of religious identity during colonial times as a causal agent of extant terrorism. While the colonial government created and imposed monolithic identities on various religious groups in the subcontinent, they began to systematically exploit the differences between groups in order to secure their own rule. As incipient nationalism emerged during the latter part of the 19th century into the early 20th century, the British Empire's concern for the stability of their own rule caused them to pursue their Machiavellian tactics even more aggressively.

While Muslims had earned Britain's wrath during the 1857 Rebellion, Britain's favor began to shift back towards the Muslim elite during the beginning of the 20th century. This change occurred as the Indian National Congress, which was dominated by Hindu leaders, evolved into a nationalist organization that challenged British hegemony. The colonial regime allied itself with Muslim leaders in order to weaken the Indian demand for more home rule, culminating in the creation of the Indian Muslim League in 1906. But when British administration portrayed the Congress as a Hindu party and the League as a representative of Muslim interests, they created a dangerous schism between the two imagined communities and collapsed the political into the religious.

THE INDIAN NATIONAL CONGRESS AND THE MUSLIM LEAGUE

Allan Octavian Hume founded the Indian National Congress (Congress) in 1885. His implicit aim was to create a dialogue between the educated Indian elite and the British Empire and to prevent Indian natives from engaging in violence or advocating for self-rule. The logic was that a pro-Government Indian organization could serve as an intermediary between the imperial power and its subjects. Ironically, the foundation of the Congress is considered a key event in

---

104 Bernard S. Cohn, "From Indian Status to British Contract," *Journal of Economic History* 21, no. 4 (1961): 613.

the opposition movement against British rule in India. The Congress evolved from a loyalist grouping of upper class elite intellectuals, including primarily Hindus but also Muslims, Parsis, Christians, and some sympathetic British, into a nationalist organization. The loyalist agenda of Congress is evident in Robert Hume's description:

> Despite the apparent outward unity in all the deliverances of the Congress there has been a growing cleavage of sentiment and aim between the radical and conservative sections in the community. This cleavage recently came to a clash and a rupture in the Congress movement itself. The Moderate party has as its goal only the desire for a larger measure of home rule like that in Canada and Australia, together with loyal connection with British supremacy in a world empire. The Extremists would omit the last half of the twofold program of the Moderates, though without openly advocating any early separation from British connection.[105]

The Congress was an elite organization of intelligentsia supported by wealthy merchants and lawyers. It supported obedience to the Raj while championing support for the class interests of its benefactors, jobs for Indians in colonial government, and an Indian voice in legislative matters. Early Congressmen were products of Britain's desire to create native administrators to ease the burden of colonial administration. Thomas Maccaulay (1800-1859) expressed in his 1835 "Minute on Indian Education" the colonial need for "a class who may interpret between us and the millions whom we govern; a class of persons, Indian in blood and colour, but English in taste, opinions, in morals, and intellect."[106]

Indeed, such an elite group—high-caste, urban, educated in England, detached from the common natives, and having more in common with the colonial masters than with traditional Indian society—made up the first generation Congress members. This was an emerging urban middle class in terms of its material interests and perception of social status, and it endeavored to get elected nominees into colonial political bodies while striving for an expansion of jobs in the British civil service. Simple statistics show how elite these Congressmen were in relation to the rest of the Indian population at the time: in 1901, the overall literacy level was less than ten percent; meanwhile, 60 out of 86 of the leading Congressmen between 1885 and 1914 were lawyers.[107]

---

105 Robert Allen Hume, "The Indian National Congress," *Journal of Race Development* 1, no. 3 (1911): 370.
106 Quoted in Maya Tudor, *The Promise of Power: The Origins of Democracy in India and Autocracy in Pakistan* (New York: Cambridge University Press, 2013), 45.
107 Maya J. Tudor, *Twin Births, Divergent Democracies: the Social and Institutional Origins of Regime Outcomes in India and Pakistan, 1920-1958* (New York: Cambridge University, 2013), 4. The literacy rates in India were approximately 3% in 1881 and 8% in 1931, which should indicate the degree to which Congress members were elitist and unrepresentative of the population.

As the Congress members' increasing demands for more representation and more opportunities in the British controlled civil service positions were not accommodated, the group's loyalist leanings began to shift. By 1907, the Congress had split into moderate and militant factions, with the militants demanding self-rule for India. On August 4, 1914, Britain declared war against Germany and declared that its Indian colony would provide it with material support and manpower. The Indian nationalists as well as Indian princes overwhelmingly supported their imperial masters; Congress leaders believed that a British victory would mean freedom for India.[108] Instead, the end of World War I brought harsh repressive laws back into the subcontinent, including Rowlatt Act of 1919, aimed at crushing any opposition to British rule. The harsh Rowlatt Act was called the Black Act and protests against it culminated in a horrendous bloodbath in Punjab. On April 13, 1919, Brigadier Dyer ordered the massacre of hundreds of non-violent unarmed men, women, and children in Jallianwala Bagh, Amritsar whose only crime was participating in a political gathering.[109] Dyer's troops fired for ten minutes, killing 379 and wounding 1,100, according to official British figures. The dynamics of relationship between Congress and the British began to change due to a plethora of grievances against colonial policies and as well as increasing demands for self-rule. Despite its elitist membership and its history of subservience to the British Empire, Congress eventually developed into the preeminent nationalist organization in India, especially during the interwar years. Proclaiming a secular agenda, it demanded Indian independence from British occupation.

Beginning in the early part of the 20th century, under the leadership of Mohandas Karamchand Gandhi (1869–1948), better known as Mahatma Gandhi, the Congress began a fitful and drawn-out freedom movement. Indian resistance to colonial rule combined peaceful civil disobedience with mass action. Although Muslims were involved in Congress, including some at its highest levels, the majority of Congress support came from predominantly upper-caste Hindus.

Congress was ostensibly a secular organization; its rhetoric was directed toward Indians without any regard to class or religion. However, some of the symbolism used by the Congress in mass campaigns against the British was laden with Hindu imagery and mythology. Gandhi himself, the dominant Congress leader, relied heavily on Hindu symbolism in his political speeches. While other leaders attempted to clamp down on centrifugal pressures raised due to religious differences, the influence of its wealthy patrons, mostly consisting of the Hindu trading class, sometimes revealed itself in this Hindu symbolism and imagery. In response, the minority Muslims cried out against this tactic, seeing it as Hindu

---

108 Wolpert, *A New History of India*, 289.
109 Ibid., 289.

exclusivism inserted into a supposedly secular political movement. While such tactics could be described as an effort to appeal to the broad public, the majority of which was indeed Hindu, it resulted in the Muslim population's reluctance to support the Congress.[110] The British exploited this minority fear by presenting the Empire as the force that could protect minority interests.

The Congress was successful in its quest to unify its membership's competing interests against British colonial rule. To a large extent, Congress' shift in ideology and its transformation into a massive nationalist party can be traced to Gandhi's charismatic power over the masses. As the Congress began to grow, transforming from a loyalist organization into one demanding freedom, the British encouraged the formation of a counterbalancing force in the form of a comparable Muslim political party.

Even though Muslim's relatively privileged position had suffered following the 1857 Rebellion, the British nevertheless considered them a useful ally against the Hindus. As the Congress began to dominate the Indian nationalist struggle against British rule, the Muslim elite grew gravely concerned. Their most significant anxiety was the threat they perceived against their vast properties. The Muslim elite believed that the nationalist movement threatened their zamindari property interests,[111] since Congress leaders, with their socialist rhetoric and talk of land redistribution, gave the impression that they might abolish the zamindari system. Toward the end of the 19th century, efforts were made to approach the Raj authorities about representing Muslim interests. However, as Muslim interests differed based upon regional diversity and class differences, the lack of any unified "Muslim interest" made it difficult to gain any effective political traction. Ideological differences within the Muslim community also resulted in some Muslim support for Congress as the representative body of all Indians.

On October 1, 1906, a group of Muslim aristocrats and landlords met the Viceroy of India, Lord Minto, and pleaded for separate Muslim electorate, seeking representation based not on the number of Muslims but on their social status and importance. The deputation asked for positive discrimination for Muslims, arguing that Muslim power and representation *"should be commensurate not merely with their numerical strength but also with their political importance and the value of the contribution which they make to the defence of the Empire."* [112] Lord Minto, a skillful colonial administrator, advised the deputation that he supported "the

---

110 Additionally, Muslims were not adequately represented in Congress's membership itself: between 1885 and 1905, Muslims constituted between 20 to 25% of the subcontinent's population, but only 7-13% of Congress membership.
111 Zamindars were landowners with vast tracts of lands who sometimes held aristocratic and royal titles. They also had the right to collect revenue.
112 Wolpert, *A New History of India*, 278.

Mahommedan community" and would safeguard their political rights and interests. Shortly thereafter, in December 1906, the Indian Muslim League was born. The League started as a very small organization, its support mostly coming from the provinces in which Muslims were a religious minority. It was a socially conservative and elitist organization, headed by wealthy landlords and conservative Muslim intellectuals. While the league claimed that its primary mission was to protect and advance the political rights and interests of Indian Muslims, the League members' main concern was the threat that the rising nationalistic movement posed to their property. For years the League remained a loyalist lobby for the elite Muslims, and was ignored by many Muslims and Hindus alike.

The Raj's cultivation of the alliance served them well, as the Muslim League enthusiastically and openly supported the British Raj. The British Government, through the Indian Council Act of 1909, conceded to the Muslim League's demand for a separate electorate in limited local governance, the so-called Morley-Minto Reforms. Some of the Muslim elite's most critical demands incorporated in the Act reserved exclusive seats for Muslims in municipal and district boards, provincial councils, and the imperial legislature. Furthermore, they stipulated that only Muslims could vote for Muslim candidates—in specific seats reserved solely for Muslims—creating separate electorates that rendered impossible any future accommodation between Hindu and Muslim communities.

The most serious implication of the Indian Council Act was that the colonial regime provided its official sanction to religious nationalism by linking religion with political representation, power, and patronage. Thomas Metcalf describes the impact of Morley-Minto reforms:

> The Morley-Minto reforms... embed[ded] deeply in Indian life the idea that its society consisted of groups set apart from each other. Most portentous was Minto's conception of India's Muslims as a distinct community who deserved representation on their own. By Minto's time, community based electorates had become ever more visibly a device to secure a base of support for the Raj in the face of an increasing nationalist challenge. Minto's 1906 creation of special Muslim constituencies was hailed as 'nothing less than the pulling back of sixty-two million people (Muslims) from joining the ranks of the seditious opposition.'[113]

David Page concludes that enfranchised members of Muslim and other communities were made to vote communally, think communally, and express their grievances communally; there was no need to collaborate with or accommodate other communities. "Muslim politicians did not have to appeal to non-Muslims;

---

113 Metcalf, *Ideologies of the Raj*, 224.

THE HISTORY OF THE INDIAN SUBCONTINENT

non-Muslims did not have to appeal to Muslims," he writes. "This made it very difficult for a genuine unified Indian nationalism to emerge."[114] Page argues that British initiatives were ultimately responsible for dividing Hindus and Muslims, pointing to the Montague-Chelmsford constitutional reforms of 1919 that institutionalized separate electorates for Hindus and Muslims and were crucial in the development of divisive politics.

The Morley-Minto reforms were followed by the Communal Award of 1932. The separate electorate created for Muslims were now expanded to Sikhs, Indian Christians, and Anglo-Indians, another step in Britain's policy of fostering communal divide in India.

The Muslim League's founding charter stated as its central objective, "To foster a sense of loyalty to the British Empire among the Muslims of India."[115] This loyalty was demonstrated by the League's refusal to participate in the anticolonial movement being spearheaded by the Congress. However, several important Muslim leaders, including Sheikh Abdullah in Kashmir, Khan Abdul Ghaffar Khan (known as the "Frontier Gandhi") in the NWFP, Mian Iftikharuddin in the Punjab, and Maulana Azad in the United Provinces all decided to work with the Indian National Congress rather than the Muslim League. Despite British support, the Muslim League was politically dormant and quiescent until the late 1930s. The League's efforts to preserve dominance and special privileges for the Muslim elite brought it in direct conflict with the Congress as the socialist members of the Congress were calling for land redistribution as well as the abolition of large landlords. Furthermore, the League's exclusionary discourse that framed political issues in terms of Muslim versus the Hindu interests created an unbridgeable conflict with the Congress as well as with other Hindus.

In subsequent chapters, we will see that this evolving divide, actively aided by the British Raj, poisoned the relationship between Hindus and Muslims to such an extent that it culminated in hatred, religious rioting, and devastating violence. This is no clearer than when one looks at the events the both preceded and followed Britain's departure from the subcontinent, and its partition of the region into India and Pakistan.

---

114 Page, *Prelude to Partition*, 260.
115 Quoted in Ali, *The Clash of Fundamentalisms: Crusades, Jihads and Modernity* (London: Verso 2002), 169.

Division of Bengal

In 1905, the British decided for reasons of "administrative efficiency" to divide the province of Bengal, with a majority Muslim population in the eastern regions and a majority Hindu population in the west. Britain's administrative move was motivated by its desire to weaken Bengali opposition to the Raj, which Britain attributed to the elite Hindu community of Bengal. Its objective was to "split up and weaken a solid body of opponents to [Britain's] rule."[116]

In a note written in February 1905 by the Indian Viceroy, Lord Curzon, and dispatched to Sir John Brodrick, the Secretary of State for India, Curzon described Calcutta, Bengal, as the center of the Indian National Congress' influence, stating, "they may one day be able to force a weak government to give them what they desire."[117] Their solution was to cut down Congress' influence by marketing Bengal's division as a means of empowering poor Bengali Muslims against the wealthier Bengali Hindus. Most educated Bengalis, both Hindu and Muslim, opposed the partition of Bengal.

The Bengali Hindu leaders accused the British of engaging in "divide and rule" tactics, portraying the partition as a deliberate attack on a "nation" that had once been united by a common history, language, and race. The Hindus also saw the partition as giving enhanced status to East Bengal (and to its Muslim population), whose peasant inhabitants had converted to Islam. Protests broke out, including rallies, petitions, and a boycott of British goods. There was intense opposition to the division, however this opposition was not embraced by a majority of the Muslim population, which consisted mostly of poor peasantry. Most Bengali Muslims supported the partition and their consequent new empowerment as a political majority in the territory of East Bengal.

The Congress entered the debate and opposed the partition, making the provincial issue of Bengal's partition a national issue. The Muslim League voiced their official support of the Bengal's partition. In Bengal, the Muslim peasantry's support of partition had more to do with their exploitation by absentee and exploitative landlords, the majority of whom happened to be wealthy Hindus. Compared to the Hindus, the Bengali Muslims were a socially backward and economically depressed community.[118] Ultimately, the strength of the opposition

---

116 Karl E. Meyer, "The Invention of Pakistan: How the British Raj Sundered," *World Policy Journal* 20, no. 1 (2003): 78; See also Anil B. Ray, "Communal Attitudes to British Policy: The Case of the Partition of Bengal 1905," *Social Scientist* 6, no. 5 (1977): 34-46.
117 Quoted in Samanth Subramanian, "The Long View: the Partition Before Partition," *New York Times*, October 3, 2011.
118 Ray, "Communal Attitudes to British Policy," 43.

movement resulted in the partition being rescinded in 1911. However, enormous damage had been done to the British rule, creating, in effect, the first significant nationalist movement against the Raj.

WORLD WAR II AND DECOLONIZATION

While the British Empire fought for its existence during the Second World War, its inclination toward the Muslim League became pronounced. In September 1939, the British declared that India would participate in British war efforts. They had not consulted any Indian politician before making this announcement, which angered Indian nationalists. However, Indian leaders reacted cautiously, providing no immediate reaction or instant rebellion against the decision. They wanted to give the British more time to see how the situation unfolded.

The Indian National Congress issued a statement that "the issue of war and peace for India must be decided by the Indian people and no outside authority can impose this decision upon them, nor can the Indian people permit their resources to be exploited for imperialist ends."[119] They then asked Britain to declare its war aims. Britain provided vague assurances to the Congress leaders that after the war, political advances towards independence would follow. The Congress challenged Britain, reminding the Raj that during the First World War, Britain had promised political advances to the nationalists, only to abandon its commitments once the war was over.

Congress' conditions for Indian participation in the war included a promise to grant freedom to India after the war was over. In a telling message that Indian freedom was not on the table, the colonial government refused to accept Congress' conditions. In response, Congress protested Britain's decision to involve India in the Second World War without consulting the natives, and the Congress provincial ministries resigned in protest by the end of 1939. In response, the Viceroy of India, Victor Hope, 2nd Marquess of Linlithgow, continued to raise the profile of Muhammad Ali Jinnah, a lawyer and politician who was quickly rising to political prominence in the Muslim world.[120] Linlithgow positioned Jinnah and the Muslim League as the sole voice of Indian Muslims, calling Congress a Hindu organization.

With Congress completely opposing the Raj's aims, Linlithgow found in Jinnah an imperial tool willing to undercut nationalist agitation that could hinder Indian contribution to the war effort. Jinnah was quite aware that his fortunes had

---

119 Devendra Panigrahi, *India's Partition: The Story of Imperialism in Retreat* (Abingdon: Routledge, 2004), 113.
120 Panigrahi, *India's Partition*, 122-123.

changed because of the Raj's needs; according to him, "After the war was declared, the Viceroy naturally wanted help from the Muslim League. It was only then that he realized that the Muslim League was a power. For it will be remembered that up to the time of the declaration of war, the Viceroy never thought of me, but of Gandhi and Gandhi alone."[121]

Shortly after Congress' provincial ministries resigned, Jinnah, in a presidential address to the Indian Muslim League given in Minto Park in Lahore on March 22, 1940, put forth what is known as the Lahore Resolution. The Lahore Resolution asked that contiguous Muslim majority areas in northwest and northeast India be turned into independent states in which the constituent units would be autonomous and sovereign.[122] Although the separate state of Pakistan was not mentioned, the Hindu press later construed the resolution as a demand for Pakistan, dubbed it "the Pakistan Resolution." Ishtiaq Ahmed, a political scientist, has claimed that Viceroy Linlithgow initiated the idea for the partition of India in order to checkmate Congress' efforts to force Britain's withdrawal from India during WWII.[123]

During WWII, colonial Britain relied heavily on the British Indian Army, the bulk of which was constituted by native Indian soldiers with a mostly British officer corps. Between May 1940 and September 1941, the British recruited 550,000 Indians to fight alongside British Allied Forces. The monthly recruitment of Indians for the war effort averaged approximately 50,000 men per month.[124]

During the war, two million Indians fought for Britain as part of the British Indian Army. Great Britain's war efforts would have suffered tremendously on both eastern and western fronts if not for the British Indian Army and the resources that were siphoned from India. In addition to the more than two million men under arms, India provided support in the form of hundreds of thousands of men working in pioneer and military labor corps.[125] Additionally, a large number of laborers were raised from eastern India. On the Assam front, the eastern part of India, almost 200,000 Nagas (tribal people from northeastern India) were deployed as porters and carriers. Various Indian princes also provided war funding, troops, and state labor corps.[126]

---

121 Quoted in Panigrahi, *India's Partition*, 123.
122 Talbot, *India and Pakistan*, 144.
123 Ishtiaq Ahmed, "Splitting India," *Friday Times*, September 20-26, 2013; See also Ishtiaq Ahmed, *The Punjab: Bloodied, Partitioned and Cleansed; Unraveling the 1947 Tragedy Through Secret British Reports and First Person Accounts*, 2nd ed. (New Delhi: Rupa, 2011).
124 Kaushik Roy, "Military Loyalty in the Colonial Context: A Case Study of the Indian Army during World War II," *Journal of Military History* 73 (2009): 504.
125 Christopher Bayly and Tim Harper, *Forgotten Armies: The Fall of British Asia, 1941-1945* (Cambridge, MA: Belknap Press of Harvard University Press, 2005), 425.
126 Ibid.

THE HISTORY OF THE INDIAN SUBCONTINENT

VICTORY MARCH, London, 19th July 1919 - © IWM
Image reprinted with permission from Imperial War Museum, Lambeth Road, London, SE1 6HZ

As the wartime confrontation between Congress and the British grew, Congress launched the Quit India movement in 1942, which started in August with large demonstrations against the colonial government. There were widespread efforts to sabotage the war efforts, as participants cut telegraph lines and ripped up railway lines. Britain's fear of a large-scale rebellion in India (which would have disrupted a major source of their war funding and supply of soldiers) when combined with the existential threat posed to it by Germany, resulted in an ironfisted response. More than 30,000 Congressmen and other political activists were thrown in prison, including Gandhi and most of the Congress high command. Congress leaders remained in prison for most of the duration of the war. Demonstrators were arrested in mass and whipped on the spot. Floggings were deemed "necessary" in order to "deter hooligans," and Viceroy Linlithgow nearly sanctioned the aerial machine-gunning of saboteurs.[127] In the end, over 90,000 Indians were arrested and up to 10,000 political protesters were killed.[128]

Within a month, the brutal crackdown had its intended effect on Indian demonstrations and acts of civil disobedience against British rule. British Prime Minister Winston Churchill, who already loathed Gandhi and the Congress and

---

127 Ibid., 248.
128 Madhusree Mukerjee, *Churchill's Secret War: The British Empire and the Ravaging of India During World War II* (New York: Basic Books, 2011), xxx.

favored the Muslim League, had a striking reaction, which was described by the British Secretary of State, Leopold Amery, as "Nazi-like attitude" towards India.[129] Churchill was greatly predisposed towards Jinnah and frequently made mention of Pakistan.

Furthermore, despite a shortage of wheat in India, Britain ordered India to supply 50,000 tons of wheat per month for British and Indian troops stationed in the Middle East and Iran.[130] Approximately 3 million people starved to death in the great Bengal famine of 1943-44, a tragedy that can be attributed to a devastating cyclone that damaged Bengal's rice harvest, war efforts on the eastern front, jaundiced colonial attitudes, as well as the revenue generation that Britain was ruthlessly extorting from Bengal.[131] Furthermore, when British Burma, on India's eastern border, fell to Japan, the British destroyed the transport network in the east that supplied rice to Bengal. Despite their knowledge of the famine and food shortage in Bengal, the British government refused to deal with the crisis and continued sending Indian food overseas. Their war effort did not take into account dying Bengalis when there were soldiers and war workers who needed to be fed. Even when the censored press in India began to use the word "famine" in July 1943, the British Cabinet was unwilling to release more than one quarter of the food demanded in India. Christopher Bayly states,

> Quite apart from the demands of war, it is difficult to escape the impression that the War Cabinet was simply hostile towards India. The prime minister believed that the Indians were the next worst people in the world after the Germans. Their treachery had been plain in the Quit India movement... Churchill's scientific adviser Frederick Lindemann thought the Bengalis were a weak race and that overbreeding and eugenic unfitness were the basic reasons for the [food] scarcity.[132]

British rulers' invidious attitude towards Congress, especially during the Second World War, as well as their use of the Muslim League to counterbalance Congress, strengthened Jinnah, the leader of the Muslim League, during the war years. The most significant push toward Hindu-Muslim discord directly resulted from the colonial imperatives during the Second World War and shortly thereafter culminated in the 1947 partition of India on a religious basis. This devastating move, born of imperial convenience, will be discussed in the next chapter. Throughout the rest of the 20th century, and through today, many disasters in the Indian subcontinent can be traced back to the consequences of the partition:

---

129 Quoted in Bayly and Harper, *Forgotten Armies*, 251.
130 Roy, "Military Loyalty in the Colonial Context," 504.
131 Bayly and Harper, *Forgotten Armies*; Mukerjee, *Churchill's Secret War*; Madhusree Mukerjee, "Wreath for an Imperial Famine," *Huffington Post*, August 2, 2013.
132 Bayly and Harper, *Forgotten Armies*, 286.

wars between India and Pakistan, the political use of Islam as a means of unifying Pakistan, border conflicts between South Asian nation states, and, eventually, the use of Jihadi politics to achieve Pakistan's political goals.

BLOODLINES: THE IMPERIAL ROOTS OF TERRORISM IN SOUTH ASIA

CHAPTER 2

DECOLONIZATION AND ITS AFTERMATH

THE PARTITION OF INDIA AND ITS IMPACT

The British Empire was irreparably weakened after World War II. With a new liberal government that was more sympathetic to the idea of Indian independence and in the face of increasing agitation against imperial rule, it began to plan its retreat from the Indian subcontinent. As with the creation of the Durand Line in 1893, the colonial government began to redraw the boundaries of India in 1947. The process was entirely under the control of the imperial government, although they allowed the natives bickering for a proper place in the coming power vacuum to offer suggestions. The process was hasty: In February 1947, Prime Minister Attlee announced Britain's intention of transferring power in British India to Indian hands by June 1948, and India partitioned in August 1947.

The power of the Empire was not formidable anymore, and it faced numerous pressures on many different fronts. Natives in several colonies were agitating for freedom. Violence was escalating and Britain's will to control it was diminishing as economic incentives to hold on to the territories faded. Britain ultimately decided to grant India independence because it was tired of policing and controlling territories so far from home. The decision was made grudgingly, it was poorly executed, and it faced resistance from conservative forces in Britain.

During the Indian nationalist struggle, the Muslim League had benefitted from colonial imperatives. As the British attempted to marginalize the Congress' anticolonial struggle, they termed it a "Hindu" organization—a charge that conveniently failed to take into account that in a country where the population consisted of almost eight Hindus out of ten citizens, a mass-based party was bound to have a majority of Hindu members. The Muslim League, which had been moribund for most of its existence and had disastrously failed in limited provincial elections of 1937, adopted Britain's colonial rhetoric, calling the Congress a "Hindu" party and portraying itself as representative of all Indian Muslims and their interests.[1] Despite the preponderance of Hindus in the Congress, its leaders

---

1   This is not to take away from the real social grievances of the Muslim communities against the Hindus, who often treated Muslims similar to Hindu untouchables. While the majority of Muslim grievances were economic, Hindu and Muslim communities also regularly clashed over

continued to declare that the Congress was a party of all communities and engaged in rhetoric of inclusiveness. This rhetoric denied the Muslim League a niche since the League was exclusively attempting to portray itself as the sole representative of Indian Muslims. If the Congress claimed to represent Muslims as well as all other communities, what could the League offer the natives?

The 1937 provincial elections demonstrated that League's claim that they represented all Indian Muslims was hollow. Despite contesting seats reserved for Muslims, it received only 4.8 percent of the Muslim vote while Congress swept the elections. The League's leader, Jinnah, was marginalized. The League and Jinnah would have remained a non-entity in India had it not been for the British attempts to use them, and in the process raise their profiles, during the World War II. Muslims constituted a substantial portion of the British Indian Army; supporting the provincial parties in Punjab as well as Jinnah could assure Britain a continual supply of the native soldiers. Another factor that catapulted the Muslim League to prominence in 1940s was its rallying cry of "Islam in danger," which was meant to mobilize the Muslim masses. As the 1937 elections had revealed, the common Muslim had shown no interest in an elite- and landowner-run organization. However, the divergent Muslim populations of the subcontinent were effectively unified by threats that a Hindu majority was mobilizing to destroy Islam now that India was about to be free from British rule.

India's diversity is noteworthy, especially when considering the success of the large-scale movement toward Muslim unification in the subcontinent during the early 20th century. Surveys in India have identified 4,599 distinct communities, 325 different languages and dialects, and about 12 distinct language families. As Gerald Larson notes, "communities within communities within communities represent fundamental and major features of South Asian social reality."[2] It was within this milieu that the British Empire had extracted, demarcated, and identified monolithic religious and ethnic groups, reducing them to Hindus, Muslims, and Sikhs. However, no distinctive community based Muslim political separatist tendencies could be observed in the common people until the tail end of the Raj.

At the elite level, the separatist thought could be traced to Sayyid Ahmad Khan (1817-1898), who had described Hindus and Muslims as two prominent nations in India. Khan's views, however, were neither widespread at the time nor

---

religious ceremonies and cow killing. However, high caste Hindu chauvinism was equally or more pernicious against the lower caste Hindus and the economic exploitation and oppression of the poor by Hindu moneylenders and large landowners was quite secular.

2   Gerald J. Larson, *India's Agony Over Religion*, SUNY Series in Religious Studies (Albany, NY: State University of New York Press, 1995), 285.

were they supported by the religious, especially the scholars from the Deoband Islamic movement.[3] The term "Pakistan" was first coined by a Cambridge student, Rahmat Ali, who had neither any standing in the Muslim elite nor any political connections in India. In fact, most Muslim politicians promptly dismissed his scheme as impractical and chimerical.[4] The first formal articulation of a demand for separate state for Muslims did not occur until March 23, 1940, at the annual session of the Muslim League in Lahore.[5] The Lahore Resolution and subsequent separatist demands were made against the backdrop of the Second World War; the Muslim League was still operating under state patronage and the Congress was locked in a struggle against the colonial state through its non-cooperation movement (1939-1942) and the Quit India movement (1942).[6] It was not until 1946 that the involvement of local Muslim religious figures became tangible and Islamic sloganeering began appearing in elections.[7] Once this process began, conservative ulema (religious scholars and clerics) from the Barelvi school of Islam mobilized, as well as *pirs* (religious divines) and *maulvis* (lower-level clerics) who campaigned for the Muslim League. Still, the leading Muslim scholars, especially from the Deoband School, including Husain Ahmad Madani and Maulana Maududi, were against the demand for a separate Muslim state.[8]

Despite the opposition of many Islamic scholars, Pakistan was achieved as a political reality in 1947 in the name of Islam. Much success could be attributed to the Muslim League's chauvinistic propaganda, which was effective in rallying the Muslim population. In the 1946 provincial elections, the Muslim League won more than 75 percent of the Muslim vote—a dramatic increase from the less than

---

3   Contemporary radical Deobandi groups, including the Taliban, sprang out of Deobandi madrasas in northeastern Pakistan. Although Deobandi Islam is the most popular form of pedagogy in the Pashtun belt on both sides of the Durand Line, the intellectual and spiritual heart of Deobandi Islam lies in the Indian city of Deoband. Darul Uloom, the first major seminary to impart training in Deobandi Islam, was founded in Deoband in 1867.

Unlike the Muslim elite who relied on loyalty to the colonial government to preserve their status, Deobandi leaders opposed British colonialism. They sought to purify an Islamic spirituality that they believed had been polluted through syncretism with Hindu practices. Despite their separatism, early Deobandis were accommodative, working with non-Muslims against the British rule in India. Deobandi ulema contributed to the formation of Jamiat al-ulama-i-Hind ("The Association of Indian Islamic Scholars") in 1919, which supported the non-violent anti-British struggle of the Indian National Congress. Most Deobandi scholars were against the demand for Pakistan or a nation state for Muslims and rejected the partition of British India.

4   Ayesha Jalal, "Conjuring Pakistan: History as Official Imagining," *International Journal of Middle East Studies* 27, no. 1 (1995): 75.
5   Talbot, *India and Pakistan*, 144.
6   Ian Talbot and Gurharpal Singh, *The Partition of India*, New Approaches to Asian History (Cambridge, UK: Cambridge University Press, 2009), 224.
7   Ahmed, *The Punjab*, 104.
8   Jamal Malik, *Islam in South Asia: A Short History (Themes in Islamic Studies)*. (Leiden, Boston: Brill Academic Pub, 2008), 370.

5 percent it earned in 1937. By portraying Hindu populations as a monolithic enemy—a tactic taken directly from the 19th century British colonial playbook—the Muslim League demonstrated just how well they could play the colonial game.

Prior to the 1946 elections, even the British Governor of Punjab was expressing concern over the dangerous implications of the League's crude use of Islam for political ends. In his dispatch to the Viceroy of India, Governor Bertrand Glancy warned about the League's incendiary use of religion, "…increasing reports of a deterioration in the communal situation, consequent on the poisonous propaganda of political parties, especially of the Muslim League, are being received from rural areas… The Muslim League orators are becoming increasingly fanatical in their speeches… travel all around the Province and preach that those who fail to vote for the League candidates will cease to be Muslims…"[9] Jinnah appealed to religious and sectarian heads, promised Sharia, and frightened Muslims by arguing that their political and social status was at risk in a postcolonial India. In an election meeting, he said, "If you do not vote for Pakistan you will be reduced to the status of Sudras (Hindu low castes) and Islam will be vanquished from India."[10] Muslims were promised that those who voted for the Muslim League would go to heaven while those who did not would be denied burial in Muslim cemeteries and suffer hellfire with non-believers.[11]

Jinnah, who had made significant efforts towards Hindu-Muslim unity in the earlier parts of the twentieth century, had made a complete turnaround. Under his leadership, the Muslim League contested the 1946 provincial elections using incendiary religious rhetoric. In their efforts to convince Muslim laypeople to vote for the Muslim League, the group began using slogans such as "*Pakistan ka na'ara kya? La Illaha Il-lilah.*" (Translation, "What is the slogan/calling for Pakistan? There is no god but Allah."). Muslims were repeatedly told that the Islam was in danger and that if they failed to vote for the League's candidates they would be excommunicated and their marriages would be annulled.[12]

In the run-up to the 1946 provincial elections, the Muslim League and Congress leaders could finally see that British colonial rule in the subcontinent was coming to an end. While the Muslim League was instrumentally using Islam, the Congress too had its share of Hindu chauvinists. However, the diverse interests

---

9   Lionel Carter, *Punjab Politics 1 January 1944-3 March 1947: Last Years of the Ministries, Governors Fortnightly Reports and Other Key Documents* (New Delhi: Manohar, 2006), 167, 171.
10 Quoted in Akbar, *Tinderbox*, 221.
11 Ibid., 220-221.
12 Ahmed, *The Punjab*, 104.

and groups present in Congress, especially the socialists and liberals, put pressure on it to uphold values of inclusiveness and secularism.[13] Thus, in contrast to the Islamic rhetoric of the League, the Congress engaged in the rhetoric of secularism.

There was a great rise in religious violence and rioting after 1945. The conversation about the upcoming political vacuum after the British departure from India was given a religious coloring, especially as the Muslim League attempted to portray itself as the sole representative of Indian Muslims. The Congress, fashioning itself as a secular and unifying force, had to face the fact that its leadership and mass base was indeed composed mostly of Hindus. Recognizing the fact, Congress leader Jawaharlal Nehru urged the provincial Congress committees in 1937 to make a special effort to enroll Muslim Congress members, rolling out a "Muslim mass contact" plan. Congress approved Nehru's plan during its October 1937 session, and its message was that Congress wanted to protect the religious, linguistic, and cultural rights of the minorities and ensure their participation in the political, economic, and cultural life of the nation.[14] The leading ulema of the Deoband School and the Jamiyat al-Ulama supported the mass contact and asked Muslims to enlist as Congress members. While the program was successful initially, the Muslim League vigorously opposed it, seeing it as a challenge to its own constituency. The plan was also described by the leading conservative theologian (and later founder of *Jamaat-e-Islami*), Maulana Abul ala Mawdudi[15], as a means of disintegrating the Muslim community, subverting the faith of the Muslim masses, and converting them to Marxism. The plan ended in 1939 with a whimper, as it did not receive the support of many factions of the Congress. The Congress conservatives were bitterly opposed to the campaign as it threatened their political dominance, and raised the chances of Nehru's Muslim, socialist, and communist allies dominating the Congress. On the other hand, some of Nehru's socialist allies were opposed to recruiting members as Hindus or Muslims, preferring to focus on peasants and workers of all communities.[16] In any case, the divide between the Hindu and Muslim communities continued to widen as the elite jockeyed for their positions in the future India.

On July 18, 1947, the British Parliament passed the India Independence Act. Less than four weeks later, the subcontinent was partitioned and colonial power was transferred to the new states of Pakistan and India, on August 14 and August 15, respectively. This partition came about because the Congress had been agitating for independence from Britain, and the Muslim elite had been agitating

---

13 Akbar, *Tinderbox*, 198.
14 Mushirul Hasan, "The Muslim Mass Contact Campaign: An Attempt at Political Mobilisation," *Economic & Political Weekly* 21, no. 52 (1986): 2273.
15 Alternatively spelled as Maududi, Maudoodi, Mawdudi, and Modudi.
16 Hasan, "The Muslim Mass Contact Campaign," 2279.

for independence from both British and majority Hindu rule. The Muslim League's argument—that Muslims needed protection from Hindu oppression—paradoxically led to the division of two Muslim majority provinces, Bengal and Punjab, with western Punjab and eastern Bengal becoming the geographical core of Pakistan.

Lord Mountbatten, the last Viceroy to India, was sent to dismantle the British Empire. Indian leaders agreed with his version of the partition plan of the Indian Empire on June 3, 1947. The provinces of Punjab and Bengal (on the western and eastern periphery of British India, with majority Muslim populations) were to be divided to create West and East Pakistan. The presence of large Hindu and Sikh minority populations in these states complicated the creation of new borders, as these minority populations were widely distributed in Punjab and Bengal and the land ownership and business interests of minority communities happened to fall in majority areas. Historical artifacts and cultural centers of certain communities also sometimes fell in areas where another community was more populous, and topographical features further confounded the simple demarcation of boundaries. Furthermore, the process of determining boundaries was made even more daunting as the Muslim League had never defined the boundaries of Pakistan in their demands and had, in fact, deliberately kept them vague.[17]

To consider the chronology: On June 3, 1947, the British announced that their final transfer of power to India had been made; a boundary commission was assembled in July and had completed its task in mid-August; and the subcontinent was divided in mid-August. This highly condensed timeline shows how abrupt of the entire partition process was. Considering that a large landmass roughly the size of Europe (excepting Russia) with almost 400 million people was to be divided, at best this could be described as an exercise conducted in reckless haste. Lucy Chester concludes that the boundary commission process was "largely an exercise in public relations" for the fading British Empire: "Abandoning India because ruling it was no longer convenient would have undermined its efforts to maintain that position and would have amounted to an admission that imperialism was exploitative and illegitimate."[18]

It was obvious to the British that the Congress and League members would not come to an agreement, so to give the appearance that the natives could not come to consensus, equal numbers of Congress and League members were chosen

---

17 Lucy P. Chester, "The Mapping of Empire: French and British Cartographies of India in the Late-Eighteenth Century." *Portuguese Studies* 16, (2000): 256-275; Stephen P. Cohen, T*he Idea of Pakistan*, 2nd ed. (Washington, DC: Brookings Institution Press, 2004), 28-29.
18 Lucy P. Chester, "Boundary Commissions as Tools to Safeguard British Interests at the End of Empire," *Journal of Historical Geography* 34, no. 3 (2008): 507.

for the commission. The British chairman made all final decisions, providing the process with the façade of objectivity when it was in fact under the complete control of the dying Raj:

> ...given that nationalist leaders of India's interim government had taken part in the negotiation that formed the commission, it allowed the British to portray partition as a joint responsibility. This pretense allowed the British to avoid shouldering (at least temporarily) most of the responsibility for the violence that accompanied partition. In doing all this, the Radcliffe Commission allowed the British to escape their South Asian responsibilities quickly by providing the hastily drawn boundary line necessary to implement partition.[19]

Punjab and Bengal were the two provinces in colonial India with clear Muslim majorities. If the rights of the minority Muslims were in need of protection from Hindu supremacy, Muslims in these two provinces certainly were in no fear of Hindu domination. The Pakistan movement had emerged under the guidance of the Muslim elite from United Provinces,[20] where Muslims were in a minority, but this area remained within India after the partition. Instead of serving the interests of Muslims who would be more vulnerable to perceived Hindu domination—the Muslim minorities in Hindu majority provinces—the partition instead divided the provinces where Muslims already controlled the provincial legislature. In effect, the creation of Pakistan placed minority Muslims in a worse situation. They were given the choice to either stay in Hindu-majority areas or to leave their ancestral homes and migrate to a new state, severing their cultural, linguistic, ethnic, and historical connections in the land.

During Britain's rule, patron-client relations in the subcontinent were dynamic. The British needed local alliances and collaborators in order to continue and expand their imperial project. Though the British had built up Jinnah's stature and propped up the Muslim League during WWII, following the war Jinnah and the Muslim League had lost their value and the British instead attempted to re-forge an understanding with their former archenemy, the Congress. This political maneuver was at its heart an attempt to impose and maintain a postcolonial relationship between Britain and the emerging successor state of India.

Pakistan had remained vaguely demarcated because the Muslim elite who had demanded Pakistan had themselves been uncertain about whether they would get a Pakistan and, if so, how it might turn out. Some have suggested that Jinnah may have used the demand for a Pakistan and an appeal to religion as a political tactic

---

19   Ibid., 508.
20   In colonial north India, the region containing Agra and Oudh was called the "United Provinces." Muslims were a small minority in the region, however, the United Provinces were amongst the primary centers of Muslim power and opulence as the seat of the erstwhile Mughal Empire.

and negotiating tool for postcolonial power sharing.²¹ There had been divisions within the Muslim elite, especially from Punjab and Bengal, and some leaders preferred to keep provincial self-rule within a weak central Indian government. Additionally, even a mere two years before the country was partitioned, it remained uncertain whether a division of India would occur, as negotiations and efforts to keep the subcontinent unified after the British departure continued well into 1947. As a result, with two months to go before the partition, it was a serious undertaking: creating new boundaries in a loose federation of dominions that had existed for centuries and dividing twenty percent of the world's population and its assets.²²

The man selected as the chairman of the boundary commission, Cyril Radcliffe, had never been to India, had no connections with India or its politics, and had absolutely no knowledge of the territories he was about to divide. Additionally, Radcliffe had no cartographic experience or experience in dividing territories. Radcliffe is said to have remarked to Mountbatten that given the vastness of India and its huge population, it would take even the most qualified arbitrator years to decide on a boundary, and even with this kind of discretion, the boundary would certainly cut across homes and populations. Radcliffe was shocked to discover that he had only five weeks to complete his work.²³ He was suddenly responsible for separating people and dividing 175,000 square miles of territory between them. His sole briefing for this enormous project consisted of a 30-minute session with the Permanent Under-Secretary in the India Office, which was conducted using a large-scale map of India. Radcliffe was expecting to be provided with sufficient time—several months—for his historically unprecedented enterprise. However, he arrived in Delhi on July 8, 1947, and was given the firm deadline of mid-August that same year.²⁴

On the surface, the terms of reference for the Boundary Commission were fairly simple: the commission was entrusted with demarcating boundaries on the basis of contiguous majority areas of Muslims and non-Muslims. However, Radcliffe's difficult work was made problematic by the confusing terms of reference on how the boundaries of the partitioned areas were to be determined. For example,

---

21 Ayesha Jalal, *The Sole Spokesman: Jinnah, the Muslim League and the Demand for Pakistan* (Cambridge: Cambridge University Press, 1995), 5.
22 Lucy P. Chester, "Parting of the Ways," *History Today* 50, no. 3 (2000): 40-43.
23 Tai Yong Tan and Gyanesh Kudaisya, *The Aftermath of Partition in South Asia*, Routledge Studies in the Modern History of Asia (London: Routledge, 2002), 85. For an overview of the Radcliffe Commission, see Lucy P. Chester, *Borders and Conflict in South Asia: The Radcliffe Boundary Commission and the Partition of Punjab* (Manchester: Manchester University Press, 2010).
24 Tan and Kudaisya, *The Aftermath of Partition*, 84-85; Anthony Read and David Fisher, *The Proudest Day: India's Long Road to Independence* (New York: W. W. Norton, 1998), 482.

besides considering contiguous majority areas of Muslims and non-Muslims, the commission also had to take into account "other factors" that remained undefined. Even the units of territory (block, village, or district level, etc.) were not defined for the commission while they were considering "contiguous areas" for division. And since only Hindu and Muslim contiguous areas were to be divided, no provision was made for the Sikh population, which was threatened to be split down the middle, with their fertile lands and holy sites going to Pakistan.[25]

Besides distributing populations based upon religion, the Congress, the Muslim League, and some Sikh leaders laid conflicting claims to territory with reference to economic, cultural, and historical factors. Demarcating some of the regions was highly contentious because of complex demographics, as Muslim, Hindu, and Sikh populations were more or less equally spread out over the districts. Furthermore, the two Indian states with majority Muslim population that were to be divided to create Pakistan were so heavily populated that any potential dividing line would have to slice through densely populated areas, severing railroads and roadways, irrigation systems, and individual landholdings. Some of the areas had evenly-distributed Muslim and Hindu populations and therefore confounded the boundary creations, others were problematic due to natural boundaries such as rivers and mountain ranges. Additionally, the Sikhs, who owned large areas in Punjab and considered Punjab their heartland, were opposed to their land being partitioned, which would bring with it their concomitant loss of political power, wealth, and access to religious sites that would now be considered part of Pakistan. The Sikh population was significantly smaller than the Hindu and Muslim populations, which meant that their interests were neglected during the partition negotiations between the British, the Congress, and the Muslim League. Virtually all of the Sikh population (approximately six million in 1941) lived in Punjab. Although Sikhs comprised only thirteen percent of Punjab's population, they controlled the best lands in the province and were, on average, considerably wealthier than the other communities. By July 1947, it was evident that the Sikhs would resort to violence if the boundary commission's favor for Muslims and Hindus negatively affected Sikh interests.

Working under impossible conditions, Radcliffe ended up with an outcome that he knew was deficient and controversial. In a letter to his stepson, he wrote "Nobody in India will love me for the award about the Punjab and Bengal and there will be roughly 80 million people with a grievance who will begin looking for me. I do not want them to find me."[26]

---

25 For an overview of the Sikh demands related to partition, see Tan and Kudaisya, *The Aftermath of Partition in South Asia*, 101-121; Chester, "Parting of the Ways," 40-43.
26 Quoted in Tan and Kudaisya, *The Aftermath of Partition in South Asia*, 94.

The boundaries created by Radcliffe generated great controversy due to the lack of consistent criteria. They were regarded as illogical, problematic, and equally unfair to both Hindu and Muslim communities. The boundary award followed no natural dividing features, cut across villages, canal systems and communication lines, and in the process, separated communities. Allegations were also made that the Viceroy, Lord Mountbatten, had influenced Radcliffe in India's favor. Mountbatten received Radcliffe's awards on August 12, two days before Britain transferred power to Pakistan and three days before the transfer of power to India. There was no time to make arrangements for mutual transfer of population or to provide security in the newly created border areas. On August 17, with the announcement of Radcliffe awards, countless people found themselves on the wrong side of the border.[27]

Large populations in Punjab and Bengal did not know in which state they would end up until the partition was already enacted, despite the monumental fact that it brought an official end to British colonial power over the Indian subcontinent, and had birthed the new states of Pakistan and India. Lord Mountbatten had held back the details of partition until August 17. Even at the very end, Britain's desire to control its subjects and its utter disregard for the long-term consequences of its colonial decisions rendered the newly created states completely unprepared for the bloodbath that ensued. When Britain postponed its release of the partition's details, its bungle was not alleviated in any way; it simply delayed the reaction of the Indian people.

It quickly became apparent that the partition created new dilemmas that most of the Hindu and Muslim elite had not previously anticipated. The Raj, though claiming to benevolently dispense independence on unworthy Indian natives, had not made adequate provisions to deal with the process and aftermath of the partition. Serious violence had preceded the partition in Punjab in March and a Punjab Boundary Force was formed on July 22 under the command of Major General Rees to maintain order. The force was said to be 55,000, strong but it neither reached that level nor was deployed. In other words, it was completely inadequate for its purposes. Not only did it have an enormous 37,5000 square mile area under its jurisdiction, its troops were also from Punjabi Muslim and Sikh communities, which were deeply antagonistic towards each other due to

---

27 For an analysis of the genocidal violence associated with the partition, see Paul R. Brass, "The Partition of India and Retributive Genocide in the Punjab, 1946-47: Means, Methods, and Purposes," *Journal of Genocide Research* 5, no. 1 (2003): 71-101.

the division of Punjab. Though Punjab was experiencing an ongoing communal bloodbath, the Boundary Force remained in barracks and was disbanded on August 29.[28]

The partition resulted in one of the most brutal and bloody forced migrations in history, as Sikhs and Hindus were evicted from newly created Pakistan and Muslims were expelled from India. The ensuing violence resulted in the massacre of between one to two million Hindus, Muslims and Sikhs; the expulsion of approximately twelve million people from their homes; the abduction and rape of over 75,000 women; and the creation of one of the largest refugee waves in history.[29] Margaret Bourke-White, an American photographer, was in India to photograph the birth of two nations in the fall of 1947 for *Life Magazine*. She described the migration of refugees in miles-long columns, as approximately five million people moved immediately after independence was declared. There were homicidal attacks on caravans, and women were abducted and raped. Trains leaving from Lahore and Delhi, packed with refugees going to the other side, arrived at their destinations filled with butchered and bloated remains of the same refugees. Hindus and Sikhs killed Muslims, and Muslims killed Hindus and Sikhs.

The enormous number of refugees posed a huge resettlement problem for India and Pakistan. Almost ten percent of Pakistan's population consisted of refugees. The religious violence unleashed by the partition was followed by a war between the nascent states over the disputed territory of Kashmir, which both India and Pakistan claimed on different grounds. This ongoing war has been a major source of terrorism in South Asia and its impact has been felt around the world. The trauma incurred by partition was so profound that relations between the two states have not yet normalized over six decades later. Communal animosities have converted to institutional and inter-state animosities, and they have worsened with time.

Several factors resulted in the eruption of large-scale violence during and after the partition. The proximate cause was Britain's disregard for the situation's potential for violence. By not knowing the exact boundaries until after the partition of subcontinent had already been accomplished, the British failed to

---

28 Ahmed, *The Punjab*, 320-322, 398-399; Talbot and Singh, *The Partition of India*, 47-48.
29 For an overview of the partition-related violence, see Ahmed, *The Punjab*; Margaret Bourke-White, *Halfway to Freedom: A Report on the New India in the Words and Photographs of Margaret Bourke-White* (New York: Simon and Schuster, 1949); Brass, "The Partition of India and Retributive Genocide, 1946-47," 71-101; Uravashi Butalia, *The Other Side of Silence: Voices from the Partition of India* (Durham: Duke University Press, 2000); Stephen P. Cohen, *The Idea of Pakistan*, 2nd ed. (Washington, DC: Brookings Institution Press, 2004); Rounaq Jahan, "Genocide in Bangladesh," in *Century of Genocide: Eyewitness Accounts and Critical Views*, ed. S. Totten, W. S. Parsons, and I. W. C. Charny (New York and London: Garland Publishing, 1997), 291-316; Penderel Moon, *Divide and Quit* (London: Chatto, Windus, 1961).

organize, or even plan for an orderly transfer of populations. Moreover, it failed to organize a police force under its British officers that was adequate to the task of countering inter-communal violence. Just as the fate and future boundaries of the subcontinent were uncertain in 1947, the positions of those serving in the British Indian Army were increasingly insecure as partition approached. It was only in April 1947 that the Muslim League had made a formal request to Britain for a division of the British Indian Army, a division that the British were initially reluctant to make.[30] Field Marshal Sir Claude Auchinleck and other senior staff opposed dividing the army, wanting instead to maintain it as a single entity for the defense of both India and Pakistan.[31] Some senior Hindu army officers agreed with Auchinleck, arguing that a division of the military would lead to conflict between India and Pakistan and also expose the nascent states to external threats.

The division of the military was based mostly upon religion and region. A Muslim soldier from a region in India could opt for the Indian Army but a Muslim from a region in Pakistan could not. Similar constraints applied to Hindu soldiers. After the partition, Pakistan inherited most of the Muslim component of the army although many opted to stay in India.

As different groups jockeyed for political power in the wake of Britain's departure, they relied on the same religious rhetoric that had fueled the communal hatred building since 1940. This was compounded by the uncertainty of communities in the boundary areas who did not know where they were going to end up after the partition. On August 17, when the boundary commission awards were made public, instead of bringing peace between the communities, they intensified hatred; people created a frenzy so as not to be caught on the wrong side of the border. In the end, even law enforcement and armed forces personnel participated in the bloodbath. The Baluch Regiment, entirely consisting of Muslim soldiers, took part in the massacre of Hindus and Sikhs, and Sikh and Hindu troops killed many Muslims.

IDEATIONAL IDENTITIES AND THE ORIGIN OF CONFLICT IN SOUTH ASIA

Before and after the partition of the subcontinent, India and Pakistan created sharply contrasting self-images based on irreconcilable ideological foundations. Pakistan saw itself as the homeland for all Muslims in South Asia, whereas India saw itself as a secular state without any role for religion in its polity. Several layers

---

30 Hasan-Aaskari Rizvi, *Military, State and Society in Pakistan* (New York: St. Martin's Press, 2000), 52.
31 Ibid., 53.

of adversarial identities were created and shaped before and after the subcontinent was decolonized. After the partition, these identities hardened, making the conflict between the two states violent and intractable.

The Congress had been agitating against British rule since the early twentieth century, was regarded as a nationalist organization, and saw the Muslim League as a loyalist organization that preferred British rule to India's freedom. The contrast between the two organizations' identities became increasingly adversarial as each gained political power and readied for the British departure. The Raj's special treatment of the Muslim League during World War II and the Raj and League's extremely divisive pre-partition politics created further acrimony between the Congress and the League, especially in the years from 1945-1947. The rhetoric of Hindu reactionaries regarding the partition—who predicted the dissolution of Pakistan and its reabsorption into India—further created feelings of hostility and insecurity in Pakistan. Thus, the two neighboring nation states with seemingly irreconcilable interests and conflicts not only evolved with strongly adversarial identities; their unique geographical, cultural, and historical ties going back centuries made it impossible for India and Pakistan to simply ignore each other. The two countries came into being in a state of existential rivalry, each questioning the legitimacy of the other, and the results of this adversarial genesis still bear bitter fruit for South Asia and the rest of the world.

The Muslim nationalism that resulted in Pakistan's creation was based upon Muslim separatism and contributed to the creation of adversarial religious as well as separatist identities. Conversely, the Congress had created a big umbrella secular identity representing all Indians, which was non-reconcilable with Pakistan's religious-separatist identity. The ideologically conflicting goals put the nation states on an immediate collision course. Distrust and hatred progressively worsened as the nascent states went to war over Kashmir shortly after gaining freedom from the British.

Pakistan's identity has resulted in the perpetuation of conflict with India because, as Nasr states, "Pakistani identity has largely evolved not in terms of any indigenous cultural or civilizational values but in contradistinction to the idea of India."[32] This contradistinction has caused unremitting hostility between the two states, as evidenced by the following statement from Pakistani dictator General Zia-ul Haq. Explaining why Pakistan maintained a position of hostility and conflict with India, Zia stated:

---

32 Vali Nasr, "National Identities and the India-Pakistan Conflict," in *India-Pakistan Conflict: An Enduring Rivalry*, ed. Thaza V. Paul (New York: Cambridge University Press, 2005), 179.

Turkey or Egypt, if they stop being aggressively Muslim, they will remain exactly what they are—Turkey and Egypt. But if Pakistan does not become and remain aggressively Islamic, it will become India again.[33]

In the newly created state of Pakistan, the distinct cultures and histories of Baloch, Bengalis, Punjabis, Sindhis, and the people of NWFP clashed with the culture of the new ruling class. The elite who usurped power in Pakistan did not come from the regions that constituted Pakistan; in fact, the leadership of the Muslim League predominantly came from regions that had remained in India after the partition. They spoke a different language (Urdu) and were culturally and ethnically distinct from the natives. This understandably created tension within the nation: "newcomers" were now dominating state politics.[34] From its very inception, Pakistan was confronted with a paradox: the state that was created on the basis of the "two-nation" theory was facing separatist and secessionist forces on linguistic and ethnic grounds, which threatened to negate the legitimacy of Pakistan's formation. If Muslims in the subcontinent believed that they deserved a nation of their own, Baloch, Pashtuns, and Sindhis in Pakistan might also demand their own separate nations as well. Kapur argues, "Without the cementing influence of Islam and anti-Indianism, Pakistan would likely have degenerated into civil war among the Punjabis, Balochis, Pashtuns, and Sindhis."[35] Without a concrete and unifying ideology to guide the newly created state, Pakistan increasingly relied on Islam as its sole cement. Instead of focusing on governance, infrastructure development, and developing an alternate functional political ideology, Pakistan unified behind Islam. Conflict with India has become a crutch that prevents a real political project from being actuated in Pakistan.

Ironically, sectarian violence, religious strife, and ethnic conflicts have resulted from Pakistan's own ideational identity,[36] which since its inception has doggedly attempted to impose a unitary state over its diverse populations. The cycle viciously perpetuates itself as disaffected groups in FATA, Baluchistan, Sind, and elsewhere rebel against the state and provide assistance to militant jihadi groups fighting the state. Pakistan then uses brute force to suppress provincial agitations and again

---

33   As quoted in Atif Shafique, "The Case for Constructivism in Analyzing the India-Pakistan Conflict," E-International Relations, September 7, 2011.
34   Cf. Christophe Jafferlot, "Islamic Identity and Ethnic Tension," in *A History of Pakistan and Its Origins*, ed. Christophe Jafferlot (London: Anthem Press, 2002), 9-38; Nasr, "National Identities and the India-Pakistan Conflict"; Jean-Luc Racine, "Living with India: Relations between Pakistan and India," in *A History of Pakistan and Its Origins*, ed. Christophe Jafferlot (London: Anthem Press, 2002), 112-133; Phillips Talbot, "The Subcontinent: Menage a Trois," *Foreign Affairs* 50 no. 4 (1972): 698-710; Talbot and Singh, *The Partition of India*.
35   Ashok Kapur, "Major Powers and the Persistence of the India-Pakistan Conflict," in *India-Pakistan Conflict an Enduring Rivalry*, ed. T. V. Paul (New York: Cambridge University Press, 2005), 142.
36   The term "ideational" in this context is related to a self-created conceptual identity.

must fall back on Islam as a unifying banner. This tactic, which is sometimes effective, also has been adopted by militant groups claiming that they are more Islamic than the state itself.

The partition of colonial India was and continues to be the defining event of modern India and Pakistan. From a humanitarian perspective, the partition of India proved disastrous for the subcontinent, especially in the period immediately following independence. From a political and geostrategic perspective, the decision to partition India has led to consequences that have affected the entire global community.

KASHMIR AND PARTITION

One of the most damaging, bitter, and dangerous legacies of partition—one that continues to have a debilitating impact in South Asia—is Kashmir's unresolved status.[37] Kashmir continues to occupy the center stage of an almost seven-decade long dispute between India and Pakistan, as both countries lay claim to the former kingdom of Jammu and Kashmir. It has been suggested that India and Pakistan's ongoing dispute over Kashmir lies at the heart of the conflicts entangling Afghanistan, India, and Pakistan.[38] The ongoing, low-intensity conflict that has lingered since 1947 has been the proximate cause for three wars between India and Pakistan and has the potential to ignite nuclear confrontation between the two states.[39] As I will show, Pakistan's institutional use of terrorism as a state strategy can be directly related to the conflict over Kashmir.

During the partition of India, the status of subcontinent's 562 princely states, which largely had been ruled autonomously by regional kings under British dominion, had to be determined. In theory, with the lapse of British rule the princely states were free to accede to either India or Pakistan or to become independent states; in reality, the last option was not on the table. Lord Mountbatten told the rulers of the princely states to accede to either India or Pakistan after evaluating two main criteria: geographical contiguity to India or Pakistan and the wishes of

---

[37] The pre-partition princely territory of Jammu and Kashmir remains divided between India and Pakistan. For simplicity, I call the Indian-held territory "Kashmir" and the Pakistan-controlled territory "Pakistani Kashmir" or "PK."

[38] For an overview, see Ganguly, *Conflict Unending*; Alastair Lamb, *Incomplete Partition: The Genesis of the Kashmir Dispute, 1947-1948* (Karachi: Oxford University Press, 2002); S. Paul Kapur, "The Kashmir Conflict: Past, Present, and Future," in *The Routledge Book of Asian Security Studies*, ed. Sumit Ganguly, Andrew Scobell, and Joseph C. Liow (London: Routledge, 2010), 103-114; Thaza V. Paul, "Causes of the India-Pakistan Enduring Rivalry," in *The India-Pakistan conflict: An Enduring Rivalry*, ed. T.V. Paul (Cambridge: Cambridge University Press, 2005), 3-24; Victoria Schofield, *Kashmir in Conflict: India, Pakistan, and the Unending War* (New York: St. Martin's Press, 2000).

[39] There have been four wars if the Kargil conflict is included.

their subject populations. Thus, to avoid fragmenting India or Pakistan, those states that fell in Pakistani territory would accede to Pakistan, while those that fell deep within Indian territory would join India. Similarly, primarily Hindu states would join India and primarily Muslim states would join Pakistan.[40]

Kashmir was in a unique situation as its territory abutted both India and Pakistan. The majority of its population was Muslim, but its ruler, Hari Singh, was a Hindu. When the time for independence came, Hari Singh decided to join neither India nor Pakistan, hoping to keep Kashmir independent. A strong Kashmiri regional movement, the National Conference, had close ties to the Indian National Congress and was not inclined to join Pakistan. The most eminent Kashmiri nationalist leader, Sheikh Abdullah, was committed to a process of land reform and redistributive justice and was a strict anti-monarchist. He was against joining Pakistan and instead favored Kashmir's independence.

In constitutional terms, Kashmir's ruler had the legal right to choose whether to accede to India or to Pakistan. In cases where the ruler did not share the faith of a large majority of his population it was assumed he would nevertheless go along with the wishes of the people.[41]

After the partition, Hari Singh was pressured by both India and Pakistan to accede to their dominions, but he continued to vacillate. Pakistani leadership strongly desired a union with Kashmir. Hari Singh himself was a brutal and unpopular ruler, and after the Britain's departure, brewing unrest against the king emerged as an uprising in the Poonch region of Kashmir. Pakistan sought to transform this unrest into a full-blown revolt against Hari Singh by supporting thousands of tribesmen as they launched an attack on Kashmir. Their objective was to overthrow the king and ensure that Kashmir would accede to Pakistan, and by supporting an internal uprising and an external tribal militia attack, Pakistan could avoid direct appearance of involvement. This combination was initially successful as the invading tribes captured a key city and moved towards Kashmir's capital, Srinagar, in October 1947. Pakistani military regulars guided the tribesmen during their push towards Srinagar, referring to their invasion as "jihad" and claiming they were liberating Kashmir from Hindus for Muslims.[42] Believing his regime was about to be overthrown, Hari Singh panicked and asked for India's help against the intruders; it was promised in return for Kashmir's accession to India. Desperate to save his kingdom, Hari Singh joined the Indian Union on

---

40 Bose, *Kashmir: Roots of Conflict, Paths to Peace*, 306; Paul, "Causes of the India-Pakistan Enduring Rivalry," 103-114.
41 For a discussion of the Kashmiri ruler's indecision to accede to India or Pakistan, see Schofield, *Kashmir in Conflict*, 28-33.
42 S. Paul Kapur and Sumit Ganguly, "The Jihad Paradox: Pakistan and Islamist Militancy in South Asia," *International Security* 37, no. 1 (2012): 119

October 27 in return for India's military aid. Pakistan did not accept the accession and sent in troops, and the first war over Kashmir broke out between India and Pakistan. It lasted until the United Nations brokered a cease-fire in January 1949. When the war ended, approximately one-third of the Kashmiri territory was under Pakistan's control with the remainder under Indian control. But this was merely the beginning of a long and deeply destructive conflict between India and Pakistan.[43]

The Indian government considered Maharaja Hari Singh's signed accession papers a legally binding contract that made Kashmir a part of India. Meanwhile, Pakistan argued that since Kashmir was a Muslim-majority state, it rightfully belonged to Pakistan. Pakistan also pointed out that India's refusal to hold a plebiscite for the Kashmiri people (which would allow them to decide whether they wished to join India or Pakistan) rendered the accession undemocratic. Both countries were determined to possess the country by any means.

The dispute was more than territorial; it was an existential conflict between the two nation states. Since Pakistan separated itself from the secular, multicultural, and multi-religious India, positioning itself as the home to Muslims in the continent, the loss of Muslim Kashmir became a symbol of shame to Pakistan's ruling elite. Furthermore, as the second largest Muslim nation in the world, Pakistan wished to claim leadership of the Umma, the global Muslim community. Due to their defeat in the first war for Kashmir, Pakistan was unable to lay claim to such a prestigious global position.

Kashmir lies at the center of an identity-based conflict, one that has the power to threaten the legitimacy of a state's existence, whether that state is India or Pakistan. In India's case, its secular ideational identity is nullified if the majority Muslim state of Kashmir is given to Pakistan. Similarly, if Muslim Pakistan, with its ideational identity as the homeland for South Asia's Muslims, cannot incorporate Kashmir in its territory, the reason for its creation becomes questionable. This quandary lies beneath the conflict between India and Pakistan.

When the subcontinent was divided, India's military strength was substantially greater than that of Pakistan as the military infrastructure and units of the old British Indian Army had been divided on a 7:3 ratio in India's favor. Despite its weaker military position, Pakistan was not deterred from its adventurism in Kashmir. Colonial attitudes had shaped Pakistan's conception of its military's capabilities, giving it an unrealistically optimistic outlook regarding Kashmir. The Pakistani elite and military leaders had inherited the prejudices of Raj officials,

---

43 For a discussion of Kashmir's centrality in India-Pakistan conflict, see Ganguly, *Conflict Unending*.

who had very condescending views of Hindu military abilities and a very high opinion of martial prowess of Muslims. The 18th and 19th century ideas about the Muslim and Punjabi "martial races," as opposed to the weak and effeminate caste Hindus, had permeated the psyche of the Pakistan Army. This opinion has been rather neatly stated by Pakistani General Akbar Khan, whose ideas reflected those of the Pakistan Army's elite:

> In the remotest of our villages, the humblest of our people possess a self-confidence and ready willingness to march into India – a spirit the equivalent of which cannot be found on the other side…. In India, in the absence of homogeneity, a penetration in any direction can result in separation of different units geographically as well as morally because there is no basic unity among the Shudras, Brahmins, Sikhs, Hindus and Muslims who will follow their own different interests. At present, and for a long time to come, India is in the same position as she was centuries ago, exposed to disintegration in emergencies.[44]

Contrary to the colonial perceptions of the Pakistani armed forces, the first full-scale war had resulted in a stalemate. The UN-brokered ceasefire did not moderate Pakistan's irredentist goals, and Pakistani leadership remained committed to taking over the entirety of Kashmir through the use of diplomatic as well as military pressure on India.

In Pakistan there remained a strong belief that the country would be "incomplete" without Kashmir. In the words of Pakistan's then foreign minister Zulfikar Ali Bhutto:

> If a Muslim majority can remain a part of India, then the raison d'etre of Pakistan collapses…. Pakistan is incomplete without Jammu and Kashmir both territorially and ideologically. It would be fatal if, in sheer exhaustion or out of intimidation, Pakistan were to abandon the struggle, and a bad compromise would be tantamount to abandonment; which might, in turn, lead to the collapse of Pakistan.[45]

The Indian government also remained intransigent, refusing to cede any ground on Kashmir and disregarding the wishes of Kashmiri people and their leaders as it steadily tightened its grip on the disputed territory. Pakistan's identity as the homeland of the Muslims of the Indian subcontinent, especially in terms of Kashmir, was not complete; consequently, Pakistani leadership continued to frame its goals as religious. The wishes of Kashmiri natives did not figure in either Indian or Pakistani calculations—they were mere pawns in the state-building projects that were taking place on both sides of the subcontinent's newly-drawn boundary.

---

44 Ganguly, *Conflict Unending*, 20.
45 Ibid., 32.

Kashmir's continuing importance to Pakistan is demonstrated by General Musharraf's September 19, 2001 address to Pakistan. Musharraf explained that the decision to support the United States served Pakistan's national interests because failure to do so would jeopardize their cause in Kashmir and endanger Pakistan's nuclear installations. While Musharraf addressed Pakistan's protection of its nuclear installations, these endeavors have been a direct consequence of its obsession with counterbalancing India's military superiority. Praveen Swami has called Pakistan's pursuit of nuclear weapon a means of *"creating a shield behind which the jihad in Jammu and Kashmir could be pursued without inviting Indian retaliation."* [46] Musharraf's claim elucidates that Kashmir is one of Pakistan's foreign policy raisons d'être.

Since their creation, both India and Pakistan have made possessing Kashmir a foundational part of their national identities.[47] It is important to India for many different reasons. First, because Kashmir is the only Muslim-majority province in India, losing it would damage India's identity as an inclusive secular state. Allowing Pakistan to take over Kashmir would imply that minority groups could not thrive in India. Second, India views Hari Singh's agreement to its annexation as legally binding. Third, according to India, the partition was completed in 1947 and any territorial concession to Pakistan would constitute a second partition. And finally, India also feared that relinquishing Kashmir would lead to separatist tendencies in other parts of the country, destabilizing or even fragmenting India.

Pakistan, on the other hand, has considered itself territorially and ideologically incomplete without Kashmir because it has regarded itself as the homeland for the subcontinent's Muslims. If Pakistan accepted Indian control of Kashmir, it would mean that Muslims could live and thrive in a Hindu-majority India, thus negating the necessity for Pakistan's creation. Because both nations have seen control of Kashmir as essential to their respective national identities, the conflict was irreconcilable.

Both arguments are flawed. For India, it was not then, nor is it now, essential to retain Kashmir in order to validate India's secular credentials. More than 140 million Muslims live in India, spread across many regions.[48] What validates its pluralistic polity is how the Indian state treats these Muslims, not that it retains

---

46 Praveen Swami, *India, Pakistan and the Secret Jihad: The Covert War in Kashmir, 1947-2004* (London: Routledge, 2006), 141.
47 Cohen, *The Idea of Pakistan*, 36; Sunil Dutta, "Clash of Identities: the Reason for India-Pakistan Conflict?" *Pakistan Daily Times*, May 21, 2012.
48 An Indian Census from 2001 listed the Muslim population of the country as 138 million, or 13.4% of its total population. Government of India, Ministry of Home Affairs, Office of the Registrar General and Census Commission, "Distribution of "Population by Religion," 2001, Table 21.

Kashmir. Similarly, the argument that Pakistan's claims as the state for Muslims in the subcontinent was fallacious even in 1947, let alone now, as a third of British India's Muslims chose (or resigned themselves) to remain in India after the partition. These Muslims do not live in Pakistan; why is it necessary for Kashmiri Muslims to be incorporated into it? (This particular line of argumentation was further weakened when East Pakistan broke away from Pakistan to become Bangladesh in 1971.) Regardless of logical flaws, the ideological power of these arguments has been harnessed by the nationalistic enterprises of both India and Pakistan for the last 67 years as the two states celebrated their 67th year of independence in August 2014. While India has been content with the status quo in Kashmir, Pakistan never accepted the existing facts on the ground since 1947.

Kashmir also provided Pakistan with a convenient distraction from its failure to develop a consolidating ideology (outside of Islam) that could constitute genuine nationalism. When the new government was faced with regional, ethnic and linguistic divisions (Balochi, Bengali, Punjabi, Sindhi, Urdu); religious conflicts (Sunnis versus Shias, Sunnis versus Ahmadiya); ethno-nationalist conflicts (as in Baluchistan, Bengal, the NWFP, Punjab, and Sindh), it instead conveniently chose to focus on a never-ending oppositional conflict. As such, Kashmir became a nucleus for the state-building project in Pakistan. The Indian government faced similar regional and linguistic conflicts and dealt with them in a ham-fisted manner, using brutal force in case of separatist demands in Punjab and the northeast. However, to its credit, India also managed to diffuse several such conflicts by creating new linguistic based states, for example Andhra Pradesh for Telugu speakers was created from Madras in 1953 and Haryana and Himachal Pradesh were carved out for non-Punjabi speakers from Punjab in 1966.

Pakistan first heavily invested in its proxy war capabilities when it utilized militants and non-state actors during the anti-Soviet jihad in Afghanistan. However, its use of non-state actors as tools of state policy dates back to 1947.[49] Pakistan has consciously and strategically used irregulars to achieve its political and military objectives. The use of non-state actors as tools of asymmetric warfare against stronger adversaries—for instance, the Soviet Union and India—is a policy that took shape at Pakistan's birth. By using non-state actors to fight its proxy wars, Pakistan provided itself with plausible deniability (however tenuous) and allowed it to avoid full-scale, direct combat wars with larger and better-equipped enemies.[50]

---

49 Kapur and Ganguly, "The Jihad Paradox," 111-113.
50 Ibid., 123-124, 132.

Pakistan's first engagement in proxy and asymmetric warfare culminated in the first India-Pakistan war. In October 1947, Pakistan mobilized tribal militias to invade and seize Kashmir. Pakistan used irregular fighters, as well as regular fighters drawn from its military, paramilitary, and intelligence agencies who disguised themselves as irregular fighters. Pakistan has never acknowledged its official involvement in the conflict that spanned from October 1947 to May 1948, describing the incursion by Pakistan-supported irregulars as an indigenous movement. This was just the beginning of a pattern where Pakistan relies on denials and half-truths as it participates in proxy warfare in Afghanistan, Kashmir, and India. Similarly, even when confronted with evidence of its support of militant jihadis and reliance on terrorism for its foreign policy, Pakistan has almost always refused to acknowledge its role.

Pakistan and India engaged in several multilateral and bilateral negotiations between 1949 and 1965. Due to their entrenched positions, however, there had been no possibility for compromise. After the first Indo-Pakistan war, Pakistan supported numerous covert cells within Indian-administered Kashmir. Plans to arm and train a Kashmiri militia were hatched in Pakistan and resulted in several attacks in Kashmir.[51] This use of militants formed the basis of a planned attack in 1965. In 1965, Pakistan formulated "Operation Gibraltar" to infiltrate Kashmir, stoke anti-Indian sentiment, and stir up a rebellion, expecting Kashmiri Muslim support. The Pakistan Army planned to use this as an opportunity to invade and seize Kashmir in a plan called "Operation Grand Slam." Volunteers were trained to infiltrate Kashmir, and military and paramilitary personnel accompanied these irregulars to provide support and guidance. Pakistan dispatched approximately 30,000 infiltrators into Indian-administered Kashmir to set up bases, engage in sabotage, and foment a wider indigenous insurrection. However, the plan failed. Kashmiris did not support Pakistan's aims nor did they rise up against India. Instead, they notified Indian authorities of Pakistani infiltration. Though Operation Gibraltar itself failed, Pakistan launched a full-scale attack on September 1, starting its second full-scale war over Kashmir. This war, too, failed to wrest Indian-controlled Kashmir and ended up in a stalemate.

Six years after the 1965 war, in 1971, India and Pakistan engaged in another direct war. This war resulted in a devastating loss for Pakistan as it was dismembered and East Pakistan seceded to form Bangladesh. This particular incident will be treated in detail in the next chapter of this book. Suffice it to say, one critical lesson Pakistan learned in 1971 was that direct conflict with India would be catastrophic because India possessed a much stronger military. As a result, Pakistan gave the

---

51 Ganguly and Kapur, "The Sorcerer's Apprentice," 49-50

strategy of waging war with proxies and irregulars a place of even more prominence in its security posture. When the Soviets invaded Afghanistan in 1979, Pakistan's use of proxies and militant jihadis to fight asymmetric warfare against Soviet forces would again reinforce its reliance on irregular non-state agents. This too will be discussed in detail in a subsequent chapter.

While the focus on an-all Afghan resistance during the Afghan War (1979-1988) redirected Pakistan's attention from its proxy war in Kashmir, its obsession with Kashmir continued. Pakistan began using the American aid to build up its armed forces so it might confront India in the future. Its intent was to use the Soviet-Afghan War as a smoke screen so it might renew and expand its militant campaign in Kashmir; this is clear from Pakistani dictator General Mohammad Zia-ul Haq's private description, comparing the war in Afghanistan to the jihad in Kashmir.[52] The importance of Kashmir to Pakistan and to Zia is also reflected in an interview given by the Amir of Jamaat-e-Islami, Pakistan-administered Kashmir, Maulana Abdul Bari. Zia told Bari in a meeting in early 1980 that the reason Pakistan would participate in the American-sponsored war in Afghanistan was to prepare for a larger conflict in Kashmir. The general reportedly told Bari that he would be able to divert significant amounts of weaponry provided by American support to Kashmir. In return, Bari was asked to have Jamaat-e-Islami work with the Pakistan Army.[53]

Within Kashmir, Pakistan first supported the Jammu and Kashmir Liberation Front (JKLF), a Kashmiri secessionist group. While the Afghan War continued across the Durand Line, in 1984, the Director General of ISI, Lieutenant General Akhtar Abdur Rehman, held several meetings with the JKLF leadership in which he offered them assistance.[54] Pakistan agreed to provide JKLF with military and financial support to fight in Kashmir. Pakistani support included helping with JKLF recruitment, publishing of propaganda material, and providing military and financial backing.

While several high profile acts of terrorism in Kashmir occurred in 1983-1986, a large-scale rebellion against India erupted in Kashmir in 1989. It is no coincidence that this occurred just after the Afghan War drew to a close.

Indian action contributed to Kashmiri resentment and rebellion. During the 1987 Kashmiri elections, the Muslim United Front (MUF), an alliance of several religious-political parties, contested the elections on the grounds of blatant ballot

---

52 Arif Jamal, *Shadow War: The Untold Story of Jihad in Kashmir* (Brooklyn: Melville Publishing House, 2009), 109.
53 Ibid., 109-110.
54 Ibid.

rigging in favor of Delhi-backed rulers (including forcible takeover of the polling stations), ballots stamped in favor of Delhi-backed candidates, and that Delhi supporters were stopping the vote count if opposition candidates took the lead. As the ballots were being counted, it was apparent that MUF's Yusuf Shah was winning by a landslide. However, Yusuf Shah's opponent was declared the winner, and when MUF supporters dared to protest, Yusuf Shah and his election manager, Mohammad Yasin Malik, were arrested and imprisoned without formal charges or an appearance in court.[55]

Yusuf Shah, who should have been a member of the opposition in Kashmir assembly in 1987, took on a new name, Syed Salahuddin (the name of the legendary Muslim warrior, Saladin, who fought against the Christian Crusaders) and emerged as a new avatar. He is currently the chief of Hizb-ul-Mujahideen (HM), a group with an Islamist agenda that advocates Kashmir's accession to Pakistan. Yasin Malik became a member of the JKLF, although unlike Yusuf Shah, Malik rejected supporting Pakistan and remained committed to the goal of an independent and sovereign Jammu and Kashmir.[56]

While the eruption in Kashmir was clearly tied to genuine popular grievances against India's oppressive policies, Pakistan effectively used the situation to turn the rebellion into a full-fledged insurgency and re-deployed many jihadis from Afghanistan to Kashmir.

Pakistan's attitude towards JKLF underwent a change since the Front was a genuinely nationalist Kashmiri organization and not radically Islamist. The objective of the Front was to achieve independence for Kashmir, not to join Pakistan. The JKLF maintained that neither India nor Pakistan had any legal claim to Kashmir, recognizing the solution to the conflict in Kashmir as a merging of all the parts of the state into a single sovereign nation. These conflicting goals caused tension between Pakistan and the JKLF and in early 1990s Pakistan shifted its support from the Front to HM.[57] Despite HM's irredentist posture, members were native Kashmiris and thus less prone to indiscriminate and vicious attacks in Kashmir. Pakistan solved this issue by deploying radical militant organizations with no Kashmiri members into Kashmir. The most prominent of these Pakistan-based organizations included *Lashkar-e-Taiba* (LeT), *Jaish-e-Mohammad*, and

---

55 Bose, *Kashmir*, 49.
56 Ibid., 50.
57 Kapur and Ganguly, "The Jihad Paradox," 127.

Harkat-ul-Ansar. The militants were provided with large scale support by the Pakistani military, including weapons, training, and logistical support to cross the Line of Control into India.[58]

Lashkar-e-Taiba was formed, with the assistance of the ISI, as the militant wing of the Pakistani *Markaz al-Dawa wal-Irshad* (the "Center for Proselytization and Preaching," or MDI) in 1987. Abdullah Azzam formed the MDI with help from Hafiz Muhammad Saeed and Zafar Iqbal, and its mission was to apply the lessons learned from the Afghan jihad to the struggle against Kashmir and India. The center trained Kashmiri insurgents to fight alongside the mujahideen in order to provide them with combat experience. Camps were set up in Afghanistan's Kunar Province; additionally, the ISI trained MDI operatives in its own camps as well.[59] The MDI supported the Afghan jihad by establishing militant training camps in the Paktia and Kunar provinces in Afghanistan. Both the MDI and LeT benefited from CIA funding that was channeled through the ISI during the Afghan jihad. Lashkar-e-Taiba is said to be closely associated with Pakistani intelligence agencies.

After the Soviets departed from Afghanistan, MDI and LeT focused on liberating Kashmir from India, and a majority of LeT's violent actions were limited to Kashmir throughout the early 1990s. After 9/11, LeT reorganized just before the United States designated it a Foreign Terrorist Organization, when Hafiz Saeed created *Jamaat-ud-Dawa* (JuD) and transferred all of the LeT's assets to it. It is believed that JuD and LeT are practically the same organization.[60] LeT has created a vast infrastructure in Pakistan for training militants whereas JuD conducts fundraising and militant recruitment. Most recruits come from the Punjab region of Pakistan. LeT has conducted several daring operations where its operatives' mission is to kill as many targets as possible. Of all the radical groups nurtured by the ISI, LeT is considered the deadliest, as well as affiliated with al Qaeda. There are other militant groups fighting in Kashmir that are based in Pakistan and have links to al Qaeda; some of these include Harakat-ul-Mujahideen, based in Muzaffarabad and Rawalpindi and aligned with Jamiat-I Ulema-I Islam; *Jaish-e-Mohammed* is also aligned with *Jamiat-I Ulema-I Islam*; and *Hizb-ul-Mujahideen* is associated with *Jamaat-e-Islami*.[61]

---

58 See Alexander Evans, "The Kashmir Insurgency: As Bad as It Gets," *Small Wars and Insurgencies* 11, no. 1 (2000): 69-81; Ganguly, *Conflict Unending*; Rathnam Indurthy, "Kashmir Between India and Pakistan: An Intractable Conflict, 1947 to Present," 2011.
59 Riedel, *Deadly Embrace*, 32.
60 For an analysis, see Fair, "Lashkar-e-Tayiba and the Pakistani State," 29-52.
61 See K. Alan Kronstadt and Bruce Vaughn, "Terrorism in South Asia," US Congressional Research Service Report (2004), 1-30.

These Pakistan-based militant organizations, termed *mehmaan mujahideen* ("guest holy warriors") in Kashmir, were unconcerned about the impact that their insurgency was having on the Kashmiri people and became increasingly brutal. By the mid-1990s, with extensive military, financial, and logistical support of Pakistan, *Lashkar-e-Taiba* and *Jaish-e-Mohammad* became the leading militant groups in Kashmir, launching attacks against prominent military as well as civilian targets. Pakistan-backed militants systematically eliminated those seeking independence rather than union with Pakistan, effectively placing the insurgency in Kashmir under the control of groups pursuing Islamabad's agenda.[62] The insurgency indicated to Pakistan that their goals could be achieved through a low-intensity conflict. A sustained asymmetric campaign, Pakistani leadership believed, would drain Indian resources and erode its military advantage at relatively little cost to Pakistan.

Indeed, Pakistan's support of a large number of insurgent groups in Kashmir and its adoption of low-intensity conflict did blunt the advantages that India enjoyed due to its greater size, power, and economy. Pakistan's low-intensity strategy proved to be highly effective. Based on Kashmiri government documents, between 1990 and 2011, a total of 43,460 people were killed in Kashmir; of these, 21,323 were militants and 5,369 were members of the security forces.[63] There were over 5,000 acts of violence by militants in 1993 alone, including bombings and arson. As the violence spiraled out of control, India was forced to deploy more than a quarter of a million soldiers and security personnel in Kashmir. While India has not released the official number of troops, in 2007 Lieutenant General Panag mentioned the presence of 337,000 troops in Kashmir, which would raise the number of security forces to over 400,000 when paramilitary forces and state police numbers were included.[64] Opponents maintain that 600,000 Indian troops are stationed in Kashmir. The insurgency has created a climate of fear and caused serious damage to India's economy, and India's heavy-handed response to it, which has included human rights violations, has damaged India's reputation.

While the violence in Kashmir continued through Pakistani proxies throughout the 1990s, in 1999, India and Pakistan came close to a full-scale war over Kashmir. That year, Pakistan's Northern Light Infantry (NLI) made an incursion into Kashmir near the Indian town of Kargil. The area was rugged; its harsh terrain,

---

62   See also, Evans, "The Kashmir Insurgency," 69-81; Howenstein, "The Jihadi Terrain in Pakistan," 28-31; Swami, *India, Pakistan and the Secret Jihad*.
63   Randeep S. Nandal, "State Data Refutes Claim of 1 Lakh Killed in Kashmir," *Times of India*, June 20, 2011. These numbers are contested and are highly likely to be underreported. A coalition of pro-independence and pro-Pakistan group, the Hurriyat Conference, claims that between 1989 and 2002, 80,000 were killed during the insurgency.
64   Praveen Swami, "Kashmir: Fewer Troops, More Peace," *The Hindu*, January 12, 2014.

high altitude, and thin air made military operations taxing and expensive. Both the sides engaged in partial winter retreats from their forward northern areas, which were too dangerous to man in winter. Each year, after the snowmelt, each side reclaimed and restocked their posts. In Kargil in March and April of 1999, the Pakistan Army had planned to capture vacated Indian posts long before Indian troops returned. This became the flashpoint of a major battle between India and Pakistan. Pakistan anticipated that the element of surprise and their tactically superior high ground location would prevent India from dislodging the NLI troops before the onset of winter. Once the Pakistani forces were in place and access to the high posts were frozen, Pakistan could restock its own forward posts and lock in its territorial gains across the Line of Control. Pakistani planners, however, did not expect India to escalate the counteroffensive to the level that it did.

The infiltrating force had camouflaged itself in local clothing and used local dialects on radio to pretend they were local jihadi militants. Initially India believed that jihadi militants had made the incursion; later it became clear that the NLI had been involved in the operation. Pakistan used this ploy to convince Indian forces that the intruders were civilian Kashmiri militants struggling to liberate Kashmir from Indian control and that its regular army had not crossed the Line of Control. Christine Fair maintains, "The Pakistan army hoped that the mujahideen façade would last long enough to obtain some territorial gains even if eventually the truth would be discerned."[65] Even after it was discovered that the invasion involved Pakistan armed forces, Pakistan was hesitant to concede the NLI's involvement, which would be tantamount to committing an act of war. The admission was made four years later in 2003.

The conflict started when Indian soldiers attempted to retrieve their posts in May and came under fire near Kargil. India launched a major counteroffensive, using air strikes to support the soldiers fighting at very high altitudes. The two sides battled intensely for two months at altitudes ranging between 12,000 to 17,000 feet. Escalating the stakes even further, India mobilized its troops in other locations along the India-Pakistan border, even positioning its navy for a blockade around Karachi. Pakistan came under increasing international pressure to pull back its troops from the Indian side of Kashmir. The operation turned into a major military crisis and it took the United States' intervention to bring the situation to a stop. The United States received intelligence that Pakistan had been making nuclear preparation, and on July 4, President Clinton demanded that Pakistan's prime minister, Nawaz Sharif, immediately withdraw all Pakistani troops. In the

---

65 C. Christine Fair, "Militants in the Conflicts: Myths, Realities, and Impacts," in *Asymmetric Warfare in South Asia: The Causes and Consequences of the Kargil Conflict* (New York: Cambridge University Press, 2009), 233.

end no territory exchanged hands, however, the conflict was significant as both India and Pakistan had exploded nuclear weapons in 1998 and both the sides were nuclear-armed states. [66]

While probably neither side was prepared to begin a nuclear war, Peter Lavoy states, "we now know that Indian troops were within days of opening another front across the [Line of Control] and possibly the international border, an act that could have triggered a large-scale conventional military engagement, which in turn might have escalated to an exchange of recently tested Indian and Pakistani nuclear weapons."[67]

Though forced to give up the posts it has captured, Pakistan saw the operation as a success. General Pervez Musharraf claimed, "Considered purely in military terms, the Kargil operations were a landmark in the history of the Pakistan army. As few as five battalions in support of the freedom fighter groups were able to compel the Indians to employ more than four divisions," deplete their artillery sources from strike formations, and force them to "mobilize their entire national resources, including their air force."[68]

The Kargil crisis was one link in the chain of India-Pakistan crises related to Kashmir. Like the others, it did not result in any resolution and only prompted both countries to prepare for their next war. After the cessation of hostilities in Kargil, India and Pakistan relations worsened and both sides ramped up the production of nuclear weapons and missile delivery systems as well as their conventional conflict capabilities.

As Pakistan and India have continued their battle over Kashmir, they have treated the people of Kashmir as pawns in a battle centered on identity and ideology. Indian Kashmir has experienced an authoritarian centralized government, where regional demands for autonomy are seen as "anti-national" and are crushed in a manner befitting the Raj in colonial India. India has treated Kashmir no better than a colony. The short-term expediencies of keeping Kashmir in India—including the authoritarian behavior of the central government and its blatant interference in governance (such as rigging elections and denying autonomy)—have understandably alienated Kashmiris.

---

66   For a discussion of Kargil conflict's significance in India-Pakistan conflict, see Peter R. Lavoy, "Why Kargil Did Not Produce General War: The Crisis Management Strategies of Pakistan, India, and the United States," in *Asymmetric Warfare in South Asia: The Causes and Consequences of the Kargil Conflict*, ed. Lavoy, Peter (New York: Cambridge University Press, 2009), 171-204.
67   Lavoy, *Asymmetric Warfare in South Asia*, 2.
68   Ibid., 8.

On Pakistan's side, its use of irregulars and proxies, pursued under the garb of Islam, is directly related to its successful use of Islam during the short Pakistan nationalist struggle. The rhetoric of Islam was employed with full force in 1945 and was a success for the Muslim League. Naturally, Pakistan has employed Islamic rhetoric and militancy in Kashmir as it has approached other oppositional conflicts.

East Pakistan's Secession and the India-Pakistan War of 1971

When British India was divided into Pakistan and India in 1947, the western part of Punjab became West Pakistan and the Bengal province in the east became East Pakistan. Dominated by the Punjabi elite, West Pakistan inherited its colonial military culture. Due to the circumstances of its creation, Pakistan soon came to be dominated by its military and bureaucracy, with West Pakistan as the dominant half, greatly influenced by large landlords with close connections to the military.

While India and Pakistan came into being with adversarial identities, the nascent Pakistan itself began with adversarial identities coming from its eastern and western wings and from other conflicting populations. The first significant oppositional identity within Pakistan was between the migrants (called "*mohajirs*"), or the refugees from India, and indigenous groups, each of which had its own conception of what Pakistan meant.[69] The *mohajirs* compared their migration to the Muslim exodus (*hijrat*) led by the Prophet Muhammad, using this myth to seek pre-eminence as the "real'" Pakistanis. Differences also existed between the East Pakistan and West Pakistan. The better-educated migrant communities soon dominated Pakistan's institutions, which were mostly concentrated in the west. The west, dominated by Punjabis, absorbed the preeminent Muslim League political leadership, which came from the United Provinces and spoke Urdu.[70] Urdu had been used as a key marker of Muslim identity by Muslim separatists due to its Persian and Arabic lexicon; soon it became the state language of Pakistan. Bengali, however, was the mother tongue of over half the Pakistani population. East Pakistan comprised 56 percent of Pakistan's population, and there almost everyone spoke Bengali. Only approximately one percent of the population in the East regarded Urdu as their first language.[71] Despite the fact that only a small minority of Pakistanis in both the East and West wings of Pakistan spoke Urdu, the elite in the West chose it as the national language, causing great resentment.[72]

---

69 Farzana Shaikh, *Making Sense of Pakistan* (New York: Columbia University Press, 2009), 48-52.
70 Ibid, 50-53.
71 Talbot, *India and Pakistan*, 254.
72 For a discussion of the language controversy, see Mussarat Jabeen, Amir Chandio, and Zarina Qasim, "Language Controversy: Impacts on National Politics and Secession of East Pakistan," *South Asian Studies* 25, no. 1 (2010): 99-124.

The government brutally crushed the language riots that erupted in 1952 in East Pakistan. By making Urdu the official language of Muslims in Pakistan even though it was only spoken by seven percent of its population, Pakistan's elite not only denied the existence of other major indigenous languages and peoples, including Bengali, Sindhi, Punjabi, Pashto and Balochi, they also sowed the seeds of discord within the new nation state.

Besides the linguistic conflict, the West Pakistani elite had also absorbed the British colonial attitude that the Bengalis were an effeminate and weak race. The Urdu-speaking migrants believed that their version of Islam was superior to that of the Bengalis. Since most of the Bengali Muslims were converts from Hinduism and Bengali Islam was suffused with local Hindu rituals, the elite from the West held them in disdain. This ideational and adversarial identity of pure Islam in the West and doubt regarding Bengali Muslim's "Muslimness" resulted in two significant consequences: the 1971 civil war which resulted in East Pakistan's secession to create Bangladesh, and West Pakistan's (the remaining Pakistan) increasing use of Islam as a means of justifying its existence.

The adversarial relations between the East and the West wings had a colonial basis. Thomas Macaulay (1800-1859), famous for his 1835 *Minute on Indian Education*, had described the Bengalis as a weak-minded people who had been historically trampled upon by men of more hardy breeds. The Bengalis, deliberately denied representation in the Imperial Army and subsequently in the Pakistan Army, were still treated like colonial subjects, even in Muslim Pakistan. In Cohen's words, "Further, the army's overwhelming Punjabi-Pathan officer corps had never accepted the idea that Bengalis were militarily equal to them in terms of their "'martial' qualities, so by assuming that half of Pakistan's citizens were militarily inferior, they also implied over half the country comprised lesser Pakistanis." [73] Pakistani dictator Ayub Khan (1907-1974) possessed incredibly naïve and racist views towards Bengali Muslims and his views were shared by Pakistan's ruling elite.

---

73   Cohen, *The Idea of Pakistan*, 73-74.

In Ayub Khan's words:

> East Bengalis... It could be no exaggeration to say that up to the creation of Pakistan, they had not known any real freedom and sovereignty. In addition, they have been and still are under considerable Hindu cultural and linguistic influences. As such they have all the inhibitions of downtrodden races and they have not yet found it possible to adjust psychologically to the requirements of the new born freedom... their popular complexes, exclusiveness and... defensive aggressiveness... emerge from this historical background.[74]

The Punjabi-dominated military continued the racist colonial pattern of recruitment, excluding Bengalis from Pakistan Army and thus from the elite social strata. Eight years after independence, only fourteen out of 894 high-ranking officers in the Pakistan Army were Bengalis. The Pakistani Navy had seven Bengali officers out of a total 593. Discrimination persisted: in 1965, almost twenty years after independence, the Pakistan Army had 6,000 officers but only 300 were of Bengali origin. The overall percentage of the Punjabi component of Pakistan Army in 1947 was 77%, with Pashtuns representing 19.5% of the troops. Civil services were similarly dominated by the western part of Pakistan.[75] This composition can be directly traced to British discrimination against Bengali soldiers following the 1857 Rebellion.

Bengali Muslims not only faced discrimination among the military-bureaucratic elite of the newly emergent Pakistan, but the resources of East Pakistan were also exploited by the Punjabi elite in the West at the expense of development in the East. Reminiscent of the British, who began their colonial project in Bengal by extracting excessive revenue from Bengal and shipping it to London, impoverishing the once-wealthy province, Bengal was treated as a revenue source by the West. In effect, the establishment of Pakistan, instead of bringing freedom, simply replaced British supremacy with a Punjabi civil-military elite at the head of its East wing.[76] The Punjabis and Pashtuns, favored by the British and labeled the "martial races," would not share power with Bengalis, creating the perception that East Bengal was really just a colony of Pakistan. Bengalis protested for the recognition of their language, economic neglect, and low representation in civil and military services; their grievances were ignored or repressed by the regime in West Pakistan.

---

74 M. Ayub Khan, *Friends Not Masters: A Political Autobiography* (New York: Oxford University Press, 1967), 187.
75 Jafferlot, "Islamic Identity and Ethnic Tension," 48.
76 For a discussion of the ways in which the Punjabs overshadowed other units in post-colonial Pakistan, see Tai Yong Tan and Gyanesh Kudaisya, *The Aftermath of Partition in South Asia*, 204-219.

Bengali resentment was further peaked when during the 1965 war against India, military dictator Ayub Khan's failed to deploy sufficient resources for an eastern defense, stating that the defense of Pakistan lay in the West.[77] This provincial attitude that East Pakistan could be sacrificed to India to save West Pakistan, was just one example of why the Bengali Muslims grew increasingly alienated from the West.

Pakistan's first national general elections, held in December 1970, resulted in an absolute sweep by the East Pakistan-based Awami League party, led by Sheikh Mujibur Rahman. The Awami League won 160 of the 162 seats in East Pakistan, whereas the Pakistan People's Party, led by Zulfikar Ali Bhutto, won 81 of the 131 seats in West Pakistan.[78] With its absolute majority in the national assembly, the Awami League looked forward to forming the government. However, the West Pakistan-based power brokers, with Bhutto in the forefront and the military behind, refused to allow the Awami League to form its democratically elected government. The Western Pakistanis and the Punjabi and Pathan-dominated Pakistan Army found it intolerable to hand power over to the Bengalis.[79]

The talks between Mujibur Rahman, Zulfikar Ali Bhutto, and General Yahya Khan broke down on March 25, 1971, and the Awami League was given no chance to form the government. Mujibur Rahman was arrested after midnight and the West Pakistani troops began a crackdown during the dark of night.[80] On March 26, 1971, Bangladesh declared independence. Twenty-four years after Pakistan was created, half of it had sloughed off its connection with South Asia's Muslim homeland. Many Awami League leaders fled and took refuge in India and a government-in-exile was formed in April. A war of liberation broke out. Remarkably, the declaration of independence by the Bangladesh government in exile merited no response from India, who did not extend their official recognition of the government-in-exile until December.

Once again, the Pakistan Army had revealed its entrenched colonial attitudes. The "martial" Punjabi Muslims and Pathans believed that the cowardly Bengalis would quit their rebellion at the first sign of chastisement. The "traitorous" minority Hindu population of East Pakistan and enemy Indians were also believed to be responsible for the revolt. Western Pakistan's decision about how to solve the problem was also grounded in imperial history: the Bengali and Hindu problem in East Pakistan would be taken care of with brute force. According to Oldenburg:

---

77 Cohen, *The Idea of Pakistan*.73-74.
78 Hamza Alavi, "Bangladesh and the Crises of Pakistan," *Socialist Register* 8, no. 8 (1971): 291.
79 For a detailed analysis of the events leading to the civil war after the 1970 elections, see R. Sisson and L. E. Rose, *War and Secession: Pakistan, India, and the Creation of Bangladesh* (Berkeley: University of California Press, 1991).
80 Wolpert, *A New History of India*, 387.

On the ground, army officers, too, operated with a theory of how the killing and driving out of the Hindus would help save Pakistan. Anthony Mascarenhas reports that "senior military and civil officers in Dacca and Comilla" told him that "we are determined to cleanse East Pakistan once and for all of the threat of secession, even if it means killing off two million people and ruling the province as a colony for 30 years."[81]

The night of March 25, 1971, became infamous for beginning of Operation Searchlight, a brutal massacre that targeted, among others, unarmed members of the Bengali intelligentsia and academia. These figures had led the linguist and nationalist movement in East Pakistan and therefore were to be systematically executed. Dacca University was shelled, and teachers, intellectuals, Awami League members, and important members of the Hindu minority were targeted and slaughtered by the Pakistani military, which had been beefed up with 80,000 additional troops flown from West Pakistan. All of this was done on the part of the Pakistan Army in order to silence Bengali voices demanding more autonomy and better treatment. The violence and brutality was so savage that up to 20 million people fled their homes, and at least ten million refugees ended up in India. By September 1971, India was spending some $200 million every month to feed the refugees in its territory.[82] There has been significant controversy over the number of Bengalis killed in the pogrom, but it has been estimated that the Pakistani armed forces killed between 300,000 and 3 million people in Bangladesh.[83] Rudolph Rummel has estimated the number killed by Pakistani armed forces to be closer to 1.5 million.[84]

It is ironic that the colonial-created identity of Islam as a unified monolithic grouping of people oppositional to the Hindus came apart in the homeland created for South Asia's Muslims. West Pakistani soldiers, fueled by the myth about Bengali inferiority that they had inherited from their colonial predecessors, showed no hesitation in massacring students, intellectuals, and civilians for months. As the events of 1971 demonstrated, it was easy for the Punjabi- and Pathan-dominated Pakistan Army to slaughter Bengalis wholesale without regrets and indeed with a joyful sense of killing. Anthony Mascarenhas, who covered the 1971 war, noted,

---

81 Philip Oldenburg, "'A Place Insufficiently Imagined': Language, Belief, and the Pakistan Crisis of 1971," *Journal of Asian Studies* 44, no. 4 (1985): 729.
82 Wolpert, *A New History of India* 389.
83 For an overview, see F. Bhattacharya, "East Bengal," in *A History of Pakistan and its Creation*, ed. Christophe Jafferlot (London: Anthem Press, 2002), 39-60; Jahan, "Genocide in Bangladesh," 291-316; Oldenburg, "A Place Insufficiently Imagined," 711-733; Sisson and Rose, *War and Secession*; S. Rahman, "Bangladesh: Political Culture and Heritage," in *Government and Politics in South Asia*, 6th ed., edited by Y. K. Malik, M. Lawoti, S. Rahman, A. Kapur, R. C. Oberst, and C. H. Kennedy (Boulder: Westview Press, 2008), 235-250.
84 Rudolph J. Rummel, *Statistics of Democide: Genocide and Mass Murder Since 1900*, LIT Verlag Münster, 1998.

"in the army mess at night I heard the otherwise honourable men, all 'good chaps,' joking about the day's kill and with a friendly rivalry keeping track on the top score."[85]

The March crackdown and the civil war continued until November. The army also began systematically purging the East of minority Hindus, whom it considered traitors, by either killing them or driving them out of the country.[86] A *Mukti Bahini* (liberation force), composed of Bengali civilians, military defectors, and paramilitary defectors formed and engaged in guerilla warfare with Pakistani forces. India fully encouraged the Bangladesh liberation movement and provided support and training to the *Mukti Bahini* during the war of liberation against West Pakistan.

Though India had been covertly aiding Bangladeshi liberation groups for months, it changed the scope of its involvement in November. Earlier, Indian units would engage in what they described as defensive responses to the Pakistani shelling of Indian territory, or in some cases East Pakistan territory held by *Mukti Bahini*, by cross-border strikes and withdrawals. After November 21, the Indian forces fortified themselves near the Pakistani positions, establishing operational bases in East Pakistan.[87] Pakistan was uncertain whether Indian forces were engaging in a limited campaign or readying for an all-out attack. On December 3, the Pakistan Air Force was ordered to strike at targets in northwestern India, marking the commencement of the third Indo-Pakistan war. India justified its intervention in the East based on humanitarian principles: it wanted to end the bloodshed in East Pakistan. In reality, Indian goals were much broader, as they viewed the conflict as a window of opportunity to weaken Pakistan by dividing its eastern and western halves. India also needed to end the tremendous economic pressure that the large refugee population amassing in the Indian state of Bengal was creating.

The 1971 war was different from the previous Indo-Pakistan wars of 1947 and 1965 in that it began in East Pakistan and it was quick and decisive. By December 17, it had ended in a complete rout of Pakistani forces, with India taking 90,000 prisoners and East Pakistan seceding to become Bangladesh.[88] The war of 1971 made it clear to the Pakistani military that they could not win a conventional war against India. This could be seen as a turning point in Pakistan's Kashmir strategy; not wanting to engage in direct and hazardous wars with India, Pakistan's strategy

---

85 Anthony Mascarenhas, *The Rape of Bangla Desh* (Delhi: Vikas Publications, 1971), 118.
86 For an overview, see, Alavi, "Bangladesh and the Crises of Pakistan," 289-317; Gary J. Bass, *The Blood Telegram: Nixon, Kissinger, and a Forgotten Genocide* (New York: Knopf, 2013); Mascarenhas, The Rape of Bangla Desh.
87 Sisson and Rose, *War and Secession*, 5.
88 Ḥaqqānī, *Pakistan: Between Mosque And Military*, 87.

shifted to "death by a thousand cuts" via covert asymmetric warfare. At the same time, their defeat in 1971 led to Pakistan's determined quest for nuclear weapons to neutralize India's conventional military superiority.[89]

The 1971 War further entrenched Punjabi dominance within Pakistan's military. Additionally, since the army had employed Islamic rhetoric to assert its superiority over Bengali Muslims (who were belittled as cowardly converted Hindus), the Islamic chauvinism that the Punjabi Army employed actually acted as a catalyst for Pakistan's radicalization.[90] After its eastern half seceded, the only unifying identity left for Pakistan was Islam; unfortunately, this tactic has been utilized with continually disastrous results in Pakistan's relations with India, Afghanistan, and even its ally the United States.

Pakistan came into being as an "insecurity state."[91] It was flanked on the eastern border by India, whom it perceived as its existential enemy. Not only was India significantly larger and possessed a stronger military, Pakistan also lacked an adequate industrial base because most of the industrial regions fell into Indian territory. Pakistan was left with just 10 percent of British India's industrial power following partition. The immediate war and stalemate in Kashmir also heightened Pakistan's sense of being surrounded by enemies. There were territorial disputes regarding resources, including sharing river water with India. Pakistani leaders believed that India aimed to undo partition and reabsorb Pakistan into India. Additionally, on its western flank, Afghanistan had opposed Pakistan's entry into the United Nations and had expressed claims over Pakistan's Pashtun areas, which it argued had been artificially divided by the Durand Line.

One of Pakistan's grievances was its apparent lack of legitimacy: after the partition of the subcontinent, India was considered the true inheritor of the British Raj, whereas Pakistan was viewed as a secessionist state carved out of British India. Pakistan institutionalized security (against India) as a state priority, justifying this move by pointing to claims made by Rightist Indian leaders, that Pakistan would not survive and would ultimately be re-incorporated into India. Thus, the nascent state was faced with the antipathy of its neighbors, threats to its security, and economic pressures that challenged its survival.

---

89 Itty Abraham, *South Asian Cultures of the Bomb: Atomic Publics and the State in India and Pakistan* (Bloomington: Indiana University Press, 2009), 28.
90 Haqqānī, *Pakistan: Between Mosque And Military*, 3.
91 Thomas P. Thornton, "Pakistan: Fifty Years of Insecurity," in *India and Pakistan: The First Fifty Years*, ed. Selig S. Harrison, Paul H. Kreisberg, and Dennis Kux (Cambridge: Cambridge University Press, 1999), 171.

Pakistan's insecurity and its sense of disadvantage worsened with time and heightened greatly with the secession of half of its population in 1971. As Pakistan's creation was based on the argument that Muslims of South Asia were a unified "nation" and could not coexist with Hindus, the secession of the eastern half of Pakistan negated the "two nation" hypothesis and with it the reason for Pakistan's creation.

Instead of realizing that draconian and divisive decisions that its dictatorial western half made had caused the secession of its eastern wing, the Pakistan that remained instead became more reliant on political Islam for its identity. Pakistan's absolute adherence to state identity at the price of denying the identities of its many people continues to fan centrifugal forces within the nation. However, the state project asserting an Islamic mono-culture-sans-ethnicity became even more hardened after 1971. Under General Zia, Pakistan's Islamic identity was based on militant religious extremism. The Islamic state ideology of Pakistan evolved into Zia's "Islam as state," an ideology that underpins its tactic of using the Taliban, JI, LeT, and other Islamic militant groups to achieve state objectives.

It can be argued that Pakistan's denial of the cultural and political rights of its own people is a major factor in its present political and ideological crisis, and that part of this denial translates into anti-Americanism and a consistent supply of willing soldiers in terrorist training mills. The denial can be connected to Britain's colonial project, which relied on centralizing power, creating monolithic groupings in the subcontinent, and flattening differences in diverse communities. Though imperial project was long ago taken over by its colonial successor states, it still creates conflicts that we can see over six decades later.

CONFLICT ON THE WESTERN FRONT: AFGHANISTAN

While Pakistan battled on its eastern front from its inception in 1947, another conflict was being fought on its western boundary. Pakistan's conflict with Afghanistan was not as intense and bloody but it significantly shaped Pakistan's future. And when the Soviets invaded Afghanistan in 1979, the conflict took a broader international dimension.

Mohammad Daoud Khan (1909-1978), Afghanistan's Prime Minister from 1953-1963, was a Pashtun and a paternal cousin and a brother-in-law of the Afghan king Zahir Shah. He had been a key figure in the Afghan government since 1933, but in 1973 Daoud overthrew Zahir's monarchy and became the President of Afghanistan (1973-1978). Though he belonged to the royal family, Daoud saw himself as a radical Pashtun reformer dedicated to creating a strong state.

As mentioned in an earlier chapter, since the creation of Pakistan, Daoud had supported reunification of the Pashtun people across the Durand Line in Pashtunistan. This would have resulted in territorial loss for Pakistan, but in Daoud's opinion the "Pathans in Pakistan were entitled to claim independence if they chose to do so and that the Afghans, as the same people, had the right to promote the Pashtun cause."[92] Afghanistan-Pakistan hostilities had been apparent since 1949, and as early as 1949 and 1950 the neighbors had engaged in border clashes.[93]

Daoud's irredentist rhetoric stirred up animosity in Pakistan. In 1961 Pakistan closed its consulates and trade offices in Kabul; in response, Afghans broke off diplomatic relations with Pakistan, an action that culminated in the formal closure of its border. As a land-locked country, Afghanistan's border closure cut off the custom revenues and the export route of its produce east. The Soviet Union was an attractive option in the north that could help with Afghanistan's transit problem and it now almost had a monopoly on trade with Afghanistan as Afghanistan's main trading partner.[94]

The post-World War II period in Afghanistan was characterized by modernization and an assertive middle class. The number of schools increased by 400% between 1950 and 1965.[95] Kabul University became a center of political radicalism and radical politics flourished in Kabul as leftists and conservatives vied for dominance.[96] As the educated urban middle class that were largely distanced from the religious groups flourished, so did the fundamentalist groups focused on an Islamic revival. With an increased Soviet influence in Afghanistan, conservative Muslim factions became concerned about the effects of communism. Tahir Amin indicates that the first "nucleus" of a fundamentalist movement was formed by a group of professors in 1957, including Professor Ghulam M. Niazi, Professor Abdul Rasul Sayyaf, Dr. Saeed M. Musa Tawana, and Professor Burhanuddin Rabbani, with some of the members deeply influenced by the Egyptian Muslim Brotherhood and Pakistan's Jamaat-e-Islami.[97] For instance, the leader of Afghan Islamists and the founder of Afghan Jamaat-i-Islami, Burhanuddin Rabbani,

---

92   Quoted in Victoria Schofield, *Afghan Frontier: At the Crossroads of Conflict* (London: Tauris Parke Paperbacks, 2003), 259. Pathan, Pashtun, Pakhtun, Pakhtoon are interchangeably used.
93   Amin Saikal, *Modern Afghanistan: A History of Struggle and Survival* (London: IB Tauris, 2004), 120.
94   Schofield, *Afghan Frontier*, 260.
95   Tahir Amin, "Afghan Resistance: Past, Present, and Future," *Asian Survey* 24, no. 4 (1984): 376.
96   Thomas Barfield, *Afghanistan: A Cultural and Political History*, Princeton Studies in Muslim Politics (Princeton: Princeton University Press, 2012), 213.
97   Amin, "Afghan Resistance," 377, 385.

had studied at Egypt's al-Azhar University, had a close relationship with senior Egyptian Muslim Brotherhood figures, and had translated the writings of the Muslim Brotherhood's ideological grandfather, Syed Qutb, into Dari.[98]

The Muslim Youth, the youth component of the fundamentalist movement, was founded in 1968 and included, amongst others, Gulbuddin Hekmatyar. The movement established connections with other fundamentalist movements, including the Muslim Brotherhood, Jamaat-e-Islami, and several Iranian groups. The youth group's influence increased as the fundamentalists won an overwhelming victory in Kabul University Student Union elections of 1973.[99] Many members of the Kabul Islamists would later join Osama bin Laden in Afghanistan after 1996.

Afghan communists had formed the People's Democratic Party of Afghanistan (PDPA) in 1965 under the leadership of Nur Muhammad Taraki and Babrak Karmal. Two years later, the party split into two factions. The *Khalq* ("Masses") faction, which was largely Pashtun, was under the leadership of Taraki and Hafizullah Amin and recruited Pashtuns from the Afghan military. The *Parcham* ("Banner") faction consisted of mostly Persian speaking people and its center of power was largely localized in governmental bureaucracy and educational institutions. *Khalq* was more predisposed towards overthrowing the old order and bringing quick change whereas *Parcham* was willing to cooperate with progressive forces and the ruling elite. The communists as well as the fundamentalists were centered in Kabul: they had a limited rural political base, were from relatively wealthy backgrounds, and were almost all university educated.[100]

Daoud had used the support of intellectuals and communists, particularly the *Parcham* party led by Babrak Karmal, when he staged the coup in 1973. Daoud considered the fundamentalist his serious rivals for power and believed they were infiltrating the army to overthrow his regime. In concert with the *Parcham*, the only effective rival to fundamentalist groups on campuses, Daoud's government began its focused attack on fundamentalists. Amin estimates that between 1973 and 1978, communists under the Daoud regime killed approximately 600 members of the fundamentalist movement. Many fundamentalists fled to Pakistan in 1974-75.[101]

Pakistan, worried about Daoud's rhetoric surrounding Pashtunistan, welcomed these fundamentalist leaders. Pakistan first provided weapons to radical Islamist parties in 1973, supplying weapons to Shias and to Islamist parties in order to

---

98 Jason Burke, *Al-Qaeda: Casting a Shadow of Terror* (London: I. B. Tauris, 2003), 63.
99 Ibid., 63-65.
100 Barfield, *Afghanistan: A Cultural and Political History*, 168-169.
101 Amin, "Afghan Resistance," 378.

execute a rebellion against the Daoud government.¹⁰² The fundamentalists were provided help, including training. Pakistan gave the leaders of the future jihad against the Soviet invasion, Burhanuddin Rabbani, Gulbuddin Hekmatyar, Muhammad Yunus Khalis, Ahmad Shah Massoud, Din Muhammad, Abdul Qadir, Abdul Haq, and others, monthly allowances, arms, ammunition and training in sabotage and explosives. Pakistan's President Zulfikar Ali Bhutto himself established an ISI Afghan Cell that trained 5,000 Islamists in guerrilla war in secret camps in Peshawar.¹⁰³

With the assistance of Pakistan, the fundamentalists launched an insurgency in Afghanistan in 1975, calling for a general uprising to topple the godless and communist-dominated Daoud government. Insurgency was launched in four provinces; the most prominent was in the Panjshir Valley and was led by Ahmad Shah Massoud. The insurgency, however, failed to generate any local support and was crushed.¹⁰⁴

Daoud began to reach out to other countries, including Iran and Saudi Arabia, to reduce Afghan dependence on the Soviet Union. He improved relations with Saudi Arabia, ending their support of Daoud's Islamist opponents and making the Islamists completely dependent on Pakistan. In order to wean the Afghanistan military from its dependence on the Soviet Union, army officers were sent to train in Egypt and India.¹⁰⁵

The communists were disillusioned as they discovered that Daoud was no socialist and thus began a campaign against him. In April 1978, the united factions of PDPA overthrew the Daoud regime, murdering Daoud. The new government was formed with the *Khalq* faction leader Nur Mohammad Taraki as the Prime Minister and *Parcham* faction leader Babrak Karmal as the Deputy Prime Minister.

The new government in Afghanistan was soon beset by dissent and struggle; many across Afghanistan resisted the PDPA regime. Taraki, who was highly regarded in Moscow, was murdered on September 14, 1979, and Hafizullah Amin took his place as Prime Minister. With the rebellious countryside becoming difficult to control, the regime appeared ready to collapse. To stabilize the situation, the Soviet tanks rolled into Afghanistan in December 1979, marking the beginning

---

102 Michael V. Bhatia and Mark Sedra, *Afghanistan, Arms and Conflict: Armed Groups, Disarmament and Security in a Post-War Society*, Contemporary Security Studies (London: Routledge, 2008), 44.
103 Amin, "Afghan Resistance," 378; Bhatia and Sedra, *Afghanistan, Arms and Conflict*, 44.
104 Amin, "Afghan Resistance," 378. For an overview, see Barfield, *Afghanistan*; Bhatia and Sedra, *Afghanistan, Arms and Conflict*; Nabi Misdaq, *Afghanistan: Political Frailty and External Interference*, Routledge Studies in Middle Eastern History (London: Routledge, 2006).
105 Barfield, *Afghanistan*, 216; Schofield, *Afghan Frontier*, 274.

of a ten-year Soviet occupation. Amin was killed and the Soviets installed Babrak Karmal as the President of Afghanistan under their military occupation. The ensuing resistance and war was devastating for the Afghan people.[106]

While Afghanistan has a diverse ethnic population with various tribal, regional, and sectarian schisms, all Afghans united against the Soviet invaders, creating a widespread rebellion. In the beginning the resistance was not effective, and until 1984 the Soviet forces had the upper hand. Despite their losses, the resistance continued to improve their guerrilla tactics against the PDPA and Soviet forces and they eventually inflicted heavy damages. The resistance and the concomitant Soviet response became increasingly violent, creating a massive humanitarian crisis: 5 million out of 12 million Afghans became refugees. Shortly thereafter, the United States began to pass weapons to rebels through an arms pipeline in Pakistan, just across the Durand Line. Saudi Arabia pledged to match all U.S. contributions in 1984 and the U.S. arms assistance grew to over $630 million per year between 1986-1990. Saudi funds were channeled through a Swiss bank account shared with the United States.[107] All covert assistance was regulated and disbursed through Pakistan's intelligence agency, the ISI. Pakistan parceled out the assistance and set up training camps that would eventually train approximately 80,000 Mujahideen in various skills, including sabotage, demolition, urban terrorism, and the construction of improvised explosives.[108]

As a consequence of the Soviet invasion, Afghan opposition groups concentrated in the Pakistan border region just east of the Durand Line in Peshawar. In June 1981, the Islamist opposition groups joined to form the *Ittehad-i-Islami Mujahideen-i-Afghanistan*, (Islamic Unity of Afghan Mujahideen, IUAM). In March 1982, the IUAM split into a union of fundamentalist organizations, the Group of Seven (IUAM-7) and a union of traditionalist organizations, the Group of Three (IUAM-3). In May 1985, the two groups rejoined to recreate as an organized opposition: the Peshawar Seven.[109]

The group consisted of radical Islamists, all Deobandi Sunni Muslims, who were called Fundamentalists:
- Hizb-i-Islami (HI), led by Gulbuddin Hekmatyar, a Pashtun
- Jamiat-i-Islami (JIA), led by Burhanuddin Rabbani, a Tajik (this also included Ahmad Shah Massoud and Ismail Khan)

---

106 For an overview, see Gilles Dorronsoro, *Revolution Unending: Afghanistan, 1979 to the Present*, CERI Series in Comparative Politics and International Studies (London: C. Hurst & Co., 2005).
107 Bhatia and Sedra, *Afghanistan, Arms and Conflict*, 44.
108 Ibid., 45; Dorronsoro, *Revolution Unending*, 209.
109 Michael A. Gress and Lester W. Grau, *The Soviet-Afghan War: How a Superpower Fought and Lost* (Lawrence: University Press of Kansas, 2002), 53.

- Hizb-i-Islami (HIK), led by Yunus Khalis, a Pashtun
- Ittihad-i-Islami party (The Islamic Union for the Liberation of Afghanistan, or IUA), led by Abdul Rasul Sayaf, a Pashtun

The traditionalist conservatives, called Traditionalists, consisted of:
- Mahaz-e-Milli Islami (the National Islamic Front of Afghanistan, or NIFA), led by Pir Syed Ahmad Gailani, a Sufi Pir and a Pashtun
- Jebh-e-Nijat-i-Milli (The Afghanistan National Liberation Front, or ANLF), led by Sighbatullah Mujaddidi, a Naqshbandi Sufi
- Harakat-e-Inqilab-e-Islami (The Islamic Revolutionary Movement, or IRMA), led by Maulana Mohammad Nabi Mohammedi [110]

Hizb-i-Islami pursued an Islamic state in Afghanistan and sought to spread the message of Islam around the world. The majority of HI followers were Pashtuns and Tajiks. Hekmatyar, an Islamic purist, was a detribalized Pashtun from Kunduz with a narrow base of support, and was recognized as unscrupulous, cruel, and authoritarian.

Rabbani's JIA shared the same goals as Hekmatyar's HI and included Tajiks, a smaller group of Pashtuns, Turkmens, and Uzbek adherents. Rabbani was a Tajik who was recognized as pragmatic and flexible.

Maulavi Mohammad Yunus Khalis, a Pashtun from Paktia province, had split from Hekmatyar's HI to form HIK. Khalis had a radical Islamic agenda inspired by the Deoband school of Islam. Mullah Omar, the future leader of the Taliban, fought under Khalis's mujahideen.

Abdul Rasul Sayyaf's Islamic Union for the Liberation of Afghanistan was formed in 1982 and was financed almost entirely by Saudi Arabia. It had no territorial base and was known for its extreme Wahhabi and anti-Shia ideology.

Mujadidi's Afghanistan National Liberation Front sought to establish an Islamic state based on justice, equality, and observance of Sharia law. The ANLF was open to all Muslims and did not discriminate based on their political and religious views.

The National Islamic Front of Afghanistan was lead by Gailani, associated with the Sufi order of Qadiriya, and its followers were mostly Pashtuns.

---

110 The resistance group information is from Gress and Grau, *The Soviet-Afghan War*; John Cooley, *Unholy Wars: Afghanistan, America and International Terrorism*, 2nd ed. (London: Pluto Press, 2000); and Angelo Rasanayagam, *Afghanistan: A Modern History; Monarchy, Despotism or Democracy? The Problem of Governance in the Muslim Tradition*, rev. ed. (London: I.B. Tauris, 2005).

The Islamic Revolutionary Movement was founded in 1973 in Baluchistan, and most of its followers were Pashtuns.

TABLE 1. THE SUNNI PARTIES

Name of Party	Leadership	Organisation	Ideology	Recruitment
Hezb-i Islami	Islamist (Gulbuddin Hekmatar)	Bureaucratic	Islamist	Educated class
Jamiyat-i Islami	Islamist, clerical (*mawlani* Rabbani)	Bureaucratic	Islamist	Islamist
Harakat-i Enqelab	Clerical (*mawlani* Nabi)	Clerical	Fundamentalist	*ulema*
Jebhe-yi Nejat	Patrimonial (*pir* Mujaddidi)	Patrimonial	Conservative	*khan*
Mahaz-i Melli	Patrimonial (*pir* Gaylani)	Patrimonial	Conservative	*khan*
Hezb-i Islami	Patrimonial	Patrimonial	Fundamentalist	*khan*
Ettehad	Clerical (*mawlani* Sayyaf)	Patrimonial	Fundamentalist	Educated class

Source: Dorronsoro, Revolution Unending, 151.

TABLE 2. THE PRINCIPAL SHI'ITE PARTIES

Name of Party	Leadership	Organisation	Ideology	Recruitment
Shura	Clerical (*sayyed* Beheshti)	Clerical	Conservative	Hazara, *sadat*
Nasr	Clerical (*shaikh* Mazari)	Clerical	Islamist	Hazara *ulema*
Sepah	Clerical (*skaikh* Akbari)	Clerical	Islamist	Hazara *ulema*
Harakat-i Islami	Clerical (*shaikh* Mohseni)	Clerical	Conservative	Shi'ite *Khan*
Mustazaffin	Islamist (Engineer Hashemi)	Bureaucratic	Islamist	Educated class

SSource: Dorronsoro, Revolution Unending, 151.

TABLE 3. AFGHAN SUNNI PARTIES BASED IN PESHAWAR

Party	Leader	Ethnic Origin	Ideology	Share of foreign funding
1. Hezb-i-Islami Hekmatyar	G. Hekmatyar	Ghilzai Pashtun	Islamist	Received largest share
2. Jam'iat Islami (JI)	B. Rabanni	Tajik	Islamist	Received second largest share
3. Itehad Islami Afghanistan	A.R. Sayyaf	Half Ghilzai Pashtun	Islamist	Received third largest share
4. Hezb-i-Islami Khalis	M.Y. Khalis	Ghilzai Pashtun	Islamist	Received small share
5. Mahaz Meli Islami (NIFA)	S.A. Gailani	(Qaderia)	Sufi (moderate)	Received larger share of moderates
6. Harakat Inqlab Islami	Muhammadi	Ghilzai Pashtun	*Ulama* (moderate)	Received smaller share of moderates
7. Jabhe Najat Meli (NLF)	S. Mujadedi	(Naqshbandi)	Sufi (moderate)	Received smallest share of funds

Note: One to four Islamist parties; five to seven moderate parties; of the two, moderates got less of the funds

Source: Misdaq, *Afghanistan*, 151.

TABLE 4. AFGHAN SHI'AH PARTIES

Hezb-i-Wahdat (HW)	K. Khalili	Shi'ah Hazarah	Islamist	Islamist, comprised of eight small Iran-backed groups
Harakat Islami (HI)	A. Muhsseni	Shi'ah Qizelbash	Islamist Moderate	Moderate, based in Iran, later in Pakistan

Source: Misdaq, *Afghanistan*, 151.

It must be understood that the traditionalist and fundamentalist groups were not very different in their conception of Islamism; none of the factions advocated a democratic or secular state. The only difference between the groups was that some were relatively worse than the others in terms of authoritarian tendencies. Hekmatyar, whose mission was to set up a theocratic Islamic state in Afghanistan, led the most intolerant of the factions. Hekmatyar was bitterly opposed to democracy and capitalism, which he described as social poisons, and routinely denounced the United States as the Great Satan.[111] The seven organizations were joined by their anti-Soviet enmity but did not share a common political or ideological platform. Their unions were temporary, forced by the efforts of the CIA and ISI.[112] Shia groups claiming to follow Khomeini gathered loosely under Hizb-i-Wahdat (the "Unity Party") and remained aloof toward the Sunni groups.

---

111 Ted G. Carpenter, "The Unintended Consequences of Afghanistan," *World Policy Journal* 11, no. 1 (1994): 78.
112 Gress and Grau, *The Soviet-Afghan War*, 56.

While the fundamentalist groups are often given much attention, the Afghan resistance actually began as a grassroots movement. As William Maley points out, "This is frequently overlooked... But the bulk of Afghan Muslims who initially took up arms against the USSR and its clients were not Muslim intellectuals, but practitioners of what one might call 'village Islam.'"[113] This resistance was more of a traditional warfare than the jihad preached by the fundamentalist groups.

A large Afghan refugee contingent in Pakistan (2.7 million people in 1983 up to over 3 million in 1988) and in Iran (1.2 million people in 1983 to 2.7 million in 1988) provided a reservoir of manpower for resistance against the Soviets.[114] The resistance was financed and armed primarily by the contributions of the United States and Saudi Arabia, but the Gulf States as well as private contributors also provided substantial support.

In 1980, Umar Babrakzai led an attempt to establish a unified resistance against the Soviet invasion, calling for a national jirga that would operate outside the framework of political parties. Babrakzai hailed from a renowned family from the Zadran tribe in the Paktia Province. Resistance to the Afghan government had started early in Paktia and had been disciplined and well organized. While Paktia organized its own jirga to coordinate resistance in the province, their success provided the impetus to Babrakzai and other Paktia leaders to send delegates to Peshawar to lay the groundwork for a national jirga. On May 9, 1980, 916 representatives convened in Peshawar. To ensure representation from all of the provinces and groups, two individuals per province and four representatives from nomadic tribes were selected to serve in the Shura-yi-enqelab ("revolutionary council"). While the seven Islamic parties were slated to have a representative in the revolutionary council and had initially supported the national jirga, six of them, all but Gailani's Mahaz, boycotted the meeting.[115]

Fearing the dilution of their political influence, the Islamist parties sabotaged the national effort. However, Pakistan's opposition to the jirga played the biggest role in sabotaging any unified Afghan national resistance. Zia's regime feared losing its control over the large representative coalition of Afghan resistance as it might outgrow Pakistani control and also impact Pakistani Pashtuns in the border area. In any case, Zia was already engaged in Islamization of Pakistan and was committed to Islamic parties, so he mainly supported Hekmatyar's Hizb-I Islami.

---

113 William Maley, *The Afghanistan Wars*, 2nd ed. (New York: Palgrave Macmillan, 2002), 60.
114 Rasanayagam, *Afghanistan: A Modern History*, 111.
115 David B. Edwards, *Before Taliban: Genealogies of the Afghan Jihad* (Berkeley: University of California Press, 2002), 261.

The opposition of the Islamic parties and Pakistan government shut down another attempt made toward a national jirga fifteen months later in Baluchistan. David Edwards concludes:

> The parties balked at accepting the jirgas for understandable reasons. Their leaders reasoned, probably accurately, that if the people of Afghanistan were able to choose the form in which they would conduct their war against the communist government, political parties would lose out—in all likelihood to some moderate coalition led by Zahir Shah and a collection of ex-ministers, courtiers, and mainstream religious figures like Gailani and Mujaddidi. The failure of the two jirgas, however, ensured that there would be no independent and united national front. It also brought an end to the one institution that Afghans had always been able to count on in times of national emergency to bring consensus and reconciliation among warring factions.[116]

Pakistan's self-serving interests caused attempts to bring the resistance under a unified national banner to fail. Afghan nationalists and the people of Afghanistan suffered as a result, and the continued infighting and rivalries between the Islamic groups prolonged of the war. Additionally, because the ISI raised the prominence of radical Islamists, the nature of the resistance was transformed from a nationalistic war against invaders into a transnational anti-communist and anti-Western jihadi venture. After the war, the intra resistance rivalries and Pakistan's interference resulted in a devastating civil war, culminating in a rise of the Taliban. This devastating result will be discussed in the next section of this book.

The United States did not attempt to prevent fundamentalist control over the resistance, nor did it encourage support for King Zahir Shah or other moderate elements. This is not to say that perceptive individuals in the U.S. administration were unaware of the dangers of supporting the fundamentalists. Elie Krakowski, an adviser to then Assistant Secretary of Defense Richard Perle, strongly supported sending aid to the Afghans but was opposed to giving the ISI complete authority in its allocation. Krakowski insightfully argued that building up Afghan fundamentalists would damage long-term U.S. regional interests in the Persian Gulf and in the Middle East. However, "no one at State was interested… and the agency was definitely against putting pressure on the Pakistanis."[117] Krakowski criticized the CIA's "pandering" to the ISI, warning of the dangers that would arise as a result of its desire not to disturb valuable ties that went beyond the Afghan War. "The agency was interested in a variety of things there… They were collecting lots of interesting stuff on the Soviet Union and other things."[118]

---

116 Ibid., 262.
117 Quoted in Cordovez and Harrison, *Out of Afghanistan*, 164.
118 Ibid.

In 1982, Sheikh Abdullah, the Commissioner of Afghan Refugees for the Government of Pakistan, with oversight over Afghan political activities in Peshawar, declared that only the seven Islamic parties would be allowed to operate in Afghanistan. Prior to the restriction, there were over a hundred small Afghan parties with offices in Peshawar. Pakistan's decision decreed that Islamic parties alone were authorized to receive assistance from Pakistan and other international donors. Furthermore, it meant that all refugees would have to receive a membership card from one of the Islamist parties in order to live in registered camps and receive tents, rations, and other assistance.[119] This decision made all Afghan refugees dependent on the Islamists.

Pakistan backed the Afghan Islamist movements as they shared an ideological solidarity with Pakistan. Pakistan furthermore played a key role in eliminating and marginalizing the Maoist or nationalist movements within the Afghan resistance who threatened its domination of the Afghan resistance groups. Groups that would potentially support the creation of Pashtunistan, like the nationalist movement Afghan Mellat, were provided with no aid, and several of Mellat's members in particular were reportedly assassinated by Hezb-i Islami in Peshawar.[120] Sazman-i Azadibakhsh-i Mardomi Afghanistan (SAMA, or "The Organisation for the Liberation of the Afghan People") and other Maoist-influenced groups that fought the PDPA regime inside Afghanistan, also received no assistance from Pakistan. Maoists as well as other leftist opponents of the Soviet invasions were instead victims of assassinations by Hizb-i-Islami.[121] Hizb-i-Islami was also implicated in assassination of a number of Afghan liberals during the 1980s, Hekmatyar's forces were reportedly responsible for the assassination of leading secular figures in the Afghan exile community, including Mina Keshwar Kamal, the founder of the Revolutionary Association of the Women of Afghanistan, and Sayd Bahauddin Majrooh, the publisher of the Afghan Information Center Monthly Bulletin. Ted Carpenter attributes Majrooh's murder to a survey he published that Hekmatyar found provoking. It had showed that a vast majority, 72 percent, of Afghan refugees preferred the exiled Afghan King Zahir Shah to any of the Peshawar leaders as the future head of state of a liberated Afghanistan.[122]

While Jamiat-i-Islami was led by Tajiks, Michael Griffin writes, "The remaining six hailed from the eastern Ghilzai or 'minority' Pashtun clans, an indication that the ISI was not addressing solely the Soviet threat as it drew up plans for the resistance, but the danger to its own borders of arming an alliance that included

---

119 Edwards, *Before Taliban*, 267.
120 Dorronsoro, *Revolution Unending*, 212.
121 Dorronsoro, *Revolution Unending*, 212.
122 Carpenter, "The Unintended Consequences of Afghanistan," 79.

the 'royal' Durranis of the south."[123] Not one leader of a recognized party was from Durrani Pashtun tribes. While this decision was based on calculations that a post-Soviet Afghanistan would have a sympathetic, non-Pashtunistan oriented government, Griffin concludes that "removing the Durrani from a central role in the Peshawar-based resistance was a recipe for postwar anarchy, when Tajik, Uzbek and Hazara had been primed by combat for a greater share of power after centuries of Pashtun hegemony." Besides not recognizing any Pashtun nationalist parties, Pakistan also did not allow King Zahir Shah to contact the resistance in Pakistan.[124]

Even among the Islamist parties, Pakistan parceled out more funding to the most conservative Islamist groups, those run by Hekmatyar, Rabbani, and Sayaf. The privileged access that Hekmatyar's Hizb-i-Islami enjoyed can account for its increased prominence and strong presence in the refugee camps. It received more than half of the armaments and cash that came in for the anti-Soviet resistance.[125] In return, Hekmatyar demonstrated himself to be the undisputed champion of Pakistan's interests in Afghanistan during the resistance years. Pakistan had its reasons to support Hekmatyar as its candidate for ruling Afghanistan. Hekmatyar, a Pashtun from northern Afghanistan, did not want to seek the establishment of Pashtunistan. Hekmatyar also disapproved of Afghanistan's close relationship with India and was willing to settle border disputes between Pakistan and Afghanistan on terms favorable to Islamabad. Pakistan's policymakers probably considered his emphasis on transnational Islamic fundamentalism as a suitable diversion from the Pashtunistan issue.[126]

The Peshawar-based Islamists would probably have remained on the fringe of Afghan politics without Pakistan's support. However, with it they were able to dominate the Afghan refugee and exile communities, becoming more influential than many of the Afghan military commanders battling the Soviet forces. By directing the majority of the aid to fundamentalist Afghan groups, Pakistan distorted the influence and politics of the Afghan resistance, greatly inflating the importance of the fundamentalist groups. The popular following of the fundamentalist groups in Afghanistan was modest at best; this held true for the three million Afghan refugees in Pakistan as well. However, with these groups controlling the money channeled through ISI, they became a formidable political force.[127]

---

123 Michael Griffin, *Reaping the Whirlwind: The Taliban Movement in Afghanistan*, rev. ed. (London: Pluto Press, 2003), 20.
124 Burke, *Al-Qaeda*, 69.
125 Griffin, *Reaping the Whirlwind*, 19.
126 Ibid.
127 Carpenter, "The Unintended Consequences of Afghanistan," 78-79.

There was some international concern expressed over Pakistan's choice of Afghan factions. Representative Donald Ritter, in a hearing before the Subcommittees on Europe and the Middle East and Asian and Pacific Affairs, Committee on Foreign Affairs on March 7, 1990, criticized Washington's choice:

> We should keep in mind that the seven political leaders of the Peshawar-based parties were not in any way chosen by the Afghan people but by President Zia ul-Haq. Some of the moderate parties have a legitimate following among the Afghan people, whose brand of Islam has never been marked by fanaticism. The fundamentalist parties, on the other hand, were creations of Pakistan and in one case Saudi Arabia. Zia and his friends in the ISI have sought to put Hekmatyar in power.[128]

In contrast, the Reagan administration did not show any concern about Pakistan channeling aid to fundamentalist factions in Afghanistan. In fact, Pakistan's control over Afghan resistance was so absolute that it selected the so-called Afghan leaders who met with American representatives.

The ISI has firm grip on Pakistan: its directors, even after retirement, have been among the most powerful figures in the nation.[129] A majority of ISI personnel are drawn from Pakistan's military, and all of its ranking officers are military personnel who serve for a fixed tenure and are then rotated out. Headed by a lieutenant general, most ISI chiefs feel that their loyalty is to their fellow generals rather than to the civilian administration.[130] During the Afghan War, the power of the ISI expanded substantially. Besides funneling weapons and money, the ISI personnel presided directly over the strategy sessions of Afghan resistance groups. The ISI planned combat operations for the resistance groups as well as accompanied the mujahideen inside Afghanistan as advisers. Brigadier General Mohammad Yousaf directed Afghan operations for the ISI. Yousaf stated:

> There were eleven Pakistani teams of three men each operating inside Afghanistan, generally consisting of a major and two junior officers dressed like Afghans. Playing a role similar to that of Special Forces advisers in the U.S. Army, they guided local commanders "on all aspects of military operations," conducted training activities, and prepared intelligence reports.[131]

While U.S. funding went to the fundamentalist factions, Sayyaf's *Ittehad-e-Islami*, which had virtually no networks in Afghanistan, was primarily funded by Saudi Arabia and the Gulf States. The Saudis favored Sayyaf due to his Wahhabi leanings. Many foreign volunteers also were drawn to *Ittehad-e-Islami* because of

---

128 Quoted in ibid., 78.
129 For a discussion, see Zahid Hussain, *Frontline Pakistan: The Path to Catastrophe and the Killing of Benazir Bhutto* (London: I.B. Tauris, 2007).
130 Owen Bennett-Jones, *Pakistan: Eye of the Storm* (New Haven: Yale University Press, 2002).
131 Cordovez and Harrison, *Out of Afghanistan*, 161.

its Wahhabi-influenced beliefs, including Osama bin Laden. The power of Gulf funds was evident when Sayyaf created his own refugee camp called "Sayyafabad." Jason Burke described it as "a well-provided refugee camp and complex of warehouses, military bases, mosques and medressas at Pabbi, east of Peshawar, that was to become a crucial location for Islamic militants after the Soviet war."[132]

ZIA, AFGHANISTAN, UNITED STATES, AND THE GESTATION OF FUTURE TERRORISM

In 1976, Pakistan's Prime Minister Zulfikar Ali Bhutto appointed General Mohammad Zia-ul-Haq (Zia) as the nation's Chief of Army Staff, passing over six other generals who had greater seniority. Zia was considered a mediocre general who was publicly obsequious to Bhutto, who in turn believed that Zia was a loyalist religious simpleton. According to John Schmidt, "If anything, [Zia's] patent religiosity actually recommended him to Bhutto, who was advised that a pious general was less likely to challenge civilian authority."[133] Bhutto, however, had made a grave mistake. His handpicked commander of the Pakistan Army revealed himself to be a ruthless and power-hungry ideologue who overthrew the civilian government in 1977 and eventually hanged Bhutto in 1979. Zia ruled Pakistan with an iron fist for eleven years until his death in a military plane crash on August 17, 1988.

In his first address to the nation as the dictator of Pakistan, Zia proclaimed his plan to create an Islamic state. As Rizvi says, "The Zia regime was the first instance in Pakistan's history when the ruling generals openly declared themselves to be conservative-Islamic in their orientations and cultivated close ties with the political groups of the right, especially those Islam-oriented parties that were prepared to support martial law… The military government felt that a cooperative interaction with these elements would help to legitimize their rule [and] undercut the support base of their adversaries…"[134]

Since the country's inception, Pakistan's rulers have invoked Islamic ideology to legitimize their authority and control their opponents. In order to legitimize his military regime, Zia used the same tactics. Zia's Islamization was a ploy to consolidate his power rather than to establish a genuine Islamic order. Despite the rhetoric of Islam's prominence throughout Pakistan's political history, the role of Islam had never clearly been defined nor accepted. Because of this lapse, state leaders could use Islam to legitimize their authoritarian bureaucratic-military

---

132 Burke, *Al-Qaeda*, 99.
133 John R. Schmidt, *The Unraveling: Pakistan in the Age of Jihad* (New York: Farrar, Straus, Giroux, 2011), 62.
134 Rizvi, *Military, State and Society in Pakistan*, 174.

regimes and still continue in their secular ways. As Olivier Roy states, "When General Zia embarked on a policy of Islamization after his coup d'état in 1977, his opponents could criticize him only for imposing an excessively narrow vision of Islam; they could not challenge the fundamental principle."[135] Zia, a conservative Deobandi Sunni Muslim, was portrayed as an Islamic ideologue, staunchly committed to the Islamization of the Pakistan Army and society. However, despite his rhetoric or his overt demonstrations of piety, his attempts to bring Islam to Pakistani society and military were expedient and flexible. Daeschel concludes,

> Some authors have interpreted Zia's Islamisation policies as the work of convinced Islamic revolutionaries in uniform who used the military as a vehicle in order to fulfill their dream of an Islamic state. Others have rejected this view by suggesting that Islamisation was the outcome of power politics alone. According to them, religious sentiments were consciously manipulated and utilised to keep a military regime in power. As such, Islamisation had nothing to do with ideological convictions. The second approach appears more convincing than the first.[136]

However, whether Zia's Islamization was contrived or sincere, it shaped the politics and future of Pakistan in tangible ways. Zia's Islamization significantly impacted Pakistan's military and its relations with Islamic parties, as well as religious violence in Pakistan within the Muslim communities, and between Muslims and other communities. Another major effect of Zia's rule was how Islamic Afghan factions were supported, funded, and trained, while other factions were undercut, during the Soviet-Afghan War. Zia's regime attempted to co-opt Islamic parties domestically, causing a rise in sectarian violence. His regime's involvement in the jihad against the Soviet forces gave rise to religious militancy.[137]

There was a rise in Deobandi influenced madrasas during Zia's rule. Between 1983 and 1984 alone, approximately 12,000 madrasas were in operation. Talbot concludes, "This has been a crucial element in providing support for jihadist and sectarian groups... many propagated an increasingly violent sectarian and jihadist version of Islam."[138] Zia's enduring legacy is reflected from the fact that by 1988, there were approximately 8,000 official religious schools and 25,000 unregistered ones, many of them clustered along the Afghanistan-Pakistan frontier.[139]

---

135 Olivier Roy, "Islam and Foreign Policy: Central Asia and the Arab-Persian World," in *A History of Pakistan and its Origins*, ed. Christophe Jafferlot (London: Anthem Press, 2004), 137.
136 Markus Daechsel, "Military Islamisation in Pakistan and the Spectre of Colonial Perceptions." *Contemporary Southeast Asia* 6, no. 2 (1997): 141
137 For an overview, see Ian Talbot, "Religion and Violence: the Historical Context for Conflict in Pakistan," in *Religion and Violence in South Asia: Theory and Practice*, edited by J. R. Hinnells and R. King (New York: Routledge, 2007), 147-163; Ahmed Rashid, *Taliban: Militant Islam, Oil And Fundamentalism In Central Asia*, 5th ed. (London: I. B. Tauris, 2000).
138 Talbot, "Religion and Violence: the Historical Context for Conflict in Pakistan," 151.
139 Coll, *Ghost Wars*, 334.

A vast majority of madrasas are run on charity from the public (dependent on zakat, "alms"; *khairat*, "charity"; and *atiyat*, "gifts"; etc.).[140] However, Zia's government tried to gain sway over the madrasas in the 1980sby controlling the distribution of *zakat* funds, shifting the dynamics of which madrasas were financially supported. Even though most Pakistanis follow the Barelvi tradition of Islam, most of the madrasas who received funds under Zia's regime were fundamentalist Deobandi.

Funding for such schools also came from Saudi Arabia, which encouraged conservative Sunni interpretation of Islam. This state-sponsored Sunni Islamization resulted in an escalating conflict with the Shia community. Zia's *Zakat* Ordinance of 1980 exacerbated the Shia-Sunni conflict by making *zakat* compulsory. The Shias rebelled; according to their beliefs, the state could not make alms collection compulsory. The overwhelming opposition by the Shias forced Zia to exempt them from the *zakat* tax, which enraged Sunni orthodoxy. With the state's encouragement of extremist organizations, militant anti-Shia sectarian organizations began sprouting up across Pakistan. For example, the *Sipah-e-Sahaba* Pakistan (SSP) was founded in September 1985 to counteract the rising solidarity of the Shia community. Support from the Zia regime and the Saudis strengthened the SSP, a strong group that would later engage in terrorist acts and violent sectarianism. Some Sunni began to deny that Shia were true Muslims, setting the stage for further violent sectarian conflicts. In response to what they saw as Sunni imperiousness, some Shias formed the *Tehrik-e-Nifaz-e-Fiqh-e-Jafria* (TNJF) to protect the their separate religious identity.

Zia's relations with the United States had not started on a positive note. Zia's military overthrow of Pakistan's elected leaders in 1977 coincided with the Jimmy Carter's presidency in the United States. With his concern for human rights and democracy, Carter had a less than favorable attitude towards developments under Zia's dictatorial regime. On March 18, 1978, following a sham trial, the imprisoned Prime Minister Bhutto was sentenced to death. There was a worldwide outcry and many world leaders, including the Pope, asked for clemency for Bhutto. Disregarding international outrage, Zia had his former benefactor hanged on April 4, 1979.

Besides Carter's emphasis on promoting democracy and human rights, the United States was also concerned about Pakistan's development of nuclear weapons. Despite issuing threats that if Pakistan continued with its nuclear program the

---

140 Tariq Rahman, "Madrasas: the Potential for Violence in Pakistan," in *Madrasas in South Asia: Teaching Terror?* Routledge Contemporary South Asia, ed. J. Malik (London: Routledge, 2007), 71.

United States would cut off economic assistance, the U.S. administration was convinced that Pakistan wanted to continue its nuclear program in order to achieve nuclear parity with India.[141] The United States' warning was ineffective. Zia's remained committed to counterbalancing India's military superiority and moved Pakistan's nuclear weapons program to full speed. In April 1979, the U.S. government suspended aid to Pakistan. U.S.-Pakistan relations continued to worsen when, on November 21, 1979, Islamist groups in Pakistan burned down the U.S. embassy, killing four people. Pakistani authorities took an unimaginable four hours to respond; by the time authorities arrived, the rioters had already left.[142]

By 1979, Zia's martial law regime was facing international isolation and a crisis of legitimacy. However, Zia's fortunes improved when the Shah of Iran, the autocratic key regional ally of the United States, was overthrown. An Islamic Republic under the leadership of Ayatollah Ruhollah Khomeini replaced the monarchy, and the new Iranian government was hostile to the United States. The United States lost access to critical intelligence agency facilities in Iran, but Pakistan's strategic location next door made it a suitable replacement for the sites that had been used to spy on the Soviet Union. Zia increased his leverage with the United States by allowing it to install electronic monitoring facilities in Pakistan's northern border areas, which were adjacent to Soviet Central Asian missile testing and anti-satellite launch sites.[143] The CIA provided Pakistan with technical assistance and equipment to improve their electronic interception capabilities.

Just over a month after the rioters in Pakistan burned down the American embassy, the Soviet Army invaded Afghanistan to install Babrak Karmal as the president. Suddenly the United States' perception of Pakistan was transformed from a medieval tyranny to an indispensable ally. With the Soviet Army just west of the Durand Line, Pakistan had become a frontline state. President Carter called Zia and offered to bolster Pakistan's security. In a speech regarding Afghanistan, made on January 4, 1980, Carter affirmed, "We will provide military equipment, food and other assistance to help Pakistan defend its independence and national security against the seriously increased threat from the north."[144]

The Zia regime decided to oppose Soviet intervention by providing clandestine support to Afghan insurgents. As soon as they did this, the Carter administration conveniently forgot about its prior concerns regarding Pakistan's nuclear weapons program, its Islamization project, its dismal human rights record, and the bleak

---

141 Kux, *The United States and Pakistan, 1947-2000*, 226.
142 Ibid., 242.
143 Cordovez and Harrison, *Out of Afghanistan*, 56.
144 Quoted in Kux, *The United States and Pakistan*, 247.

prospect of democracy in the country. Instead, the Carter administration focused on turning Afghanistan into the Soviet Union's own Vietnam War. The U.S. approach was to make the cost of invasion so high that it would deter the Soviets from future similar adventures. On January 14, 1980, the State Department declared that over the span of two years it would offer $400 million in military and economic aid to Pakistan. The Carter administration also planned to seek authority from Congress to waive sanctions on Pakistan—sanctions that had been declared due to its pursuit of a nuclear program. Recognizing that his bargaining position was strong, on January 18 Zia declined the aid as "peanuts," stating, "... it is terribly disappointing. Pakistan will not buy its security for $400 million," an amount that would "buy greater animosity from the Soviet Union, which is now much more influential in this region than the United States."[145]

Zia also dismissed Carter's offer of $400 million because he knew that Carter was headed for defeat in the U.S. presidential elections. He anticipated that Reagan, with his strident anti-communist views, would be a much more promising source of aid. Zia's gamble proved astute: in January 1981 the new Reagan administration quickly upped the U.S. government's aid offer from $400 million to $3.2 billion. Beyond military and economic aid, the Reagan administration decided to ignore Pakistan's nuclear program as long as Pakistan did not explode a bomb.[146] The Reagan administration also decided to sell Pakistan state-of-the-art, nuclear capable F-16 fighter-bombers. Pakistan did not face the same criticism it had from the Carter administration; the Reagan administration completely ignored issues of Pakistani democracy and its pursuit of nuclear weapons.

Even during the Carter administration, while the United States and Pakistan had failed to arrive at an agreement on military and economic aid packages, the CIA and ISI expanded their collaboration in Afghanistan. Within days after the Soviets entered Afghanistan, Carter had approved a covert action program to provide weapons and supplies to Afghan resistance fighters. The operational rules for funneling aid to the Afghan resistance through ISI were worked out during the Carter presidency and continued, unchanged, during the Reagan presidency. The CIA was to supply weapons, equipment, and munitions, which would be distributed through the ISI. The weapons training, too, was imparted by American trainers to the ISI, which, in turn, trained the Afghan mujahideen. In order to mask U.S. involvement, the CIA procured and supplied only the types of weapons that the Soviets or the Soviet-bloc countries used. In some cases, the mujahideen were given vintage World War I equipment.[147] While it was the sole

---

145 Quoted in Kux, *The United States and Pakistan*, 249.
146 Ibid., 257.
147 Ibid., 252.

conduit for weapons, Pakistan denied any role in providing military supplies to the mujahideen. Pakistani Foreign Minister, Agha Shahi, proclaimed on March 5, 1980, "Let it be stated categorically that Pakistan is determined not to allow itself to become a conduit for the flow of arms into Afghanistan."[148] The port of Karachi was the arrival point for the supplies and from there they were transported by rail to a military supply depot in northern Pakistan. At the depot, called the "Ojiri Camp," shipments were broken down and trucked to Peshawar, with some supplies going to Quetta. Factions approved by the ISI and headquartered in Peshawar received the supplies. The factions then forwarded the supplies to the fighters in Afghanistan, crossing west over the Durand Line through the mountains, often utilizing mule trains. Brigadier Mohammad Yousaf, assigned to the Afghan Bureau of ISI (1983-1987) claimed, "During my four years some 80,000 Mujahideen were trained; hundreds of thousands of tons of arms and ammunition were distributed, several billion dollars were spent on this immense logistic exercise and ISI teams regularly entered Afghanistan alongside the Mujahideen."[149] Besides controlling the supplies, another Pakistani requirement was that the CIA was not allowed to deal directly with the Afghans. This precaution was taken so that Pakistan could maintain total control over who could receive aid.

The covert aid given to the mujahideen was separate from the economic and military aid that the United States provided to Pakistan yearly. This spending went up from $161 million in 1981 to over a billion dollars in 1984 and Saudi Arabia continued to match the U.S. contributions. The covert aid was controversial for several reasons. There were concerns that the ISI personnel were skimming off sizable chunks of supplies for profit or for official Pakistani use. However, the most controversial issue surrounding the covert aid given to the Afghan resistance was the selective manner in which the ISI distributed it, giving the largest share to the most fundamentalist factions. Since the United States had agreed to rely completely on ISI for disbursement of covert aid, it could not control how it was parceled out. However, despite critics' concerns that providing weapons and aid to the extremists empowered them at the expense of moderates, "There was little apparent CIA concern that the ability of the fundamentalists to hand out weapons gave them a potent form of political patronage, strengthening their standing and weakening that of more moderate Afghan groups."[150]

---

148 Ibid.
149 Mohammed Yousaf and Mark Adkin, *Afghanistan: The Bear Trap: The Defeat of a Superpower* (Havertown, PA: Casemate, 2001), 4.
150 Kux, *The United States and Pakistan*, 1947-2000, 275.

Pakistan called the ISI-directed war against the Soviet Army a jihad, terming the insurgents *mujahideen*.[151] John Schmidt described their use of jihad terminology as, "the very same tactic that had been used by the Ayub government during the 1965 war with India when the irregular forces that were infiltrated into Kashmir were also referred to as mujahideen… The primary difference between the 1965 precedent and the Afghan example is that in the Afghan case the most important insurgent groups actually did have a religious pedigree."[152]

The ISI created several training camps in the tribal areas of the Pakistan-Afghan frontier. These camps were both the assembly points for training volunteers who wished to fight in Afghanistan as well as transit points for moving weapons and supplies. As a result of this localization, the boundary areas were radicalized. Marvin Weinbaum and Jonathan Harder conclude:

> The support for the mujahideen in 1980s prepared the ground for a gradual radicalization of the population in the NWFP and tribal agencies, as well as a widening of the differences among Pakistan's ethnic groups. The population of the border regions was under heavy social pressure and coercion to support the mujahideen, and opposition was very difficult since the insurgency carried the dual banners of Islam and self-determination and had the backing of the Pakistani state… Economic and social deprivation of young Afghan refuges made their camps a fertile recruiting ground for the mujahideen.[153]

By 1986, the ISI had established large and sophisticated secret infrastructure for training fighters along the Afghan border. Specialized training camps for explosives, urban sabotage, car bombing, anti-aircraft weapons, and land mines were set up and thousands of graduates were trained, hailing from regions as diverse as Afghanistan, Egypt, Algeria, Palestine, Tunisia, and Saudi Arabia.[154] Steve Coll comments:

> Ten years later the vast training infrastructure… built with the enormous budgets endorsed by NSDD-166 (National Security Decision Directive "US Policy, Programs, and Strategy in Afghanistan")—the specialized camps, the sabotage training manuals, the electronic bomb detonators, and so on—would be referred to routinely in America as "terrorist infrastructure." At the time of its construction, however, it served a jihadist army that operated openly on the battlefield.[155]

The open operation of the jihadist army Coll mentions was approved and financed by the United States, with Saudi Arabia contributing equal funds.

---

151 Schmidt, *The Unraveling*, 71.
152 Ibid.
153 Marvin G. Weinbaum and Jonathan B. Harder, "Pakistan's Afghan Policies and Their Consequences," *Contemporary South Asia* 16, no. 1 (2008): 32.
154 Coll, *Ghost Wars*. 272.
155 Ibid., 270.

The vast majority of guerillas who fought against the Soviet and PDPA forces were Afghans. As the war progressed, fighters from other Muslim nations started arriving in Pakistan to support the jihad; many of the foreign volunteers shared Wahhabi beliefs. The frontier town of Peshawar, which once was a part of Afghanistan before it was absorbed into British India, became not only the headquarters of various Afghan guerilla forces but also a gathering point for international jihadis. The ISI welcomed the foreign volunteers, as they were willing to pursue Pakistan's foreign policy agenda not only in Afghanistan but also in Kashmir. Jihadis fighting in Kashmir were trained in the Afghanistan camps run by the ISI.[156] Describing the campaign as a "global jihad," Ahmad Rashid states, "Between 1982 and 1990, the CIA, working with the ISI and Saudi Arabia's intelligence service, funded the training, arrival, and arming of some thirty-five thousand Islamic militants from forty-three Muslim countries in Pakistani madrasas to fight the Soviets in Afghanistan."[157]

During his Islamization campaign in Pakistan, Zia had established the International Islamic University in Islamabad in 1980, inviting radical Islamists to come study and teach there. Those admitted to the university included Egyptian Arabs from the Muslim Brotherhood and Muslim separatists from the Philippines and Burma. The students' Islamic education included moving from the Islamic University to Peshawar and then to military training camps in Afghanistan to fight the infidel communists.[158]

Abdullah Azzam (1941-1989) was one of the scholars who taught Quran and Arabic at the International Islamic University. Azzam, a very influential Sunni Islamic scholar, had called Muslims everywhere to jihad, asking them to help the Afghan mujahideen against the Soviet invaders. Born in Palestine, Azzam had become a member of the Muslim Brotherhood in his teens. He completed his doctorate in Islamic jurisprudence at the historic center of Islamic learning, the al-Azhar University in Cairo, Egypt. In Egypt Azzam came in touch with the family of the famous Islamist Syed Qutb, Ayman al-Zawahiri, as well as Sheikh Abdel Omar Rahman, the blind Egyptian preacher and the spiritual leader of Egyptian *al-Gamaa al-Islamiyya*.[159] In the late 1970s Azzam taught at the King Abdul Aziz University in Jeddah, Saudi Arabia, where Osama bin Laden was enrolled as a student, and in 1979, Azzam moved to Islamabad. Shortly after the Soviet invasion, Azzam moved to Peshawar to help with the Afghan jihad. He was assassinated there in 1989.

---

156 Ibid., 383.
157 Rashid, *Descent into Chaos*, 38.
158 Shahzad, *Inside Al-Qaeda and the Taliban*, 132.
159 Burke, *Al-Qaeda*. 73.

Abdullah Azzam was considered the spiritual father of the Afghan Arabs and inspired Osama bin Laden to devote his time, energy, and resources to the Afghan jihad. Thomas Hegghammer describes Azzam as "the first modern ideologue of transnational jihad... By mobilizing foreign fighters to Afghanistan in the 1980s ... Azzām played an important role in making jihad go global."[160] In 1984, Azzam published a fatwa (religious ruling) called "Defense of Muslim Lands." The fatwa called for all Muslims around the world to support the Afghan jihad, deeming it a religious duty. His writings persuaded Arab volunteers to travel to Afghanistan and help fight the Soviet occupying forces. To support these Arab fighters and coordinate and facilitate the flow of Afghan Arabs to and from Afghanistan, Azzam set up *Maktab al-Khidamat* (MAK, or "Services Bureau") in a house that bin Laden rented.[161] Osama bin Laden, who had moved his whole household to Peshawar in 1986, became an important funding source for Azzam, providing twenty five thousand dollars a month to keep their office running.[162] When he recruited Arab volunteers, Azzam promised them that bin Laden would pay for the expenses of any Arab who would fight in Afghanistan.[163] Based on Abdullah Azzam's writings and al-Jihad magazine, Kim Cragin concludes that in 1985, MAK leaders began to look beyond Afghanistan and other parts of the Muslim world, seeing their activities in the context of broader revolutionary objectives, including rescuing the Palestinians from Israeli occupation and overthrowing secular Arab regimes.[164]

The bulk of foreign volunteers came from Saudi Arabia, Yemen, Egypt, and Algeria, with smaller numbers coming from Indonesia, Philippines, Malaysia, Chechnya, Iraq, Bosnia, and elsewhere. The arrival of radical Islamists from Egypt, including Mohammed Shawky al-Islambouli (brother of Anwar Sadat's killer) and Ayman al-Zawahiri further bolstered radicalism in Pakistan.[165] Osama bin Laden was profoundly shaped by the Afghan jihad. According to Fawaz Gerges, Azzam was of particular importance to bin Laden: "Abdullah Azzam, a charismatic Jordanian of Palestinian descent, provided ideological and theological guidance and became a driving force behind bin Laden's entry into the jihad environment. Bin Laden looked on Azzam as a spiritual father and mentor, and fell under his

---

160 Thomas Hegghammer, "Abdallah Azzam and Palestine," *Welt des Islams* 53, no. 3-4 (2013): 354.
161 R. Kim Cragin, "Early History of Al-Qa'ida," *Historical Journal* 51, no.4 (2008): 1051; Fawaz A. Gerges, *The Far Enemy: Why Jihad Went Global*, 2nd ed. (Cambridge: Cambridge University Press, 2009), 69.
162 Lawrence Wright, *The Looming Tower: Al-Qaeda and the Road to 9/11* (New York: Vintage, 2007). 103.
163 Coll, *Ghost Wars*, 290-291.
164 Cragin, "Early History of Al-Qa'ida," 1052.
165 Burke, *Al-Qaeda*, 76.

spell."¹⁶⁶ Bin Laden developed close relationships with many other fundamentalists headquartered in Peshawar, including Sayyaf, Jalaluddin Haqqani, and Yunus Khalis.

The United States had no issue with Arab volunteers arriving in Pakistan; instead, it looked favorably upon Arab recruitment drives and saw the movement as akin to an international brigade of volunteers broadening the coalition of countries involved in the anti-Soviet jihad. In fact, the CIA explored how Arab participation in the jihad might be increased as more volunteers continued to arrive during 1985-86. While Abdullah Azzam stridently denounced the United States, he travelled extensively there to raise money and recruit young Muslims to the cause. In 1986, Azzam opened an office in Tucson, Arizona.¹⁶⁷ He was also the leading recruiter for the Afghan jihad at the al-Kifah Afghan Refugee Center in Brooklyn, New York. The center was known as the "Al-Jihad" center to those who worked there.¹⁶⁸

With increasing aid, supplies, weapons, and training, the resistance began to turn the war in their favor from 1986-87, especially after receiving specialized weaponry from the United States, including shoulder-fired anti-aircraft missiles ("Stingers"). The combined U.S. and Saudi fiscal year aid in 1986 (excluding the aid from other Gulf countries and private donors) equaled $940 million, exceeding over $1.2 billion in 1987. Michael Bhatia and Mark Sedra conclude:

> Ultimately, at the conclusion of US assistance, the mujahideen received $6–8 billion of material assistance involving: 400,000 rifles (Chinese type 56/59 AK-47), SAMs, Italian anti-personnel mines, 100,000 .303 Indian rifles, 60,000 old rifles and 8,000 light machine guns from Turkey, and 100 million rounds of ammunition, of which 30 million were from the Pakistan Ordnance Factory. Total of 80,000 mujahideen trained in Pakistan; 5,000 Arab mujahideen trained by governments and Islamic charities were sent to Afghanistan.¹⁶⁹

Approximately 13,400 Soviet soldiers were killed in Afghanistan. Mounting losses turned Soviet public opinion, and the arrival of reformist Mikhail Gorbachev led to the USSR's departure from Afghanistan. As Soviet forces began withdrawing from Afghanistan, Pakistan began setting up for its long-desired mission west of the Durand Line: planting a pliant ruler in Afghanistan. "As the Soviets withdrew, Gulbuddin Hekmatyar—backed by officers in ISI's Afghan bureau, operatives from the Muslim Brotherhood's Jamiat-e-Islami, officers from Saudi intelligence, and

---

166 Fawaz A. Gerges, *The Rise and Fall of Al-Qaeda* (New York: Oxford University Press, 2011), 272.
167 Coll, *Ghost Wars*, 288; Wright, *The Looming Tower*, 17.
168 Mahmood Mamdani, *Good Muslim, Bad Muslim: America, the Cold War, and the Roots of Terror* (New York: Pantheon, 2004), 135.
169 Bhatia and Sedra, *Afghanistan, Arms and Conflict*, 68.

Arab volunteers from a dozen countries—was moving systematically to wipe out his rivals in the Afghan resistance."[170] Thus began a concerted plan to eliminate his rivals as the Soviet soldiers were pulling out of Afghanistan. As mentioned above, the Afghan poet and philosopher Majrooh, the publisher of the most influential bulletin promoting traditional Afghan royalist and tribal leadership, was killed after publishing a survey that a vast majority of Afghan refugees supported exiled King Zahir Shah rather than any of the Peshawar-based mujahideen, including Hekmatyar.[171] Coll suggests that, "The hit was interpreted among Afghans and at the CIA's Islamabad station as an early and intimidating strike by Hekmatyar against the Zahir Shah option for post-Soviet Afghanistan."[172] Similarly, Ahmed Shah Massoud, Massoud's half-brother, was killed around the same time, an incident that Massoud's brothers believed to be the handiwork of the ISI's Afghan cell.

The Soviet withdrawal was completed by February 15, 1989, leaving behind a weak PDPA regime in the hands of Mohammad Najibullah. Afghanistan's victorious resistance, however, did not bring peace to Afghanistan. The people had pushed out the Afghan communist regime and its Soviet patrons but it was a Pyrrhic victory; Afghanistan quickly became involved in an internecine war amongst the mujahideen. Even after the Najibullah government was toppled in 1992, serious bloodletting continued between various mujahideen factions. Pakistan continued to attempt to install a pro-Pakistan Islamist government in Kabul. It eventually succeeded in 1996, this time with a new fundamentalist movement called the Taliban.

In April 1992, Najibullah's government disintegrated and Kabul was taken over by mujahideen led by Ahmad Shah Massoud. The mujahideen declared Afghanistan an Islamic state; many Afghans welcomed the takeover, hoping for the end of a devastating war that had lasted almost a decade. However, from 1992 to 1996, Kabul became the scene of even more catastrophic violence.

Massoud, in alliance with Uzbek warlord Abdul Rashid Dostum, had successfully seized power in Kabul. Other Mujahideen groups competed for spoils as they occupied the suburbs surrounding Kabul. The city was divided among different factions into 12 sectors. The Iranian-backed *Hezb-i-Wahdat* occupied 30 percent of the capital. Hekmatyar's forces waited south of Kabul to launch an attack on their former allies.[173] Saikal comprehensively describes the reasons for factional fights between the mujahideen:

---

170 Coll, *Ghost Wars*, 333.
171 Ibid., 334.
172 Ibid.
173 Saikal, *Modern Afghanistan*, 213.

> As the collapse of the Najibullah government approached, the Mujahideen remained as fragmented along ethno-linguistic, tribal, sectarian and personality lines as ever. The Pakistan-based leaders of the seven main Sunni Islamic Mujahideen groups had failed to agree on a common political platform... Not one of the groups or their respective leaders had managed to develop a national profile or a nationwide following. Most groups functioned as fighting militias within specific localities from which their leaders originated, and enjoyed support substantially along lines of ethnic or tribal identification...[174]

An attempt was made to create a coalition representing all the mujahideen groups, resulting in the Peshawar Agreement of April 24, 1992. The Peshawar Agreement was forged between the Pakistan-based Mujahideen leaders. Sighbatullah Mujaddidi was chosen to head a two-month transitional government to be followed by a longer-term interim coalition government headed by Burhanuddin Rabbani. However, Hekmatyar and his ISI patrons worked against the Peshawar Agreement, even though the post of Prime Minister had been allocated for the *Hezb-i-Islami*. In August 1992, Hekmatyar attacked Kabul with rockets, killing 1,800 civilians and destroying the southern parts of the capital. In January 1994, Hekmatyar, in a coalition with other mujahideen commanders, launched another major assault on Kabul, destroying even more of the city (almost half) and killing approximately 25,000 people. Pakistan would do its utmost to install its client in Kabul. Amin Saikal concludes, "Had it not been for the ISI's logistic support and supply of a large number of rockets, Hekmatyar's forces would not have been able to target and destroy half of Kabul."[175]

However, despite Pakistan's support, as well as the other alliances he had made, Hekmatyar ultimately was unable to defeat Rabbani and Massoud. Even five years after the Soviet departure and two years after the fall of Najibullah government, Pakistan was unsuccessful in their mission to install a client regime in Afghanistan. To Pakistan's dismay, new Islamic government leaders, especially Massoud, emphasized Afghan independence from Pakistan. Despite its major investment in the proxy wars and the other ways it had interfered in Afghan affairs over the years, Pakistan failed to realize its regional ambitions. It was time to replace Hekmatyar with a new agent, and this new agent was the Taliban.

The Taliban were militant Sunni Islamists trained in the madrasas of Pakistan. Steeped in ultra-orthodoxy and trained for militant *jihad*, the Taliban wanted to make Afghanistan a puritan Islamic Emirate. They were led by Mullah Mohammad Omar, a militant who had fought under *Hezb-i-Islami* of Yunus Khalis. With ISI backing, the Taliban took over Kandahar in November 1994 and pressed towards

---

174 Ibid., 210.
175 Ibid., 220.

Kabul, soon making their way to the southern gates. By March 1995, they had begun their siege on Kabul and by September they controlled over 27 Afghan provinces out of 32.

Pakistan supported the Taliban from its inception, seeing in them a means of ending the Afghan civil war and increasing Pakistani influence in Afghanistan after the Taliban defeated the mujahideen factions. The policy to support the Taliban began under Prime Minister Benazir Bhutto and continued under Prime Minister Nawaz Sharif. However, the Pakistan Army truly called the shots, as had been the case during the Afghan jihad.[176] Pakistan pushed Hekmatyar aside to back a new organization of dedicated fanatics because it better suited their strategic goals at the time. Zia expressed this sentiment succinctly to the journalist Selig Harrison in 1988:

> We have earned the right to have a friendly regime there. We took risks as a frontline state, and we won't permit it to be like it was before, with Indian and Soviet influence there and claims on our territory. It will be a real Islamic state, part of a pan-Islamic revival that will one day win over the Muslims in the Soviet Union, you will see.[177]

While the ISI assisted by training, recruitment, and advising the Taliban militia, Pakistan advisors actively handled the logistics, including maintaining and operating the Taliban's sophisticated weapons, which included tanks and aircraft.[178] In 1996, Kabul fell to the Taliban. In May 1997, Islamabad was the first capital to officially recognize the Taliban as the legitimate government of Afghanistan. It remained one of the only three nations that recognized the Taliban, along with Saudi Arabia and the UAE.

It was in the wake of the Taliban's successful takeover of Afghanistan that Osama bin Laden arrived again in Kandahar, Afghanistan on May 18, 1996, bringing with him the core leadership of what would be known in the near future as al Qaeda. Bin Laden arrived with his three wives, his children, and about thirty of his followers. When bin Laden's plane landed on an airstrip in Jalalabad, he was welcomed by three warlords, each belonging to a different Afghan resistance faction which had fought against the Soviet forces. Maulvi Sanzoor was aligned with Sayyaf's Ittehad-e-Islami; 'Engineer' Machmud was with Hekmatyar; and Fazl Haq Mujahed was associated with Yunus Khalis' group.[179] The Afghan war commanders hoped to use bin Laden's wealth and international connections in post-war Afghanistan. From Jalalabad, bin Laden moved to a compound owned

---

176 Riedel, *Deadly Embrace*, 43, 45.
177 Cordovez and Harrison, *Out of Afghanistan*, 92.
178 Robert D. Crews and Amin Tarzi, *The Taliban and the Crisis of Afghanistan* (Cambridge: Harvard University Press, 2009), 69-70.
179 Burke, *Al-Qaeda*, 145.

by Yunus Khalis near Hadda and then further south to the Melawa Valley, where he issued his "Declaration of War Against the Americans Occupying the Land of the Two Holy Places" on August 23.[180]

Bin Laden was given sanctuary by the Taliban's chief, Mullah Omar, who was now styled *Amir al-Mo'mineen* ("Commander of the faithful").[181] According to Ahmad Rashid, "In his strategic alliance with the Taliban, bin Laden received an entire country as a base of operations. He was able to gather around him thousands of Islamic extremists and extend his operations around the world."[182] Within two years of Osama bin Laden's arrival in Kandahar, major attacks against U.S. targets were launched. U.S. embassies in Kenya and Tanzania suffered devastating bombings on August 7, 1998, killing 224 and injuring about 5,000. This happened while the Taliban openly massacred their opponents in Afghanistan.[183]

Bruce Riedel claims that Osama bin Laden had maintained a close relationship with the ISI after his first arrival in Peshawar in 1980. Osama bin Laden himself had commented that Pakistan had "some governmental departments which, by the grace of God, respond to the Islamic sentiments of the masses in Pakistan. This is reflected in sympathy and cooperation."[184] Since the ISI had carefully controlled and guarded its position in the Afghan movement, it would have been impossible for bin Laden to operate without ISI supervision. After bin Laden returned in 1996, the ISI was instrumental in developing his ties with the Taliban by setting up the first contacts between bin Laden and Mullah Omar. The Taliban allowed al Qaeda almost total freedom to operate from Afghanistan. Al Qaeda was not only planning and executing prolific operations from its base in Afghanistan, it also was training jihadis, seeding insurgencies, and supporting terrorist groups from around the world. Successful al Qaeda operations seeded, supervised, or executed from its base in Afghanistan included the bombing of the U.S. embassies in Kenya and Tanzania on October 12, the 2000 attack on the USS Cole, and the 9/11 attacks.[185]

It was the safe haven provided by the Taliban that allowed bin Laden to set up terrorist training camps and expand al Qaeda into a trans-national network with Afghanistan as its nucleus. The ISI handed the training camps they had used earlier over to bin Laden, allowing him to control all extremist groups who wanted

---

180 Ibid., 146.
181 Daniel Byman, *Deadly Connections: States that Sponsor Terrorism* (New York: Cambridge University Press, 2005), 388; Saikal, *Modern Afghanistan*, 226.
182 Rashid, *Descent into Chaos*, 15.
183 Ibid., 16.
184 As quoted in Riedel, *Deadly Embrace*, 51.
185 Byman, *Deadly Connections*, 205.

to train in Afghanistan.[186] Without the material and logistical support of ISI, the Taliban could not have taken power in Afghanistan, and, in turn, the alliance of the Taliban and al Qaeda could not have materialized.

With the massive covert operation Pakistan had conducted in Afghanistan, Islamabad had raised its value as a U.S. ally. However, Pakistan' true aim was not to assist the United States in achieving its foreign policy goals; Pakistan was following up on its own ambitions in Afghanistan and Kashmir.[187] During the Afghan War, Pakistan became the fourth highest recipient of American aid after Israel, Egypt, and Turkey, and the substantial increase in aid to Pakistan helped to revive Pakistan's moribund economy and upgrade its military.[188] Zia spun the Soviet presence in Afghanistan to his advantage in several ways. While he asked the United States for military aid, the requests for finances and weapons far exceeded the needs or capabilities of the mujahideen and thus could be diverted to strengthen the Pakistani military against its archrival, India. Jon Armajani has suggested four reasons Zia supported the mujahideen: gaining strategic depth against India, exercising influence over Afghanistan's political leadership, increasing its regional influence, and expanding its influence more broadly in Central Asia.[189] However, Zia's primary motivation always was to procure military equipment to use against India, not Afghanistan. David McGiffert, then Assistant Secretary for Defense for International Security Affairs, states that Pakistan was after "tanks and high-performance aircraft like F-16. It was perfectly clear that their orientation as far as equipment was concerned was what would be useful on the Indian border. They weren't very interested in the sort of thing we thought they needed to secure the Afghan border."[190]

Besides using the Afghan jihad to strengthen its armed forces, Pakistan used it to refine and escalate its proxy war in Kashmir. Hussain Haqqani asserts that Zia personally drew up a plan for rebellion in Kashmir in 1984, and this plan was based on the Afghan model where Islamists fighters had been provided a base, support, training, and material support in Pakistan.[191]

The impact of Zia's rule on Pakistan's society included increasing extremism and divisiveness and it has lasted long after his death. Pakistan's society was increasingly militarized, and the military, dominant within the polity since its inception, increased its grip on the state structure. The consequences of Zia's

---

186 Ibid.
187 Ḥaqqānī, *Pakistan: Between Mosque And Military*, 165-166.
188 Kux, *The United States and Pakistan*, 1947-2000, 266.
189 Jon Armajani, *Modern Islamist Movements: History, Religion, and Politics* (West Sussex: Wiley-Blackwell, 2011), 189.
190 Cordovez and Harrison, *Out of Afghanistan*, 57.
191 Ḥaqqānī, *Pakistan: Between Mosque And Military*, 273.

machinations are still being felt, not only in Pakistan but also in entire South Asia and every part of the world that has experienced terrorist violence connected to the Taliban and al Qaeda. The Pakistani officer corps became more Islamic than it was before Zia's tenure. Strong links exist between the Pakistan Army and Islamist groups. Retired ISI ranking officers have joined their previous jihadi clients and engage in anti-American jihadi rhetoric.

Zia's expressions of piousness and Islamic rhetoric should be considered within the context of justifying his military dictatorship, forging alliances to perpetuate his brand of rule and providing moral justification for exploitation of his subjects. These are all hallmarks of British colonial rule in South Asia, and they have been adroitly continued by its successor, Pakistan's military-feudal elite. However, Zia could not have done it without the support of the United States.

Pakistan's ability to sustain a proxy war in Kashmir increased greatly as a result of U.S. financial aid and the power it infused into its battered economy. Furthermore, Pakistan gained valuable experience from its experience in Afghan jihad, strengthening its covert war abilities. "Economic and military assistance that had ended with the military coup of 1977 resumed with the Ronald Reagan administration, and through the 1980s the United States was largely reconciled to allowing Pakistan's ISI to siphon off funds and supplies from those destined for the jihad in Afghanistan. Approximately $5.2 billion in overt and covert aid intended for the Afghan insurgency was passed to Pakistan from the United States during the decade."[192] As Haqqani states:

> Pakistan's critical role in the anti-Afghan jihad meant that the United States not only provided Pakistan with economic and military assistance; it was also willing to overlook several aspects of Pakistani policy. The United States ignored Zia ul-Haq's pan-Islamic aspirations even when they took on a clearly anti-Western dimension because Zia was such a staunch ally against the Soviet Union. U.S. officials tended to think of anti-Western Islamist sentiment as mere rhetoric. Zia ul-Haq's India policy, too, received scant attention in Washington, where there was little sympathy for an India widely perceived to be pro-Soviet.[193]

AFTER THE AFGHAN WAR

After ruling Pakistan for 11 years as his fief, on August 17, 1988, Zia died in a mysterious plane crash when his plane exploded shortly after the takeoff. Almost all of Zia's senior military leadership was in the plane and perished with him.

---

192 Weinbaum and Harder, "Pakistan's Afghan Policies and Their Consequences," 35.
193 Ḥaqqānī, *Pakistan: Between Mosque And Military*, 275.

The crash was believed to be an act of sabotage.[194] At the time, the Soviets had only partially withdrawn from Afghanistan. In November 1988, Pakistan held elections between the daughter of Zulfikar Ali Bhutto, Benazir Bhutto, and pro-Zia Islamic alliance led by Nawaz Sharif. Benazir Bhutto's Pakistan People's Party won the elections. The military leadership in Pakistan advised U.S. officials that it was ready to accept Benazir in power as long as she did not interfere in military matters. Additionally, an understanding was reached that Benazir would not become involved in Afghanistan or nuclear issues.[195] Thus, despite the heralding of civilian rule after eleven years of Zia's iron-fisted dictatorship, Pakistan's foreign policy remained, as it had for previous decades, strictly within the confines of its armed forces. The Pakistan Army reiterated its right to bring civilian rulers to power or remove them in order to ensure that the army's goals prevailed as state goals.

The following year was a significant year in history. The Soviet Union was undergoing reform under Mikhail Gorbachev and the Iron Curtain was falling. People were taking sledgehammers to the Berlin Wall and the Eastern Bloc was finally coming apart. America had seen its proxies defeat the Soviet forces in Afghanistan with the departure of the Soviet troops completed on February 15, 1989. George Herbert Walker Bush took over the reins of administration in Washington as President. In Pakistan, however, despite the arrival of a democratically elected leader, not much had changed on the Afghan front. The pro-Islamic ISI chief, Lieutenant General Hamid Gul, continued supporting Hekmatyar and the fundamentalists in an attempt to obtain a friendly Afghan regime in spite of the criticism of Peter Tomsen, appointed by President Bush as a Special Envoy to the Afghan Resistance. Tomsen angered the ISI by criticizing its support for Hekmatyar and inquiring about a role for the former Afghan king Zahir Shah during the transition of power in Afghanistan.[196] Ultimately the ISI interests prevailed.

In the presence of the U.S. ambassador Robert Oakley, on March 6, 1989, Prime Minister Benazir Bhutto ordered Hamid Gul to have the mujahideen attack Jalalabad. Bhutto wanted the mujahideen to capture and hold a significant Afghan city in order to demonstrate their capabilities before she would declare her support for the Afghan Interim Government formed by the Peshawar-based resistance groups. Hamid Gul said that Jalalabad could be taken in a week "if the government was prepared to allow for a certain degree of bloodshed."[197] Pakistan's

---

194 Ayesha Jalal, *The Struggle for Pakistan: A Muslim Homeland and Global Politics* (Cambridge: The Belknap Press of Harvard University Press, 2014), 257-260.
195 Kux, *The United States and Pakistan, 1947-2000*, 293.
196 Ibid., 296.
197 Ibid., 298.

interests were determining the fate of Afghanistan and its governance. While Hamid Gul had predicted the fall of Jalalabad as imminent and the mujahideen were confident of their success, they failed to capture the city. It would take three more years before the government of Najibullah would fall.

With the departure of Soviet troops from Afghanistan, the United States had achieved its objectives in Afghanistan. During the Afghan jihad, the Reagan administration had ignored warning signs regarding Pakistan's nuclear program. In January 1987, the Pakistani scientist Abdul Qadeer Khan had told an Indian journalist that Pakistan had achieved nuclear weapon capability. A month later, Zia had told Time magazine, "You can write today that Pakistan can build a bomb whenever it wishes."[198] The Pressler Amendment, passed in 1985, required the President of the United States to annually certify that Pakistan did not possess a nuclear device. Failure to obtain the certification would trigger sanctions and stop U.S. military and economic aid. Due to the concerns over Pakistan's nuclear program, the U.S. Congress had allowed the six-year waiver of sanctions lapse in the fall of 1987, temporarily halting any commitments of new aid. President Reagan, in 1986, had not only certified that Pakistan did not possess a nuclear device, he claimed that American aid significantly reduced the risk that Pakistan would acquire a nuclear device.[199] With increasing signs that Pakistan was pursuing nuclear weapons, President Reagan issued the Pressler amendment certification a second time in December 1987, allowing Pakistan to continue receiving aid despite overt signs to the contrary.

However, with the realignments occurring in the wake of changes in the Soviet Union, the fall of the Berlin Wall in November 1989, a perceived end to the Cold War, and Saddam Hussein's invasion of Kuwait in August 1990, Afghanistan had lost its importance to the United States. Concomitantly, Pakistan too lost its value to the United States as a frontline state. President Bush refused to issue the Pressler Amendment certification to Pakistan in 1990. Pakistan, which at the time was the third highest recipient of American aid, had its $564 million military and economic aid frozen. With the triggering of Pressler sanctions, all military assistance and weapon transfers were halted, including the delivery of F-16 aircrafts Pakistan had already paid for. America's close allies in the Afghan jihad were left stunned and angered. Pakistan denounced the United States' actions as unfair, discriminatory, and anti-Islamic.[200] Pakistan's leaders believed that since the Afghan War was over, the U.S. administration did not feel compelled to look the other way about Pakistan's nuclear program. A year after achieving its mission, the

---

198 Ibid., 285.
199 Ibid., 283.
200 Ibid., 308-310.

United States had washed its hands of Pakistan and Afghanistan. As Jason Burke describes it, "The State Department... was simply not that concerned by events in Afghanistan. This abandonment, particularly given the intense involvement during the 1980s, must go down as one of the most ruthless and shortsighted policies of recent times."[201] The story of jihad in Afghanistan had just begun; America could not stay away from Afghanistan for too long. Pakistan may have been shunned by the United States in 1990 but it remained a key player in the continuing wars in Afghanistan.

In "Defense of Muslim Lands," Abdullah Azzam had declared, "This duty will not end with victory in Afghanistan; jihad will remain an individual obligation until all other lands that were Muslim are returned to us that Islam will regain again: before us lie Palestine, Bokhara, Lebanon, Chad, Eritrea, Somalia, the Philippines, Burma, southern Yemen, Tashkent and Andalusia."[202]

True to Azzam's declaration, radical jihadis did not lay down their arms after the Soviet Army retreated from Afghanistan. Pakistan too did not need to be reminded of its duty to liberate Kashmir from India, to prevent the Pashtunistan issue from gathering any traction, and to undercut India's influence in Afghanistan. It was Britain's colonial legacy that led Pakistan to engage in its reckless support of radical Islamists in order to undercut any potential Afghan resistance solidarity. The Pashtunistan issue had resulted from Britain's need to secure India's frontiers in the west and its creation of Durand Line. The Kashmir conflict was a direct result of the partition of British India. Pakistan's security concerns in relation to India were congenital, emerging from the process of its birth during the partition of British India.

Pashtunistan and Kashmir are both reasons why Pakistan manipulated the Soviet incursion in Afghanistan, but there was also a historical basis for the factionalism and division in the Afghan resistance: the centralized government that the majority Pashtuns forced on the diverse Afghan ethnic populations. Pakistan effectively used these differences, just as the British colonialists had done previously, to sow discord among factions and enable its own neo-colonial interests to prevail. These expediencies unduly prolonged the war and led to deaths and misery for a vast number of Afghan people—tragic consequences that could have been avoidable. The deaths caused by the internecine warfare between the Massoud and Hekmatyar forces in Kabul alone numbered in the tens of thousands. In Kashmir, the number of deaths caused by the insurgency in the 1990s was

---

201 Burke, *Al-Qaeda*, 129.
202 Quoted in ibid., 69.

upward of 50,000, and this number excludes the unquantifiable indignities and repression that the Kashmiri people faced at the hands of both the Indian armed forces as well as the jihadi Islamists.

The death, destruction, and misery that resulted from Pakistan's pursuit of its national interests did not stop in Afghanistan and Kashmir. Pakistan's own citizens would face the effects of its use of jihadi Islamists, as sectarian violence rose during and after Zia's administration and terrorist incidents increased. As decade drew to a close and with the new millennium on the horizon, the jihadi seeds sown by Pakistan would bear the fruits of death and destruction in several other parts of the world as well.

The United States experienced terrorism inspired by the Afghan jihad on February 26, 1993, when a militant jihadi group attempted to topple the World Trade Center using a bomb. The attempt failed but caused substantial damage, killing six people and injuring over a thousand. The powerful bomb was placed in a rented van and parked beneath the Twin Towers. The bomber, Ramzi Ahmed Yousef, was initiated in the militant jihad during the Afghan War. Ramzi had intended to bring down the tower and kill 250,000 people. He was unsuccessful in this, but managed to escape on the day of bombing, fleeing to Pakistan.

Ramzi had been in the United States for six months, recruiting his bombing team, finding his first volunteers at the al-Farouq mosque in Brooklyn, "once the Maktab al-Khidamat's favorite recruiting ground for the Afghan jihad in New York."[203] Ramzi had studied computer-aided electrical engineering in Britain and had spent his summer vacation in 1989 teaching electronic bomb making skills in terrorist training camps on the frontier around Peshawar. In 1991, he had returned to training camps in Pakistan when he met with Abdurajak Abu Bakr Janjalani, with whom he went to the Philippines to train militants. Janjalani fought with the Sayyaf faction during the Afghan jihad and had set up the Abu Sayyaf group in Philippines. By mid-1992, Ramzi had returned to Pakistan, teaching bomb-making skills to jihadi militants in Pabbi, Sayaffabad, in the University of Da'wa and Jihad, and also at Sayyaf's Khaldan training camp.[204]

After fleeing New York, Ramzi went to Quetta and then on to Peshawar. In 1993, he injured himself during a failed attempt to assassinate Benazir Bhutto. In the hospital he was visited by senior Sipah-e-Sahaba leaders. (As was mentioned earlier, Sipah-e-Sahaba is a particularly violent Deobandi organization that engaged in sectarian violence against Shias in Pakistan.) The following year, Ramzi attempted to recruit Muslims in Bangkok for an attack on the embassy

---

203 Burke, *Al-Qaeda*, 101.
204 Ibid., 99.

of Israel, but the plot failed. In January 1995, Ramzi was in the Philippines, planning to assassinate the Pope. That plot also failed and Ramzi's computer was captured, revealing "Plan Bojinka," a plot to simultaneously destroy as many as twelve airplanes midflight.[205] Ramzi was arrested in February 1995 in Pakistan and eventually received the sentence of life in prison and 240 years for the World Trade Center bombing.

Khalid Shaikh Mohammad (KSM), the "principal architect" of the 9/11 attacks and Ramzi's uncle, had a similar connection to the Afghan jihad. Towards the end of the Afghan jihad, in 1989, KSM was teaching at the University of Da'wa and Jihad. KSM worshipped at the mosque where Ayman al-Zawahiri and Sayyaf occasionally preached. KSM and Ramzi were both in Philippines when the Bojinka plot was hatched.[206] With Ramzi captured, KSM was on the run and met with Osama bin Laden at his camp in Tora Bora in 1996. Bin Laden had known KSM from the time of anti-Soviet jihad, when KSM worked as Sayyaf and Abdullah Azzam's secretary.[207] KSM attempted to sell his and Ramzi's plan to bomb twelve American jumbo jets over the Pacific Ocean to bin Laden and his close companion Mohammed Atef. Bin Laden was non-committal to KSM's proposal at the time. In the spring of 1999, bin Laden informed KSM that al Qaeda had accepted his proposal, setting the 9/11 plot in motion. Bin Laden and Atef personally and individually selected the 9/11 participants while in Afghanistan. There the participants also received their tactical training before they were sent to the United States to execute the attacks.[208]

This brief chronology of just two individuals indicates how jihadi militancy during the Afghan jihad created a web of violence that would stretch from the frontiers of Pakistan all the way to the United States and elsewhere.

When Bin Laden was forced out of Sudan in 1996, he had nowhere else to go; his own country Saudi Arabia had taken away his passport. Afghanistan became his sanctuary and the Taliban his initial patrons. According to Ahmad Rashid, the strategic alliance between the Taliban and bin Laden provided bin Laden with an entire country as his base of operations. "He was able to gather around him thousands of Islamic extremists and extend his operations around the world. His main logistical support came from Pakistani extremist groups… This support base in Pakistan was to prove critical to al Qaeda's survival after 9/11."[209]

---

205 Ibid., 101.
206 Wright, *The Looming Tower*, 235.
207 Ibid.
208 Ibid.; Gerges, *The Rise and Fall of Al-Qaeda*, 85.
209 Rashid, *Descent into Chaos*, 15-16.

Within two years of moving back to Afghanistan, bin Laden had launched major attacks on U.S. targets. The first one was the August 7, 1998 truck bombing of the American embassy in Nairobi, Kenya. The suicide attack killed 213 and wounded more than 4,600. Minutes later, a second bombing of the U.S. embassy in Dar es Salaam, Tanzania, killed 11 and injured 85. The U.S. retaliated swiftly as President Clinton ordered Operation Infinite Reach on August 20, 1998. Seventy-five Tomahawk cruise missiles were launched into training camps, including those near Kandahar and Khost in eastern Afghanistan, and destroyed a pharmaceutical factory in Sudan. Bin Laden survived the missile attacks. Despite considerable U.S. pressure, the Taliban refused to hand bin Laden over to the United States.[210]

Pakistan's support for the Taliban was quite resolute. The Taliban ignored United Nations Security Council Resolution 1267, passed in October 1999, which demanded that it hand over Osama bin Laden and stop providing sanctuary to terrorists. UN Resolution 1333 in December 2000 imposed an arms embargo on the Taliban and a closure of training camps. Nevertheless, Pakistan continued to supply them with arms.

Bin Laden offered to kill Massoud so that the Taliban could take over the entire country.[211] The Taliban now had the backing of al Qaeda in their battle against Ahmad Shah Massoud's Northern Alliance forces, their unremitting enemy. The ISI and bin Laden held similar interests: a Taliban controlled-Afghanistan without the threat of Massoud, who never had been under Pakistan's control and was thought to be friendly towards India. Al Qaeda fighters, including Muslim fighters from Uzbekistan, Chechnya, and Uighurs from China fought with the Taliban forces in a September 2000 battle where the Taliban managed to capture Massoud's stronghold of Taloqan. The ISI too provided support and manpower. The Pakistani Frontier Corps managed the Taliban's artillery and communications, but "Pakistani officers were directing the Taliban campaign in league with al Qaeda and the Taliban."[212]

In its determined quest for a friendly (or pliant) regime in Afghanistan, to train jihadi militants for continued attacks in Kashmir, and to hold back Indian influence in Afghanistan, Pakistan ended up indirectly strengthening and supporting al Qaeda in Afghanistan. Pakistan's nexus with al Qaeda was known before the 9/11 terrorist attacks. Bruce Riedel asserts that in 1998, he and others in the Clinton White House were aware of Pakistan's close ties with terrorists. Commenting on the cruise missile strike intended for bin Laden at a terrorist

---

210 Ibid., 16.
211 Riedel, *Deadly Embrace*, 57.
212 Rashid, *Descent into Chaos*, 17.

training camp—which instead killed a number of ISI officers along with several Kashmiri fighters they were training—Riedel and others concluded "the fact that bin Laden was visiting a camp with ISI officers present dramatically underlined the close ties between al Qaeda's top leader and Pakistan's army and intelligence service."[213] A Defense Intelligence Agency assessment summarized the incident as follows:

> Consider the location of bin Laden's camp targeted by US cruise missiles. Positioned on the border between Afghanistan and Pakistan, it was built by Pakistani contractors, and funded by the Pakistani Inter Services Intelligence Directorate … the real hosts in the facility [were] the Pakistani ISI, [so] then serious questions are raised by the early relationship between bin Laden and ISI.[214]

On December 24, 1999, militants belonging to Harakat-ul-Mujahideen hijacked Indian Airlines Flight 814, which was traveling from Kathmandu, Nepal. The plane eventually was forced to land at Kandahar, which was controlled by the Taliban at the time. The Taliban protected the hijackers and took on the role as mediator between the hijackers and the Indian government. Riedel claims that the hijackers were assisted in gaining access to weapons in the airport by the local ISI station in Katmandu.[215] The hijackers demanded the release of 36 militants in the custody of India, with Masood Azhar on the top of the list. India released three militants, Mushtaq Zargar, Masood Azhar, and Ahmed Omar Saeed Sheikh (aka Sheikh Omar or Omar Sheikh) in exchange for the 155 hostages on the plane. The three flew with India's foreign minister, Jaswant Singh, to Kandahar where the exchange took place. After the exchange, the released terrorists were taken to Pakistan by ISI. All three were connected to militancy in Kashmir. Masood Azhar split from Harakat-ul-Mujahideen in March 2000 and formed Jaish-e-Mohammad, a group that gained notoriety by launching a daring terrorist attack on the Indian Parliament in 2001. Omar Sheikh later confessed to organizing terrorist attacks for Jaish-e-Mohammad, including the bombing of Jammu and Kashmir's legislative assembly and the attack on Indian Parliament. A court in Pakistan later convicted Sheikh for the murder of journalist Daniel Pearl.

According to Riedel, Osama bin Laden was on the ground, directing the negotiations with the hijackers behind the scene. He hosted the victory dinner when the hijackers' demands were met.[216] The hijackers and the released militants were allowed to drive to Pakistan, where the ISI took Azhar on a victory tour

---

213 Riedel, *Deadly Embrace*, 51.
214 Ibid.
215 Riedel, "Pakistan and Terror," *Annals of the American Academy of Political and Social Science* 61 (2008): 36.
216 Ibid.

around Pakistan to help raise funds for the Kashmiri cause. This hijacking episode reveals how the Pakistan-backed militants waging insurgency in Kashmir were associated with the Taliban, ISI, and al Qaeda.

On the day of the spectacular and devastating attacks of September 11, 2001, Mahmoud Ahmad, the director general of ISI, was in Washington, in a meeting with Peter Goss, chairman of the Senate Intelligence Committee. Ahmad was the part of the 1999 coup that brought General Musharraf to power and was known for his strong support of the Taliban and the militant jihadis in Kashmir. He was a powerful figure who virtually ran Pakistan's foreign policy. On September 13, Deputy Secretary of State Richard Armitage handed Ahmad a list of non-negotiable U.S. demands.[217] The United States' demands would have amounted to a deadly blow to the close relationship the ISI had with the Taliban and, in turn, with al Qaeda. In effect, the demands made by the United States were equivalent to Ahmad betraying his own intelligence agency to help destroy what the ISI had created: the Taliban. The demands were that Pakistan:

- Give blanket over-flight and landing rights for all U.S. aircraft
- Give the U.S. access to airports, naval bases, and borders for operations against al-Qaeda
- Provide immediate intelligence sharing and cooperation
- Cut all fuel shipments to the Taliban and stop Pakistani fighters from joining them
- Publicly condemn the 9/11 attacks
- End support for the Taliban and break diplomatic relations with them
- Stop al-Qaeda operations on the Pakistan-Afghanistan border, intercept arms shipments through Pakistan, and end all logistical support for al-Qaeda[218]

Secretary of State Colin Powell called General Musharraf who agreed to support each of the seven demands. However, Musharraf's discussions with the United States regarding Pakistan's stance against terrorism and the Taliban differed from discussions between Musharraf and his generals. Pakistan had serious objections to U.S. goals, specifically removing its support from the Taliban. Musharraf argued that if Pakistan did not completely cooperate with the United States, India would step in and make its bases available to the United States. However, the argument that won army support was that their cause in Kashmir might be jeopardized if they did not align themselves with the United States. Musharraf made similar

---

217 Rashid, *Descent into Chaos*, 27.
218 Dan Balz, Bob Woodward, and Jeff Himmelman, "Afghan Campaign's Blueprint Emerges," *Washington Post*, January 29, 2002.

declarations in public, "We were on the borderline of being or not being declared a terrorist state—in that situation, what would have happened to the Kashmir cause?"[219]

Musharraf understood that Pakistan could not oppose American demands but was at the same time unwilling to give up its interests. He and his command decided to accept all of the United States' demands initially without agreeing to all the details, adopting the strategy, "First say yes and later say *but…*" As Pakistan's foreign minister described this tactic of selective cooperation, Pakistan, "should indicate a generally positive disposition and negotiate details later. Such a "Yes… but" approach would allow Pakistan tactical flexibility. It could then also seek modification of U.S. policy and its expectation of Pakistan."[220]

After agreeing to support the United States, Pakistan continued to try to influence American war efforts. General Mahmoud Ahmad asked CIA director George Tenet not to insist that Pakistan sever its relations with the Taliban until Pakistan had one more chance to persuade the Taliban to hand over Osama bin Laden. Musharraf also made requests that were clearly self-serving for Pakistan and not helpful to the United States, including that the United States should not depend on the Northern Alliance and that U.S. forces could not use Indian military bases.[221] In fact, Musharraf insisted that India must not have any role in the Afghan War or the post-Taliban government in Afghanistan. Additionally, while Pakistan would help capture of al Qaeda members, Pakistani militant groups were off-limits to U.S. counterterrorism measures.[222]

On September 19, Musharraf addressed the Pakistani nation on television to explain his decision to side with the United States. He explicitly made it clear to his audience that to not do so would be to jeopardize the Kashmir cause and endanger Pakistan's nuclear installations. If Pakistan took a strong stance against the United States, India would "want to enter into an alliance with the United States and get Pakistan declared a terrorist state."[223] The fact that Pakistan had supported and enabled an organization which protected the most well-known individual enemy of the United States, Osama bin Laden, was not mentioned. Remarkably, Musharraf contravened one of the seven U.S. demands by neglecting to condemn the Taliban or al Qaeda for the 9/11 attacks. Musharraf's assertion that Pakistan's Kashmir policy would continue was tantamount to admitting that, while Pakistan would change its policy in Afghanistan, Pakistan's support for militant jihadis and

---

219 Quoted in Rashid, *Descent into Chaos*, 29.
220 Pakistan's foreign minister Abdul Sattar, quoted in ibid., 28.
221 Quoted in Rashid, *Descent into Chaos*, 30.
222 Riedel, *Deadly Embrace*, 66.
223 Rashid, *Descent into Chaos*, 28.

associated terrorism would continue in Kashmir. As Rashid notes, "The military had wrongly surmised that the 'global war on terrorism' would not include U.S. pressure to clamp down on militants in Kashmir."[224]

It was *déjà vu*: the situation that Pakistan's dictator was facing in 2001 was almost identical to the situation faced by its dictator in 1979. Both were facing a crisis of legitimacy; both were at the helm when Pakistan was facing economic crisis and economic sanctions at the time; and both used a crisis in Afghanistan, to which Pakistan had contributed significantly, for military and economic aid from the United States. Zia had used the Afghanistan crisis to ask for massive U.S. aid and changed his reputation with the United States from a ruthless dictator to a valuable ally. Musharraf too asked the United States for economic aid and as well as to lift sanctions that were imposed as a result of Pakistan's nuclear program and military coup. Musharraf also requested that Pakistan's $3 billion debt to the United States be forgiven. Dictator-by-coup General Musharraf, like dictator-by-coup General Zia, turned his reputation around and became a close ally of the United States.

Pakistan's alliance with the United States was greatly beneficial to Musharraf. His dictatorial regime now had international legitimacy, U.S. sanctions were lifted, and massive amounts of economic and military assistance started flowing into the country. The Bush administration called him a courageous and visionary leader, approbation that helped him hold on power just as Reagan's support had enabled Zia. Instead of expressing concerns about Pakistan's troubled democracy and its support for terrorists in Afghanistan, the United States praised it as an exemplary country in the fight against terrorism. In return, the United States had access to land and aerial routes to Afghanistan and could conduct its war in there.

Musharraf's decision to support the United States' "War on Terrorism" was a tactical move that did not signal any real change in Pakistan's policies.[225] It was realpolitik in action, exercised by a country that was isolated internationally after the 1999 coup, the Kargil War, and its sponsorship of a disliked militant Islamist regime in Afghanistan. The Pakistan Army had promised to support U.S. objectives in Afghanistan, calculating that the United States would shortly exit Afghanistan, after which Pakistan would be able to place a compliant regime in Kabul again. Even though Pakistan assented to supporting U.S. efforts in Afghanistan in 2001, it had such strong ties with the Taliban that throughout the initial phase of "Operation Enduring Freedom," General Musharraf implored the United States

---

224 Ibid., 31.
225 For a discussion, see Rashid, *Descent into Chaos*, 24-32.

to desist from destroying Mullah Muhammad Omar's regime in Afghanistan.[226] Unable to achieve this objective, the Pakistani military covertly assisted thousands of defeated jihadi insurgents as they crossed over to safety into Pakistani.

By the time the hijacked planes hit their targets in the United States, the following militant jihadi groups were active in Pakistan. If not created by the ISI, they were directly or indirectly supported, and provided logistical and material assistance by the ISI:

TABLE 5. SUMMARY OF MILITANT GROUPS OPERATING FROM PAKISTAN

Group Name	Sectarian Background	Regional Activities	Overlapping Membership
Al-Qaeda in Pakistan	Salafist	Has facilitated attacks inside and outside Pakistan and has planned international attacks from safe havens within Pakistan	TTP, Afghan Taliban, other Doebandi militant groups
Afghan Taliban	Doebandi	Wages insurgency in Afghanistan or Decades; enjoys safe havens in Pakistan	TTP and other Doebandi militant groups: al-Qaeda
Jaish-e-Mohammad (JM), HarKat-ul-Jihad-al-Islami (HUJI), Harkat-ul-Ansar, Harkat-ul-Mujahedeen, and similiar	Doebandi	Traditionally focused on Indian-administered Kashmir but have operated in Afghanistan (and continue to do so); factions have targeted the Pakistani state	Al-Qaeda, TTP, Afghan Taliban, Doebandi sectarian militant groups and JUI
Lashkar-e-Jhangvi (LeJ) and Slpah-e-Sahaba-e-Pakistan (SSP)	Doebandi	Historically anti-Shia, have operated in Afghanistan for decades; currently targeting the Pakistani state with the TTP and allied groups.	TTP, Afghan Taliban, al-Qaeda, other Deobandi militant groups and JUI
Hizbul Mujahdeen (HM) and al-Badr	Jamaat-e-Islami	Active in Indian-administered Kashmir	Jamaat-e-Islami
Tehrik-Taliban-ePakistan (TTP, Pakistani Taliban)	Doebandi	Targets the Pakistani state, with some commanders mobilizing fighters in Afghanistan	Afghan Taliban, Doebandi militant groups in Pakistan and possibly al-Qaeda
Lashkar-e-Tayiba (LeT)	Ahl-e-Hadith	Fights in Indian-administered Kashmir and the Indian hinterland; limited out-of-theatre operations	Although historically linked with al-Qaeda, its modern ties to the group are subject to debate

Source: Fair, "Lashkar-e-tayiba and the Pakistani State," 6.

---

226 Ashley J. Tellis, "Pakistan and the War on Terror: Conflicted Goals, Compromised Performance." *Carnegie Endowment for International Peace* (2008): 3.

Additionally, Jalaluddin Haqqani, on whose name the Haqqani Network is based, participated in the Afghan jihad as a member of the Hizb-e-Islami faction of Mohammad Yunus Khalis. His network of Deobandi fighters had joined forces with the Taliban in 1996 following the Taliban's capture of Kabul. After the Taliban was overthrown in 2001, Haqqani retreated to North Waziristan, in Pakistan's FATA.

After 9/11, when the United States demanded once again that the Taliban hand over bin Laden, threatening war if bin Laden was not given up, Mullah Omar still refused. Pakistan did not use its influence to encourage the Taliban to give up Osama bin Laden. In fact, ISI personnel advised Mullah Omar to do the opposite. Pakistan continued to support the Taliban with military and intelligence support right up to when the United States began bombing Afghanistan. The Taliban in turn continued to support Osama bin Laden, refusing to turn him over.

The close relationship between the ISI, the Afghan jihad, the Taliban, and al Qaeda is revealed by looking at the example of Pakistani Brigadier Sultan Amir, better known as Colonel Imam.[227] Imam had trained thousands of Afghan mujahideen, including Mullah Omar, who took Colonel Imam's extended three-month course in 1985. Omar addressed the colonel with the respectful title *Ustad* ("master/teacher"). In 1994, Colonel Imam acted as Mullah Omar's Pakistani advisor. Imam was observed directing Taliban assaults in 1996. According to Carlotta Gall, Mullah Omar's Pakistani intelligence advisors, especially Colonel Imam, had great influence over him. After 9/11, Colonel Imam urged Mullah Omar to ignore American demands to hand over bin Laden. Imam believed that the United States would not bomb Afghanistan for long and that it would be unable to sustain a ground war so far from home. Just as the ISI personnel had guided the mujahideen in 1980s, Imam advised Mullah Omar to redeploy to the mountains and wage a guerilla war from there. In the weeks after the 9/11 attacks, ISI chief Mahmoud Ahmad too traveled to Kandahar to have personal meetings with Mullah Omar. Ahmad, contrary to Musharraf's public posture, advised Omar to hold on to bin Laden and resist U.S. attacks. Ahmad's support for the Taliban was so obvious and troubling that the Bush administration had to demand his removal as the chief of Pakistan's intelligence. On October 7, 2001, the United States began its bombing campaign in Afghanistan. The same day,

---

227 Carlotta Gall, "Former Pakistani Officer Embodies a Policy Puzzle," *New York Times*, March 3, 2010; Carlotta Gall, *The Wrong Enemy: America in Afghanistan, 2001-2014* (Boston: Houghton Mifflin Harcourt, 2014), 20, 43-45.

Lieutenant General Mahmoud Ahmad was removed from his post. Colonel Imam remained at Omar's side even after the bombing began and Musharraf had to order him to get out.[228]

As the Taliban's Pakistani advisers were removed and its supplies were cut off, the Taliban quickly began to collapse. U.S. operations focused on al Qaeda and the Taliban, and Pakistan was told to keep Pakistani-based militants off the Afghanistan battlefield. Nevertheless, militants from all the major Pakistani jihadi groups arrived to fight with them. At the time, Pakistan was home to 58 religious political parties and 24 armed religious militias. About ten thousand Pakistani jihadis crossed into Afghanistan to support and fight alongside the Taliban.[229] Pakistan's efforts to deter these fighters from crossing into Afghanistan were inconsistent. But ultimately, Pakistan sought to prevent the Taliban's destruction by giving its leaders and members safe haven in Pakistan.[230]

As the U.S. attacks started taking their toll, the Taliban fighters scattered, with the leadership and hard core members fleeing to Pakistan. Thousands of retreating Taliban took refuge in the NWFP and Baluchistan. The tribal areas not only provided refuge from the U.S. bombing campaign, they were also used as a base of operations against the U.S. and coalition forces in Afghanistan.[231] Many relocated around the city of Quetta in Baluchistan. Osama bin Laden and the al Qaeda core also crossed the Durand Line and fled to Pakistan. The FATA area became the sanctuary of the militants escaping U.S. assault. Pakistan's major cities of Karachi, Faisalabad, and Islamabad provided refuge for many al Qaeda operatives.[232]

During their assault against the Taliban, the United States allied itself with the Northern Alliance under Massoud, who took over Kunduz on November 25, 2001, capturing about 4,000 Taliban and al Qaeda fighters. A great controversy arose when Pakistan was allowed to fly rescue planes and conduct a large-scale evacuation of Taliban and Pakistani fighters from amongst the captured enemies. The United States' consent to this plan was based on the assumption that U.S. investigators would have access to them; however, this never happened.[233] The airlift was also approved because Pakistan claimed that the trapped fighters were its intelligence agents who needed to get out. Though it claimed to be an ally of

---

228 Gall, "Former Pakistani Officer Embodies a Policy Puzzle"; Gall, *The Wrong Enemy*, 54.
229 Hassan Abbas, *Pakistan's Drift into Extremism: Allah, the Army, and America's War on Terror* (Armonk: M. E. Sharpe, 2005), 201.
230 Stephen Tankel, "Domestic Barriers to Dismantling the Militant Infrastructure in Pakistan," *United States Institute of Peace Report* 89 (2013): 7.
231 Hussain, *Frontline Pakistan*, 120.
232 Riedel, *Deadly Embrace*, 67.
233 For a discussion, see Seymour M. Hersh, "The Getaway: Questions Surround a Secret Pakistani Airlift," *New Yorker*, January 28, 2002, 36-42.

the United States in the War on Terror, Pakistan actively prevented the United States from capturing and destroying the Taliban in the wake of the September 11 attacks.[234]

At the end of 2001, the United States had overthrown the Taliban's Islamic Emirate of Afghanistan and Osama bin Laden and his core al Qaeda leaders were on the run. Pakistan, meanwhile, engaged in what might best be referred to as selective counterterrorism. While Pakistan tried to protect most Taliban members from the United States, it assisted the CIA in tracking al Qaeda in Pakistan. Leading al Qaeda members Abu Zubaydah and Khalid Shaikh Mohammad were captured in Faisalabad and Rawalpindi, respectively. By 2006, Pakistan claimed to have captured 709 al Qaeda operatives, however, these numbers were never verified because the captives were not shown to journalists or independent observers.[235] The colonial legacy of keeping the frontier areas near the Durand Line un-policed and ungoverned continued as Pakistan mostly stayed away from the FATA and other tribal areas that provided safe haven to al Qaeda members. Pakistani authorities simply denied the existence of the huge numbers of Taliban and al Qaeda members hiding in the tribal areas.

Ever since the United States began its war in Afghanistan, more and more evidence has accumulated regarding Pakistan's support and protection of militant jihadi groups. Many of these groups attacked American and allied forces in Afghanistan and launched terrorist attacks around the world. Years after the 9/11 events, militant insurgent groups continued to operate and collaborate inside the tribal areas in the FATA and the neighboring KPK in support of global as well as regional jihads in Afghanistan and Kashmir.[236] Several high-profile al Qaeda figures and other terrorists were apprehended while hiding in safe houses in Pakistan. Abu Zubaydah was captured in a safe house belonging to LeT in Faisalabad. Khalid Shaikh Muhammad was captured in Rawalpindi, home to the Pakistan Army's high command, in a secure military housing estate.[237] Khalid al-Attash, a Yemeni terrorist connected to bombing of the USS Cole, and Ramzi bin al-Shibh, a leader of the Hamburg cell, were found hiding in Karachi when arrested. And Osama bin Laden, the world's most wanted terrorist, found refuge for years in Abbotabad, a garrison town most likely under protection provided by the Pakistani military.[238] Several al Qaeda militants in Pakistan have been arrested in houses belonging to

---

234 Kapur and Ganguly, "The Jihad Paradox," 131-132.
235 Gall, *The Wrong Enemy*, 82.
236 For an overview, see International Crisis Group, "Pakistan's Tribal Areas: Appeasing the Militants." *ICG Asia Report*, Report No. 125 (2006); Vira and Cordesman, *Pakistan: Violence vs. Stability*, 1-34.
237 Rashid, *Descent into Chaos*, 225; Riedel, *Deadly Embrace*, 67.
238 Dutta, "Bin Laden, Pakistan and the End of Terrorism"; Robert Fisk, "Was He Betrayed? Of Course. Pakistan Knew bin Laden's Hiding Place All Along," *The Independent*, May 3, 2011.

Jamaat-e-Islami supporters. The effective functioning of al Qaeda after 9/11 and the attacks it executed in Pakistan and abroad would have been inconceivable without support from Pakistani extremist groups and from Islamic parties like JI. In other words, the ISI is fundamentally responsible for supporting terrorism by training and nurturing radical Islamists and terrorist organizations.

Despite overwhelming evidence of Pakistan's nexus with terrorist groups, Pakistan denies any ties with insurgent groups that attack and kill U.S. soldiers in Afghanistan and plot terror attacks against the United States and the west from Pakistani soil. Pakistan's actions, which conflict with the U.S. aims in Afghanistan, resulted in the unnecessary prolongation of the Afghan War for over a decade. Since other scholars have already extensively analyzed terrorist attacks and organizations, I will focus on the historical and strategic reasons for Pakistan's reliance on terrorism and asymmetric warfare.[239]

---

[239] For analysis of Pakistan's involvement with terrorist groups, see Jayshree Bajoria, "The ISI and Terrorism: Behind the Accusations", *Council on Foreign Relations*, May 4, 2011; Paul Cruickshank, "The Militant Pipeline Between the Afghanistan-Pakistan Border Region and the West," *Counterterrorism Strategy Initiative Policy Paper* (2010), 1-37; Fair, "Time for Sober Realism Renegotiating U.S. Relations with Pakistan," 149-172; Fair, "The Militant Challenge in Pakistan," 105-137; Fair, "Lashkar-e-Tayiba and the Pakistani State," 29-52; Gall, *The Wrong Enemy*; Ḥaqqānī, *Pakistan: Between Mosque And Military*; Howenstein, "The Jihadi Terrain in Pakistan," 28-31; Hussain, *Frontline Pakistan*; Jones, "Pakistan's Dangerous Game," 15-32; Jones, "The Terrorist Threat from Pakistan," 69-94; Isaac Kfir, "Pakistan and the Challenge of Islamist Terror: Where to Next," *Middle East Review of International Affairs* 12, no.3 (2008): 1-9; Rashid, *Taliban*; Riedel, *Deadly Embrace*.

BLOODLINES: THE IMPERIAL ROOTS OF TERRORISM IN SOUTH ASIA

CHAPTER 3

THE HISTORY OF U.S.- PAKISTAN RELATIONS

In his analysis of U.S.-Pakistan relations, Perkovich made the following observation:

> In 1957, only several years after heavy U.S. involvement in Pakistan began, President Eisenhower remarked that the military commitment to Pakistan was "perhaps the worst kind of a plan and decision we could have made. It was a terrible error, but we now seem hopelessly involved in it." Fifty-four years later, little has happened that would persuade Eisenhower to revise this conclusion. With good intentions, successive administrations and Congresses have colluded with the Pakistani Army and intelligence services to maintain their oversized, dysfunctional roles in Pakistan and South Asia.[1]

Christine Fair has argued that United States and Pakistani interests in South Asia in no way converge, and that, to the contrary, Pakistan seems vested in undermining U.S. interests in the region. She claims that in the name of the Global War on Terror (GWOT), the United States had given Pakistan approximately $27 billion in military and financial aid, a stunning amount that is in fact separate from the absurd amount that Pakistan's military overcharges the Coalition Support Funds for cost reimbursements.[2] In light of the fact that Pakistan aids and abets forces that kill American and allied military and civilian personnel in Afghanistan, and engages (directly and indirectly) in terrorism, the United States should understandably be concerned about the aid it provides to Pakistan. Additionally, Pakistan's support for militant Islamists in Kashmir and its use of terrorism as an instrument of state policy have raised qualms among U.S. policymakers. Fair points out that Pakistan, "since 2006, has openly operated against Americans in Afghanistan." Her argument raises serious questions:

> ...Pakistan is one of the biggest reasons why we are fighting the GWOT in the first place. The Pakistanis made the Taliban the effective force that they were on September 10, 2001, and Pakistan continues to undermine U.S. efforts to retard the Taliban's efforts to retake power in Afghanistan. Osama Bin Laden was safely ensconced in Abbotabad despite ten years of Pakistan assurances that he was not in Pakistan. And apart from the Taliban, Pakistan is responsible for much of the Islamist terrorism in India.[3]

---

1 George Perkovich, "Stop Enabling Pakistan's Dangerous Dysfunction," *Carnegie Endowment for International Peace Policy Outlook*, 2011.
2 C. Christine Fair, "Ten Fictions that Pakistani Defense Officials Love to Peddle," *War on the Rocks*, January 31, 2014.
3 Ibid.

On the other hand, the U.S. Department of State has openly recognized Pakistan for its cooperation in counterterrorism measures, including closing terrorist training camps in its territory. In 2004, the United States designated Pakistan a Major Non-NATO Ally.[4]

In recent years, many observers of South Asia have arrived at the conclusion that Pakistan has been supporting terrorist groups. Accusations include the ISI aiding the Haqqani network, supporting the Afghan Taliban, assisting with violent attacks and bombings in Afghanistan, providing safe haven to terrorist groups involved in the killing of U.S. and allied soldiers in Afghanistan, aiding and abetting terrorist attacks in India and Kashmir, and not doing enough to curb radical groups within Pakistan itself. These analyses have been extensively covered elsewhere.[5] Even though evidence for its complicity has been presented, Pakistan has consistently denied such accusations.

On May 2, 2011, the world's most wanted man and the head of al Qaeda was killed in a secret operation carried out by U.S. forces. While the operation was successful, it raised several troubling questions. When he was killed, bin Laden had been hiding for about five years in Abbotabad, Pakistan. Abbotabad is the home to Pakistan's elite Kakul Military Academy and several army battalions. Bin Laden's house stood within a few hundred yards of the walls of the Kakul Military Academy. It is telling that the United States chose to keep the plan secret from ISI and that information about the raid was not shared with the government of Pakistan until after the operation. The operation was a direct violation of Pakistan's sovereignty by its own patron and ally. The raid in Abbotabad shocked the people of Pakistan. The reality that Osama bin Laden had been living in a military town was scandalous enough, but that U.S. commandos were able to fly in, raid a house in a military town, and escape, caused an angry public reaction against the Pakistani armed forces and the ISI, both of which were severely criticized.[6]

---

4   United States Department of State, Bureau of South and Central Asian Affairs, "U.S. Relations with Pakistan," U.S. Department of State Fact Sheet, 2013.
5   Fair, "The Militant Challenge in Pakistan," 105-137; Fair, "Lashkar-e-Tayiba and the Pakistani State," 29-52; Haqqāni, *Pakistan: Between Mosque And Military*; Hussain, *Frontline Pakistan*; Jones, "The Terrorist Threat from Pakistan," 69-94; Kapur and Ganguly, "The Jihad Paradox," 111-141; K. Alan Kronstadt, "Pakistan-U.S. Relations: A Summary," *CRS Report for Congress*, October 21, 2011, 1-39; Rashid, *Descent into Chaos*; S. Nawaz, *Crossed Swords: Pakistan, its Army, and the Wars Within* (Karachi: Oxford University Press, 2008); Ahmed Rashid, *Pakistan on the Brink: The Future of America, Pakistan, and Afghanistan* (New York: Viking, 2012); Ashley J. Tellis, "Pakistan and the War on Terror: Conflicted Goals, Compromised Performance," *Carnegie Endowment for International Peace* (2008), 1-57; Syed S. Shahzad, *Inside Al-Qaeda and the Taliban: Beyond Bin Laden and 9/11* (London: Pluto Press, 2011); Swami, *India, Pakistan and the Secret Jihad*; Stephen Tankel, "Domestic Barriers to Dismantling the Militant Infrastructure in Pakistan," *United States Institute of Peace Report* 89 (2013): 1-59.
6   Gall, *The Wrong Enemy*, 256-257.

While there is no conclusive proof that the ISI was hiding bin Laden, retired General Ziauddin Butt, ISI chief in the government of Nawaz Sharif from 1988 to 1999, insisted in interviews that bin Laden could not have lived in hiding in Abbotabad without some higher-up being aware of it. Butt had claimed in 2011 that Brigadier Ijaz Shah, Director General of the Intelligence Bureau of Pakistan, was involved in bin Laden's safe housing.[7] Butt repeated the allegations in 2013 but later retracted his claim when Shah threatened him with a lawsuit.[8] Whatever the truth might be, Pakistan's well-established involvement in support of jihadi militants has raised serious questions about Pakistan's role as an ally in efforts against terrorism.

The *White Paper of the Interagency Policy Group's Report on U.S. Policy toward Afghanistan and Pakistan* defines the core U.S. goal "to disrupt, dismantle, and eventually destroy extremists and their safe havens within [Afghanistan and Pakistan]," and states that, "[s]uccessfully shutting down the Pakistani safe haven for extremists will also require consistent and intensive strategic engagement with Pakistani leadership in both the civilian and military spheres… [Our efforts must] enable Pakistani security forces so they are capable of succeeding in sustained counterterrorism and counterinsurgency operations."[9] While the United States' basic goals (to eliminate al Qaeda and shut down safe havens for jihadi militants) remain unchanged, the relationship between Pakistan's military establishment and various jihadi militants poses real concerns for the United States. What value is an ally who works at cross-purposes with its patron?

Following 9/11, the United States provided substantial amounts of military and economic aid to Pakistan in order to gain its cooperation for counter-terrorism measures and to cajole it away from supporting militant jihadis. Between the fiscal years of 2002-2014, direct overt aid appropriations for Pakistan, including economic aid, military aid, and coalition support funds (CSF) reimbursements to the Pakistan Army (which reimburse the army for conducting military operations to fight terrorism) totaled approximately $28 billion.[10]

---

7   Arif Jamal, "Former Pakistan Army Chief Reveals Intelligence Bureau Harbored bin Laden in Abbotabad," *Terrorism Monitor* 9, no. 47 (2011): 4-5.
8   Gall, *The Wrong Enemy*, 250.
9   The White House, *White Paper* of the *Interagency Policy Group's Report on U.S. Policy toward Afghanistan and Pakistan* (2009), 5-6.
10 Congressional Research Service. "Direct Overt U.S. Aid Appropriations for and Military Reimbursements to Pakistan: FY2002-FY2015," March 6, 2014.

The amount of U.S. aid and its significance to Pakistan can only really be measured using proper benchmarks. Pakistan's military expenditures have varied between approximately $3 billion in 1988 to approximately $5 billion in 2010.[11] Taking just the single reference point of 2005, when Pakistan received over $2.4 billion in military aid and CSF funds, it was almost equivalent to the United States paying half of Pakistan's military budget.[12] This would be equivalent to the United States getting a gift of approximately $400 billion in military aid from a patron for its 2012 military budget. Between 2002 and 2013, Pakistan received over $16 billion in military aid and CSF reimbursements.[13] This would correspond to over a quarter of Pakistan's military budget ($4 billion/year, rising to over $5 billion in 2010), equivalent to the United States getting about $200 billion for its FY 2012 military budget in gifts every year for twelve years. Considering the investment that the United States has put into its relationship with Pakistan, its returns have not been very helpful.

During the Afghan jihad, Pakistan received substantial sums of military and economic aid. Additionally, Pakistan managed all funds and arms distributions to the Afghan resistance groups, skimming off assistance sent for the war against Soviet occupation. Between 1983 and 1989, Pakistan received over $3.8 billion in overt military assistance.[14] This would correspond to America paying approximately twenty percent of Pakistan's military budget.

Azeem Ibrahim concludes, "the Pakistani military did not use most of the funds for the agreed objective of fighting terror."[15] Instead, Pakistan mostly purchased conventional military equipment that could be used in a war against India, including F-16s fighters, aircraft-mounted weaponry, anti-ship and antimissile defense systems, and an air defense radar system costing $200 million. "Over half of the total funds—54.9 percent—were spent on fighter aircraft and weapons, over a quarter—26.62 percent—on support and other aircraft, and 10 percent on advanced weapons systems."[16] Similarly, much of the military aid Pakistan

---

11   Sortable data in local and U.S. constant dollars is available from the Stockholm International Peace Research Institute, SIPRI Military Expenditure Database, http://milexdata.sirpi.org. Based on SIPRI data, Pakistan's military expenditure in constant 2010 U.S. dollars would be $3.8 billion in 1988 and $5.6 billion in 2010.
12   Guardian Data Blog, "Development Data: Sixty Years of US Aid to Pakistan: Get the Data," July 11, 2011.
13   U.S. Embassy Fact Sheet, *U.S. Assistance to Pakistan to Promote Security*. 2014.
14   Guardian Data Blog, "Development Data: Sixty Years of US Aid to Pakistan."
15   Azeem Ibrahim, "U.S. Aid to Pakistan: U.S. Taxpayers Have Funded Pakistani Corruption," Belfer Center Discussion Paper, International Security Program, Harvard Kennedy School, 2009-06, 44, 2009.
16   Ibid.

received during the Afghan jihad was used to strengthen its military in order to counterbalance India. According to Lawrence Wright, as much as half of the U.S. money given to the ISI to fight the Soviets was diverted to build nuclear weapons.[17]

Historical record indicates that the Pakistan Army was strengthened in the earlier periods of U.S.-Pakistan relations as well. Between 1954 and 1965, the United States provided Pakistan with 640 tanks, established three modern air bases, a naval dockyard, a submarine, two squadrons of B-57 bombers, nine squadrons of F-86 jet fighters, one squadron of fighter-interceptors, thirty armed helicopters, and a squadron of C-130 troop transport planes.[18]

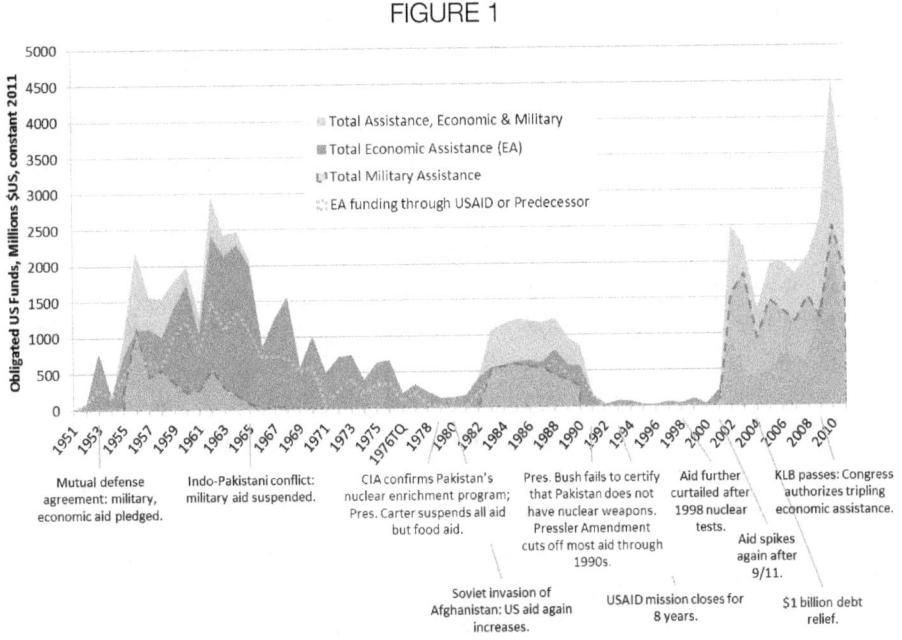

Figure 1: History of US Obligations to Pakistan from
Center for Global Development, "Aid to Pakistan by the Numbers"

Additional data on Coalition Support Funds spending should be added to the military assistance category for the years spanning from 2002–2011. While CSF is not technically foreign assistance, it has constituted the bulk of the United States' military assistance to Pakistan during the post-9/11 period. The source for CSF

---

17 Lawrence Wright, "The Double Game: The Unintended Consequences of American Funding in Pakistan," *New Yorker* 87, May 16, 2011.
18 Gary J. Bass, *The Blood Telegram: Nixon, Kissinger, and a Forgotten Genocide* (New York: Knopf, 2013), 4.

amounts can be found in "Direct Overt U.S. Aid Appropriations and Military Reimbursements to Pakistan," a report prepared for the Congressional Research Service by K. Alan Kronstadt.[19]

The current state of counterterrorism collaboration and relations between Pakistan and the United States can be best understood by examining historical relations between the two states. There has been remarkable consistency between the strained U.S.-Pakistan relations in the post-9/11 period and the relationship between the two states immediately following Pakistan's independence. Relations from the beginning were short-term, episodic, and expedient, with the United States seeking to use Pakistan as its proxy against American adversaries and Pakistan selling its services to the United States in return for its economic and military patronage.[20] These factors have not changed in the past six decades. The duplicitous role Pakistan played following 9/11, acting as a U.S. ally while also sponsoring terrorism, can be understood if Pakistan's real and imagined security needs are considered, as well as the nature of the relationship between the United States and Pakistan.

After the Soviet invasion of Afghanistan, Pakistan's policies were consistent with its ideological and strategic interests. When General Zia declared his unqualified support for the Afghan resistance, he was following in the footsteps of other Islamists who expressed great antipathy against "godless" communism. Sharing a border with the Red Army in Afghanistan, as well as the heavy flow of Afghan refugees into Pakistan, was a great economic and security burden for Pakistan. However, at the heart of Zia's decision to support the insurgency was the reality that Pakistan could exploit and reap benefits from the situation. In landlocked Afghanistan, the United States faced a hostile Iran in the west and Soviet Central Asia in the north. On the eastern and southern borders of Afghanistan, Pakistan was the only neighboring country able to provide the United States with direct access to support the insurgency against the Soviets.

While Zia's declared objectives were to aid Pakistan's Muslim neighbor and to push communism away from Afghanistan, he used his alliance with United States firstly to escape sanctions for developing nuclear weapons and secondly to seek military hardware that would help Pakistan's military to counterbalance

---

19 Center For Global Development, "Aid to Pakistan by the Numbers"; K. Alan Kronstadt and Susan B. Epstein, "Direct Overt US Aid and Military Reimbursements to Pakistan, FY2002-FY2015," Congressional Research Service, March 24, 2014.

20 For an overview, see Blom, "Pakistan: Coercion and Capital in an 'Insecurity State,'" 1-64; Robert J. McMahon, "United States Cold War Strategy in South Asia: Making a Military Commitment to Pakistan, 1947-1954," *Journal of American History* 75, no. 3 (1988): 812-840; T. C. Schaffer and H. B. Schaffer, *How Pakistan Negotiates with the United States: Riding the Roller Coaster*, (Washington, D.C.: United States Institute of Peace, 2011); Tellis, *Pakistan and the War on Terror*, 1-57.

those of India. Ultimately, Zia's strategic goal was to plant a regime in Afghanistan that would be amenable to Pakistan's directives and hostile to India. As events unfolded, all of Pakistan's goals were fulfilled: the United States ignored Pakistan's development of nuclear weapons during the Afghan War, provided over $3.5 billion in economic aid and over $3.8 billion in military aid, and sold the F-16 fighter planes that Pakistan had desperately sought. With the help of American aid, both Pakistan's economy and military were strengthened.

After 9/11, the United States once again relied on Pakistan's strategic location for its interests in Afghanistan. Iran remained beyond the reach of U.S. influence, and Pakistan once again had the opportunity to seek an alliance with the United States for military and economic aid. Additionally, Pakistan wanted to protect the jihadis it had used before and could later use in Afghanistan and Kashmir once the U.S. offensive in Afghanistan had simmered down. The United States was back in Afghanistan, but this time U.S. boots were on the ground. Once again, the interests of Pakistan did not coincide with those of the United States. Nevertheless, the two entered into an expedient relationship, overlooking their conflicting interests as each pursued its own goals. For example, when the Taliban regime collapsed in 2001, it was a satisfying success for the United States but an unmitigated strategic disaster for Pakistan: Pakistan had not only lost its ally in Afghanistan, but the new U.S.-sanctioned regime in Kabul was friendly to India.

As a rentier state,[21] Pakistan has consistently and deftly exploited its relationship with the United States since its independence; this fact is critical to understanding Pakistan's manipulative behavior, but it has not received prominent attention from political commentators.

In September 1947, when Pakistan was barely one month old, the eminent photojournalist Margaret Bourke-White interviewed Mohammad Ali Jinnah. Jinnah, called "Qaid-i-Azam" ("Great Leader") by his followers, had taken over the supreme post in the country, that of Governor-General. By not resigning the presidency of the Muslim League, Jinnah had also become the president of the constituent assembly. In effect, by making himself the head of the state, head of the sole political party, and head of the constituent assembly, Jinnah established the precedent of consolidated power and began a legacy of disregarding democratic principles—patterns that have been consistently adopted by subsequent Pakistani rulers. It was apparent in Bourke-White's interview that Jinnah had no conception

---

21 Hossein Mahdavy, "Patterns and Problems of Economic Development in Rentier States: The Case of Iran," in *Studies in the Economic History of the Middle-East: From the Rise of Islam to the Present Day*, ed. M.A. Cook (Oxford: Oxford University Press, 1970), 428. "Rentier States are defined here as those countries that receive on a regular basis substantial amounts of external rent. External rents are in turn defined as rentals paid by foreign individuals, concerns or governments to individuals, concerns or government of a given country."

about the ideology of the state he was heading, nor had he given any thought to the future constitution of Pakistan. He tried vaguely to connect democracy to Islamic ideas of social justice from the thirteenth century.[22] The rentier mentality of the leader of a nation just four weeks old was striking. When asked whether Jinnah had any plans for the industrial development of the country and whether he hoped to enlist technical or financial assistance from America, Jinnah stated, "America needs Pakistan more than Pakistan needs America."[23] Jinnah described Pakistan as the pivot of the world, "the frontier on which the future position of the world revolves," because Russia was "not very far away." This calculated desire to benefit from the U.S.-Russian rivalry could not have been more obvious as Jinnah pointed out that America was creating an anti-communist bloc by bolstering Greece and Turkey, but that Pakistan was more worthy of U.S. largesse as an anti-communist ally. In Jinnah's view, the United States should have been much more interested in lavishing Pakistan with money and weaponry because, "If Russia walks [into Pakistan], the whole world is menaced." In addition to Jinnah's promotion of Pakistan as a worthy recipient of American aid in order to keep the communists in check, Bourke-White heard similar arguments from government officials throughout Pakistan. They expressed their wish for American help in building the Pakistan Army, "Surely America will give us loans to keep Russia from walking in."[24] When asked for any evidence of Russia's supposed ill intentions towards Pakistan, there were disappointed replies. "No, Russia has shown no signs of being interested in Pakistan." Bourke-White penetratingly observes, "This hope of tapping the U.S. Treasury was voiced so persistently that one wondered whether the purpose was to bolster the world against Bolshevism or to bolster Pakistan's uncertain position as a new political entity."[25]

Bourke-White's prescience was striking when she warned the United States in 1949 of Pakistan's manipulative strategy to maximize economic aid. She connected Jinnah's belief that Pakistan could extract rent from the United States for an anti-communist alliance because of its strategic location near Russia, to Jinnah's frequently used divisive tactic during the struggle to create Pakistan. "Jinnah's most frequently used technique in the struggle for his new nation had been the playing of opponent against opponent. Evidently this technique was now to be extended into foreign policy."[26] For a poor and underdeveloped nascent nation state undergoing a devastating religious bloodbath and the forced mass

---

22 Bourke-White, *Halfway to Freedom*, 92.
23 Jinnah, quoted in Bourke-White, *Halfway to Freedom*, 92-93.
24 Ibid., 93.
25 Bourke-White, *Halfway to Freedom*, 93.
26 Ibid.

migration of millions (both of which were to continue for some time), its leader's preoccupation with seeking military and economic aid to fight a non-existing Soviet threat was nothing less than extraordinary.

The Soviet threat Jinnah and other Pakistani leaders cited in 1947 was a transparently cynical and self-serving plea to a potential patron. These leaders actually wanted the finances to build Pakistan's military and economy so it could fight its congenital enemy—India. A similar plea had been made to his former patrons, the British imperialists, during Pakistan's creation. By manufacturing an existentialist Hindu threat against Islam and Muslims, Pakistan was brought into being as a nation; conjuring an external Soviet threat for the Americans was only a logical continuation of that successful strategy. Pakistan had been created, but the Machiavellian methods used to do so had created a country without a functioning ideology and identity. British imperial patrons were traded for an American superpower patron, but the foundational identity of the nation was as victims of a powerful enemy needing a powerful patron to achieve security. This national project, which Bourke-White correctly observed in September 1947, was carried on continuously in the future, regardless of which elite ruled Pakistan.

Bourke-White also commented that Pakistan had a policy of profiting from the disputes of others. This propensity of Pakistan's elite has barely changed since 1947, as its regimes have consistently attempted to profit from disputes between superpowers. However, instead of constructively using the resources they gained, Pakistan's ruling elite has used them to destabilize neighboring states and export violence abroad. Additionally, the Pakistan-U.S. alignment was unique in terms of Cold War patron-client relationships as Pakistan worked at cross-purposes with its patron during the Afghan jihad and also after the 9/11 attacks. When the Cold War was over, Pakistan profited from the United States' efforts to curb Islamic militancy in Afghanistan, a phenomenon that Pakistan itself had created and nurtured, albeit with complicity and acquiescence of CIA. Pakistan's proxies actively attacked its patron's personnel and interests in Afghanistan.

Following its creation, Pakistan sought financial aid from the United States first. Between 1947 and 1954, its leaders repeatedly called attention to its geopolitical significance in order to coax large-scale financial and military support from Washington. Just two months after Pakistan's independence, Jinnah requested an entirely unrealistic loan of almost $2 billion for Pakistan's military, agriculture, and industrial development projects. Jinnah's request was a quid pro quo: Pakistan's alignment with the United States was offered in return for a commitment of developmental aid and military security. India was always the sole security concern for Pakistan, but Pakistani appeals for aid were always couched in virulently anti-

Soviet rhetoric since Pakistani leaders hoped to strike a responsive chord with the Truman administration. For example, one of the documents seeking American aid lists Pakistan's proximity and vulnerability to Russia as its most vexing external problem.[27]

India, on the other hand, chose a position of nonalignment in terms of its foreign policy, refusing to ally itself with either the United States or the Soviet Union. The United States initially preferred an alignment with a democratic and secular India, not with Pakistan. After India gained independence, the United States viewed it as the successor state to British India, and Pakistan as the seceding state. During the negotiations for British withdrawal and the subcontinent's freedom, the United States indicated that it preferred a unified India and was not supportive of Jinnah and the Muslim League's plans for partition.[28] Furthermore, India's large population, resources, and the international prestige Indian leadership gained during its anti-colonial struggle made India an attractive ally for the United States. Pakistan was seen as holding little promise other than the fact that some experts in the Truman administration believed that Pakistan's geostrategic location made it a more useful strategic asset.[29] On the whole, the Truman administration believed that India's emergence as a large and stable nation, sympathetic to anti-communist goals of the United States and predisposed toward the West, would greatly serve U.S. interests in South Asia. If India were to accept U.S. Cold War policies, it would enhance the United States' standing in the Third World. The newly independent India would have made a natural ally for the United States.

Indian Prime Minister Jawahar Lal Nehru dashed the Truman administration's enthusiasm with his determination to pursue a foreign policy that neither supported the United States nor kowtowed to the Soviet Bloc. Within three weeks of independence, on September 7, 1947, Nehru revealed his foreign policy approach in a radio broadcast, stating, "We propose, as far as possible, to keep away from the power politics of groups, aligned against one another, which have led in the past to world wars and which may again lead to disasters on an even vaster scale."[30] Nehru insisted that India would follow an independent policy, keeping away from the power politics of countries and blocs. After their bitter struggle against the British, the Indian public broadly supported Nehru's proposal of nonalignment. The moralistic and lofty rhetoric of the ethical duty of independence from the influence of power blocs was nevertheless pragmatic: as a nascent independent nation, India was burdened with a huge population, widespread poverty, and

---

27 McMahon, "United States Cold War Strategy in South Asia," 818.
28 Kux, *The United States and Pakistan, 1947-2000*, 12.
29 McMahon, *The Cold War on the Periphery*, 68.
30 Quoted in ibid., 37.

enormous economic and social challenges. Indian planners were seeking economic development by reaching out to both the Soviets and the United States, seeking to not alienate either one. Nehru's approach was also necessary in order to balance domestic political interests: the Congress Party, which was considered too strong to be challenged electorally in India at the time, was itself sharply divided between strong left- and right-wing factions.

This was a time of intense enmity between the United States and Soviet Union, and the United States' fears regarding Soviet expansion guided many of its Cold War policies. Virtually everything relating to inter-state relationships was viewed through the lens of U.S.-Soviet rivalry. On January 12, 1953, a New York Times article discussed the impending visit of the Secretary of State Dulles to India, Pakistan, and elsewhere in Asia. His goal "to determine to what extent their Governments are ready to cooperate in the new Administration's plans for a coordinated defense against Communist aggression in the Far East" was articulated in the same breath as he praised Pakistan.[31] By this time Nehru had already alienated Dulles, who found his neutral foreign policy naïve and had an unfavorable impression of India.[32] Indeed, U.S. officials were troubled by India's declarations of nonalignment, seeing the policy as a threat to global American interests. U.S. Ambassador Loy Henderson echoed Dulles when he concluded that Nehru's foreign policy views were not satisfactory from the United States' perspective.[33]

On the other hand, Jinnah was courting the United States even before the creation of Pakistan. In a conversation with U.S. diplomat Raymond Hare on May 1, 1947, Jinnah had suggested, "Muslim countries would stand together against possible Russian aggression and would look to the United States for assistance."[34] After Pakistan came into being, this courtship became more transparent. On December 22, 1947 a prominent Pakistani leader, Malik Feroz Khan Noon, appealed to the Truman administration:

> The US should realize three things: (1) that Pakistan is here to stay—there is not the slightest chance of any reunion with India; (2) that Pakistan will never be communistic; (3) that Pakistan is the Eastern bastion against communism as Turkey is the Western bastion. It is in the interest therefore of the US to give military and economic support to Pakistan as well as to Turkey.[35]

---

31 Kux, *The United States and Pakistan, 1947-2000*, 52.
32 Ibid.
33 McMahon, *The Cold War on the Periphery*, 62.
34 Quoted in Kux, *The United States and Pakistan, 1947-2000*, 13.
35 Quoted in McMahon, *United States Cold War Strategy*, 819.

With little else to entice its patron of choice, Pakistan offered the United States a strategic location in relation to Soviet Union. By 1949, Pakistan's near-contiguous border with the Soviet Union and its proximity to the Persian Gulf made it an ideal base for air operations against the USSR and a staging area for forces engaged in the defense or recapture of Middle Eastern oil areas.[36]

During the Eisenhower administration, Pakistan's fortune changed. Eisenhower's Secretary of State, John Foster Dulles, was a hard line Cold Warrior and truculent anti-communist. His conception of the Soviet threat in the Middle East and South Asia was not much different from the British Empire's "Great Game." To Dulles, Nehru's neutrality was immoral and naïve, whereas the armies of Pakistan and Turkey seemed like potential lines of defense against the Soviet threat. During his first visit to India and Pakistan in May 1953, Dulles' predispositions against Indian neutrality and in favor of a relationship with Pakistan were strengthened. His visit occurred a month after Pakistan's military-bureaucratic leadership dismissed Prime Minister Khawaja Nazimuddin, establishing the military's ascendance with the backing of a civil bureaucracy.[37] The new individual chosen as prime minister by the military establishment and its civil bureaucratic allies, Mohammed Ali Bogra, was weak and had no independent base of support. Bogra was known for his excessively pro-American views. In a conversation with Dulles, Bogra jokingly acknowledged that he was controlled by Washington.[38] Thus, the new Pakistani regime fawned over Dulles as it courted him for American support. The Pakistani leaders told him what he wanted to hear, affirming their anti-communism and proclaiming their support for the United States. General Mohammed Ayub Khan sold Dulles on the century-old, well-worn "Great Game" threat: that the Soviet Union planned to invade southward to reach the warm waters of the Arabian Sea. The United States must prevent this nefarious design, and would be able to do so by expanding and equipping the Pakistan Army and forming a military alliance with Pakistan in return for access to military bases in the country. U.S. Department of State memos reveal that Ayub Khan's arguments clearly established Pakistan's rentier nature in 1953. The memos document Ayub Khan's two main issues: the needs of Pakistan's army and Pakistan's willingness to ally with the United States in return for military and economic support. Ayub Khan reiterated to Dulles that Pakistan had great potential in manpower and military bases and that his government was extremely anxious to cooperate with the United States. Khan

---

36 For a review of earlier CIA Reports, Harry S. Truman Papers, U.S. Department of Defense documents, and other relevant U.S. strategic assessments regarding India and Pakistan, see McMahon, "United States Cold War Strategy in South Asia," 812-840.
37 McMahon, *The Cold War on the Periphery*, 161.
38 Ibid., 162.

argued that the United States, "which admittedly is the leader of the free world today should not be afraid to openly aid those countries which have expressed a willingness, and even desire, to cooperate with the United States."[39]

While Pakistan's appeared to be a sales-pitch for fighting communist encroachment in Asia, the salesmen's true designs were nevertheless transparent. In a memorandum deceptively titled "Assessment of the Soviet Threat to Pakistan and the Armed Forces Needed to Meet this Threat," which was delivered to Dulles on May 23, 1953 by Ayub Khan, Khan argued about the threat of a massive Soviet invasion through the mountain passes of Central Asia aimed at reaching the warm waters of the Arabian Sea. Obviously the appropriate response for the United States was to expand the Pakistan Army and equip it to block the Soviets. However, Khan also stated, "If Pakistan were strengthened by United States economic and military aid, it would result in India dropping its present intransigent attitude [on Kashmir]."[40] It was clear that despite what the United States was being sold, Pakistan's driving force behind the alliance was its stance on the Kashmir conflict. Pakistan was quite unambiguous, however, in its desire to rent its territory and armed forces to the United States.

Dulles was suitably impressed by the warm welcome and sycophancy afforded to him by the Pakistani leaders, telling the U.S. House Foreign Affairs Committee, "those fellows are going to fight any communist invasion with their bare fists if they have to."[41] In contrast, he found India's Prime Minister Nehru, with his rhetoric of neutrality and nonalignment, an "utterly impractical statesman."[42]

Besides Dulles, the Joint Chiefs of Staff and Secretary of Defense Charles Wilson also supported military assistance to Pakistan. The Pentagon cited several advantages of a pact with Pakistan; a main advantage was to "increase the defensive strength of a pro-Western state with a large military potential and a strategic location for defending the Middle East."[43] However, the U.S. ambassador to Pakistan, Horace Hildreth, provided the rather realistic projection that the aid would politically and economically help the pro-American Mohammad Ali Bogra government. Vice President Richard Nixon was also a vocal proponent of Pakistan. Nixon supported providing it with military hardware in order to defend the Middle East. How such a defense would be carried out was never

---

39 Ibid., 163.
40 Quoted in Kux, *The United States and Pakistan, 1947-2000*, 55.
41 Ibid., 56.
42 Ibid.
43 McMahon, *The Cold War on the Periphery*, 169.

clearly articulated; even the existence or nature of the threat itself was dubious. However, it was a sign of the times that an unsubstantiated threat of communism was sufficient to solicit substantial aid from the United States.

Pakistan's assiduous and opportunistic diplomacy culminated in a U.S.-Pakistan alliance in 1954, when on January 14, Eisenhower gave the go-ahead for military aid to Pakistan. The Eisenhower administration concluded that it was more important to have Pakistan on board with a nebulous idea of defending the Middle East than to preserve good relations with India. Was there any systematic attempt made to realistically assess how Pakistan could bolster Middle East defenses? Kux suggests that the concept was vague and "was more political-psychological than military in character."[44] Like the British imperialist strategy to rely on its own power and the power of the Indian Army to stop a south-facing Russian threat, "Similarly, Dulles seemed to think that the Pakistan Army (along with the military of NATO ally Turkey), backed by the might of the United States, would be able to serve as the bulwark against the Soviet threat." Kux also explains that Dulles took on the main role of promoting the idea, with little Defense Department involvement. McMahon calls the idea of using Pakistan to protect the Middle East from Soviet military sweep "almost farcical."[45]

The decision to aid Pakistan was made with full recognition that it would jeopardize United States' relations with India, a risk considered worthwhile if it meant that the Middle East was defended against Soviet incursion. The United States was given access to the southern border—the soft underbelly—of Soviet Union, and Pakistan allowed the United States to run communications intercept operations against Soviet missile test sites from monitoring stations in Badabar in Pakistan's northwest. Pakistan also provided access to Peshawar Airport, enabling the United States to fly its U-2 spy aircrafts over the Soviet Union.

Presenting its Islamic identity as an anti-communist ideology, Pakistan consistently focused on the United States as its patron of choice. Margaret Bourke-White's interviews show that as far back as 1947, Pakistan's founders and leaders were willing to use fabricated evidence of a non-existing communist threat to get aid from the United States.[46] Pakistan's intelligence community fabricated "increasingly bizarre reports" as evidence of a communist threat to Pakistan to get U.S. attention, offering itself as an "Islamic barrier against the Soviets."[47]

---

44 Kux, *The United States and Pakistan, 1947-2000*, 62.
45 McMahon, *The Cold War on the Periphery*, 338.
46 Bourke-White, *Halfway to Freedom*, 91-98.
47 Haqqānī, *Pakistan: Between Mosque And Military*, 32.

Human societies are complex systems and no significant action can be construed as having a single intended effect. As the United States made the first of many decisions to strengthen the Pakistani armed forces, little thought went into potential consequences, especially within the context of the conflict with India over Kashmir. In hindsight, U.S. military aid enabled Pakistan to engage in armed conflict with India for decades, eventually allowing it to resort to terrorism as a strategic tool. Bolstering Pakistan's army allowed the military to become the strongest institution in the country and gave it control over foreign policy, all at the expense of developing civic institutions. Pakistan's obsessive focus on security meant that it neglected to develop proper infrastructure, keeping the nation socially and materially underdeveloped. This security obsession, when reinforced by the funds coming from the United States, allowed Pakistan to engage in wars and asymmetric warfare, technologically strengthened its armed forces, and helped develop its nuclear weapon capability. Britain and later the United States came to recognize the long-term dangers of expedient decisions. What we now see in South Asia: the Kashmir conflict; the rise of Islamic militancy; an almost continuous low-intensity war interspersed with full-scale wars between India and Pakistan; the destabilization of South Asia; terrorist violence; safe haven provided to al Qaeda and other similar terrorist groups; the Pashtunistan issue; and a prolonged proxy war in Afghanistan—these are all blowback from British colonialism and the Cold War policies of the United States.

McMahon argues that between the 1950s and 1965, Pakistan exerted a substantial influence on the United States, constantly exhorting it for military aid and virtually forcing an American response.[48] Pakistan took advantage of its geographical location to seek rent from the United States and other nations and became a praetorian state.[49] Ahmed Rashid states that every Pakistani government since the 1970s has raised the threat of rising Islamic fundamentalism in Pakistan as a way of securing aid from the United States, while at the same time nurturing Islamic fundamentalists.[50] And according to Coll, the Pakistan Army has learned to extract from the United States the financial and military support that it believes it requires against India.[51] At the same time, Pakistan's generals resent their dependence on America because their core interests do not coincide with American interests and because America has been known to turn off its money and

---

48 McMahon, *The Cold War on the Periphery*, 815.
49 Blom, "Pakistan: Coercion and Capital in an 'Insecurity State,'" 11, 61.
50 Rashid, *Descent into Chaos*, 220.
51 Steve Coll, "The Back Channel India and Pakistan's Secret Kashmir Talks," *New Yorker* 38, March 2, 2009.

armament spigot at inopportune times. Though Pakistan has not always succeeded in getting its way with America, over the years it nevertheless has mastered the art of winning in their interactions with U.S. policymakers.[52]

THE UNITED STATES AS AN UNRELIABLE PARTNER

When India and Pakistan achieved independence, the emerging global conflict between Washington and Moscow was centered on the post-war sectioning of Europe. Two poor and distant states in South Asia were of little interest to U.S. strategic planning. The Eisenhower administration's interest in South Asia only emerged in the context of containing Russian imperialism. John Foster Dulles's warnings against the "Red Russian Menace" did not influence nonaligned India, which refused to join the Southeast Asia Treaty Organization (SEATO) or the Central Treaty Organization (CENTO).[53] Pakistan, however, not only accepted membership of both organizations, but also entered into a Mutual Defense Agreement with the United States in 1954.[54]

As Cohen has described, until the disintegration of the Soviet Union, Washington's South Asia policy was based on anti-Soviet prerogatives and did not pay attention to South Asia unless there was an immediate crisis or if specific U.S. interests were at stake. U.S. goals in Pakistan were limited to using Pakistan as the base of air operations against the Soviet Union and as a potential staging area for operations in case the oil fields of the Middle East came under threat. The purely instrumental goals of the United States did not include the welfare of the Pakistani masses that were impoverished and oppressed as a direct result of the Pakistan Army's obsession with India.

The United States used Pakistan as a proxy against communism and Pakistan used the United States for diplomatic, economic, and military support. During Pakistan's first engagement with the United States, it received sophisticated weaponry and economic aid, actions that the Indian government characterized as a menace to India. The U.S.-Pakistan alliance greatly antagonized India and escalated the South Asian arms race. The Soviet Union saw an opportunity to expand its own sphere of influence by offering more aid to India, which quickly

---

52 For a discussion of Pakistan's negotiation modes, see Schaffer and Schaffer, *How Pakistan Negotiates with the United States*.
53 SEATO was created as an anti-communist alliance in 1954, a Southeast Asia version of the NATO that would provide for the collective defense of its members, including Australia, New Zealand, Pakistan, Philippines, Thailand, France, United Kingdom, and the United States. CENTO (also known as the "Baghdad Pact") was also modeled on NATO and formed in 1955 as an anti-Soviet alliance and included Iran, Iraq, Pakistan, Turkey, and the United Kingdom as its members.
54 Stanley Wolpert, *Roots of Confrontation in South Asia: Afghanistan, Pakistan, India and the Superpowers.* New York: Oxford University Press, (1009), 222.

came to depend on Moscow for weapons and support to redress the imbalance of regional power that it now perceived as a result of the U.S.-Pakistan relationship.[55] After the U.S.-Pakistan Mutual Defense Agreement in 1955, Indian Prime Minister Nehru traveled to Moscow where he made a remark clearly directed toward the alliance between the United States and Pakistan: "Countries make pacts and alliances often through fear of some other country or countries. Let our coming together be because we like each other and wish to co-operate and not because we dislike others and wish to do them injury."[56]

In hindsight it seems obvious that military assistance to either Pakistan or India would escalate the region's dangerous arms race, given their unfinished business in Kashmir and their poisonous relationship. Not all American observers were in the dark about the dangers of upsetting the balance between India and Pakistan. In 1954, some influential newspapers, including the *Washington Post*,[57] opposed aid to Pakistan. Former ambassador to India Chester Bowles, Senator William Fulbright, and other opponents stressed that it was unwise to upset the larger and more important India by giving arms to Pakistan.[58] However, Washington's preoccupation with curtailing the Soviet influence blinded it to the long-term impacts of it commitment to Pakistan. The expediency of Washington's decisions was later revealed when, in the early 1960s, it began to lean toward India in order to counterbalance the Chinese influence in the region.

In the late 1950s, when China and India's border disagreements resulted in skirmishes (a later, full-scale Chinese attack on India's northeastern borders would come in October 1962), Pakistan made efforts to create an alliance with China. As China dealt a humiliating defeat to India in the 1962 war, Bhutto, Pakistan's foreign minister, continued to consolidate Pakistan's friendship with China, ceding approximately 2,000 square miles of Kashmir to China.[59] To prevent communist China from expanding its influence, the United States began sending aid to India. Just as India had vehemently protested against U.S. military aid to Pakistan in 1955, the military dictatorship in Pakistan was irate to see the United States supporting India after the 1962 war. The geostrategic imperatives of the United States were still its own number one priority; India received American military aid quite to Pakistani opposition and fury, who watched as its closest ally strengthened its most hated enemy.[60]

---

55 Wolpert, *Roots of Confrontation in South Asia*, 222.
56 Ibid., 142.
57 Most of the media responded positively to the United States' arms aid to Pakistan.
58 Kux, *The United States and Pakistan, 1947-2000*, 63.
59 Ibid., 130-134.
60 Kux, *The United States and Pakistan, 1947-2000*, 131.

Pakistani leadership was unwilling to accept that the United States had provided aid to Pakistan to buttress against the USSR while providing aid to India in order to counterbalance China. Pakistan was also bitter that the United States did not put any pressure on India regarding Kashmir and, as a consequence, it began to make more overtures toward China. At the root of Pakistan's angry reaction lay the difference between its interests and those of the United States. At that time, Washington saw India as a potential partner in containing China, whom it considered one of its major adversaries. Pakistan meanwhile considered China as a potential partner against India. Clearly Pakistan's conflicting security goals with the United States go back decades before the Taliban came in existence.

Pakistan's relationship with the United States suffered another major setback in 1965 when Pakistan went to war with India over Kashmir. In response, the United States suspended arms delivery to both Pakistan and India. Pakistani generals, expecting to receive continued support from United States, were unprepared for this response. The United States considered its action an even-handed method of preventing hostilities from escalating, while Pakistan considered it a betrayal and was, accordingly, furious. Mobs in Lahore and Karachi burned down the United States Information Service Library and American Consulate buildings, and American employees in Pakistan were stoned and chased.[61] Despite the fact that United States was the largest source of economic aid to Pakistan under the Kennedy and Johnson administrations, relations between the two countries deteriorated since the United States did not provide security assistance to Pakistan. Pakistanis felt that Washington had betrayed them.[62]

Pakistan-U.S. relations changed under the next administration. Nixon visited Pakistan five times before his election as the President and was more partial towards Pakistan, supporting the military aid package to Pakistan in 1953. In 1969, Nixon visited Pakistan and India for one day each. A tectonic shift in U.S. policy occurred as Nixon asked Pakistan's new dictator, General Yahya Khan, for help in opening up relations between the United States and China. The timing was right as both Washington and Beijing were concerned about the Soviets, and Nixon believed that positive relations with China could press the Soviet Union into a U.S.-Soviet detente. Nixon's request began a two-year-long process involving China, Pakistan, and the United States, a process that culminated in National Security Adviser Henry Kissinger's historical visit to China in 1971.[63]

---

61   Wolpert, *Roots of Confrontation in South Asia*, 148.
62   Kux, *The United States and Pakistan, 1947-2000*, 359-368.
63   Ibid., 190-192.

Nixon reciprocated for Yahya's help by doubling the United States' annual aid to Pakistan. This was ironic since the deterioration in U.S.-Pakistan relations had occurred because of China in 1965. On July 1, 1971, Kissinger arrived in Pakistan at the same time that the secret missions with China were about to culminate in success. On July 15, President Nixon announced Kissinger's trip to China, an action that was considered a political bombshell.

All of this was occurring during the same period that the West Pakistan military was massacring Bengali Muslims in East Pakistan. As the plight of millions of Bengali refugees caught widespread attention and sympathy, the House of Representatives voted to suspend all assistance to Pakistan on August 3. The next day Nixon defended his refusal to cut off aid, saying that it played a "constructive role" in the developing country and ruling any public pressure on Pakistan as "totally counterproductive."[64] The White House ignored Yahya's Bengali genocide in East Pakistan later in the year when West Pakistani armed forces butchered an estimated one to three million civilians. As Congress attempted to suspend all U.S. military aid to Pakistan, Senator Frank Church stated, "We know that the Pakistan Army, equipped mostly with American arms and led by U.S. trained officers, let loose a massive burst of violence on fellow Muslims."[65] Meanwhile, the State Department dodged any responsibility for the genocide, referring to the mass murder of the East Pakistani intelligentsia and unarmed civilians "an internal matter."[66] Senator Church eloquently described the relationship between the United States and Pakistan at the time, and the four-decade old assessment still in part describes the conflicted U.S.-Pakistan relationship:

> Military largesse, costing the United States nearly $2 billion in arms was perennially justified to the Congress and the American people as a shield to protect the Pakistanis—and the United States—against Communist aggression… Far from containing the Russian bear or the Chinese dragon, however, Pakistan has used its American-furnished military equipment first against India in 1965 and now against its own people. Indeed, in 1968, Pakistan unabashedly closed down our electronic listening post at Peshawar in order to placate Russian and Chinese feelings. By all standards, then, our military assistance policy has proved a failure—but it has been kept alive by the persistence of our arms bureaucracy, and the insistence of the Pakistan junta. When a policy goes sour but is not changed, the results are sordid.[67]

---

64 Kux, *The United States and Pakistan, 1947-2000*, 195.
65 Wolpert, *Roots of Confrontation in South Asia*, 151.
66 Ibid., 150-155.
67 Ibid., 151.

The Nixon administration refused to comment on the ongoing massacres in East Pakistan, despite the fact that about ten million Bengali refugees were fleeing across the East Pakistan border into India. Once again, India responded by moving closer to the Soviet Union, signing a Treaty of Peace, Friendship, and Cooperation on August 9, and once again, the United States' relationship with India soured. Prime Minister Indira Gandhi of India captured the spirit of the time:

> All unprejudiced persons objectively surveying the grim events in Bangla Desh since March 25 have recognized the revolt of 75 million people, a people who were forced to the conclusion that neither their life, nor their liberty, to say nothing of the possibility of the pursuit of happiness, was available to them…War could also have been avoided if the power, influence and authority of all the States, and above all of the United States had got Shaikh Mujibur Rahman released… The fact of the matter is that the rulers of West Pakistan got away with the impression that they could do what they liked because no one, not even the United States would choose to take a public position that while Pakistan's integrity was certainly sacrosanct, human rights, liberty were no less so…[68]

Leaked minutes from the Washington Special Action Group meetings on the East Pakistan crisis revealed that Nixon wanted a tilt toward Pakistan throughout the crisis.[69] India blamed the United States for failing to take any action to prevent war in South Asia. However, at the same time many in Pakistan (quite unjustifiably in light of Nixon's support) regarded the United States as an unreliable ally for failing to provide more support during the 1971 War, since the United States did not come forward directly to protect Pakistan against India. Nixon maintained a positive attitude towards Pakistan after the 1971 War; however, Pakistan's poor public image and U.S. congressional opposition limited Nixon's ability to supply Pakistan with arms. The arms embargo continued until February 24, 1975, when Washington announced that all limitations on arms transfers to Pakistan would be removed. However, military assistance grants or concessional sales were ruled out, whereas during the 1950s and 1960s, grants and concessional sales had been the mainstay of Pakistan's military aid.[70]

While relations between the United States and Pakistan remained warm during the Nixon and Ford administrations, Pakistan did not enjoy the close security relationship it had prior to 1965. Pakistan remained embittered that the United States had not come out fully to protect Pakistan in either the 1965 or 1971 Wars and had violated its commitments towards Pakistan as a SEATO member. However, major U.S. foreign policy shakeups occurring during the early 1970s—including

---

68 Quoted in Wolpert, *Roots of Confrontation in South Asia*, 154.
69 Kux, *The United States and Pakistan, 1947-2000*, 205.
70 Ibid., 215-219.

the successful opening of relations with China, the push towards détente with the Soviet Union, a winding down of the war in and withdrawal from Vietnam, the 1973 Arab-Israeli war, the oil crisis, and the Watergate scandal—pushed Pakistan's importance in the United States' eyes to the sidelines. To compensate for the loss of security assistance after 1965, Pakistan had moved towards China to supply it with military equipment and as Pakistan's security blanket against India. Pakistan continued to work Washington but proliferation concerns were working against Islamabad. The U.S.-Pakistan relationship shifted once again after 1975, as the United States became concerned over Pakistan's efforts to seek nuclear weapons. In 1976, Kissinger traveled to Pakistan to persuade Prime Minister Bhutto to drop the nuclear option, but Bhutto refused. Pakistan's relations with Washington became even more strained after the election of Jimmy Carter, and in September 1977, Zia took over control of the Pakistani government. Besides throwing Pakistan's elected leader, Bhutto, in prison, Zia also refused to alter course on Pakistan's nuclear issue. The U.S. government proceeded to suspend economic assistance to Pakistan. U.S.-Pakistan relations had chilled again, and they would not thaw again until the Soviet invasion of Afghanistan in 1979.

When Soviet troops entered Afghanistan in December 1979, the relationship between the United States and Pakistan again shifted. The United States was intent on reversing the Soviet invasion, and encouraged General Zia to initiate a covert war in Afghanistan using Islamist jihadis. A significant body of literature covers the duration and events of the U.S.-Pakistan relationship during the Afghan jihad; these can be found in the previous chapter of this book. In particular, Coll, Hussain, and Rashid provide convincing overviews of the Machiavellian tactics both the United States and Pakistan employed in order to defeat the Soviet forces in Afghanistan.[71]

The devastating impact of the Afghan War resulted in a culture of violence and religious fundamentalism in Afghanistan and Pakistan. The seeds of fundamentalist Islam, spread so casually and liberally in Afghanistan and Pakistan by successive Pakistani regimes, came to bear bitter fruit for everyone involved in the conflict. During the Afghan jihad, the Pakistani military further consolidated its grip on the state, weakening the already frail civil society. This would go on to have a major impact on the radicalization of the people of Pakistan since Pakistan's military continued to support and exploit Islamic militants, in part for the purpose of waging asymmetric warfare in Kashmir, and in part to install a compliant regime in Kabul. The emergence and spectacular victory of the Taliban in Afghanistan in 1994 can be traced to this period.

---

71 See Coll, *Ghost Wars*; Hussain, *Frontline Pakistan*; Rashid, *Taliban: Militant Islam*, Rashid, *Descent into Chaos*.

After the Soviet troops left Afghanistan, U.S.-Pakistan relations again stalled. The United States imposed sanctions on its erstwhile ally in 1990 for its nuclear program, despite the fact that it had previously and conveniently ignored warning signs of Pakistan's active pursuit and possible possession of nuclear weapons. This was a hard slap in the face for Pakistan. The Reagan administration had ignored its Islamization project and its nuclear weapon program under Zia, as well as the regime's human rights abuses and its rending of Pakistani democracy. With impunity Zia had managed to sack judges who refused to abide by his diktats, repeatedly cancel elections, impose his own brand of martial law, brutally crush his opponents as well as any cries for democracy, and jail political opponents. However, as soon as the Red Army exited Afghanistan, the United States conveniently recalled that Pakistan had pursued nuclear weapons and decided to carry through its previous threats of sanctions.

In the 1990s, U.S. military and economic aid remained out of reach for Pakistan. As discussed earlier, this was the decade when Pakistan helped a regime of medieval Islamic fanatics come to power in Afghanistan and sponsored deadly terrorist attacks in Kashmir. The drought in American material and arms largesse lasted for almost a decade until the attacks of 9/11 changed the U.S.-Pakistan relationship once again.

The shifting relationship between the United States and Pakistan is marked by significant issues. The periods when Pakistan received diplomatic as well as material support were engagements of limited focus and duration. During each engagement, Pakistan was ruled by the military or by a military-dominated government, as is visualized above in Figure 1.[72] During these engagements, as soon as the United States achieved its objectives vis-à-vis Pakistan, it lost interest in Pakistan, leaving the Pakistanis feeling betrayed.

It may be concluded that the U.S.-Pakistan relationship has been overshadowed by limited and expedient interactions and as a result has been episodic. On the American side, the relationship has been guided by Washington's global strategic goals during the Cold War and later by its need for allies in its anti-terrorism efforts in South Asia. For Pakistan, there has been a single guiding purpose: acquiring resources and support for Pakistan's enduring rivalry against India. Thus, each side seeks self-serving gains from the relationship without any genuine regard to the other's interest. To make matters more complicated, eliminating terrorism would actually work against the interests of the Pakistan Army since it would remove any incentive for the United States to provide Pakistan with military and financial aid.

---

72 Center for Global Development, "Aid to Pakistan by the Numbers."

Some South Asia experts have sought to explain Pakistan's support for terrorists as dependent upon American unreliability as an ally.[73] Such conclusions perpetuate the self-serving specious arguments that the Pakistani military and diplomats have sold for decades while exploiting the United States for military and economic aid. Pakistan has deliberately and insistently courted the United States since its inception. Since 1947, Pakistan's leaders have manipulated east-west tensions, fears of Soviet aggression, and U.S. strategic interests in the Middle East, in order to secure military and financial aid. At every sign of the United States' disillusionment, Pakistan has attempted to prove how dependent U.S. interests are on it, whether as an ally against the Soviet Union, communist aggression, or terrorism. U.S. administrations have been influenced by these entreaties since 1954.[74]

At the same time, Washington's partnership with Pakistan has also been selfish, as it uses Pakistan as a tool for achieving American strategic objectives in the South Asian region. In its quest to do so, it has indirectly subverted democracy in Pakistan, radicalized a considerable portion of Pakistani society, and destabilized South Asia. Fair describes the mutual exploitative relationship:

> By leveraging distorted narratives of the past, aggrandizing the relevance of Pakistan to US national security interests, and threatening to supplicate China or more unscrupulous partners should the United States demure, Pakistan successfully wrests expansive military, economic, and other assistance from the United States. The United States does usually get something from these transactions (e.g., ability to launch U-2 flights or more recently drones, logistical support for operations in Afghanistan), but is far from obvious that the benefits have been worth the costs paid, particularly when the transactions permit Pakistan to further invest in programs that undermine US interests (nuclear proliferation, sustained support for Islamist proxies).[75]

American interests pushed the Cold War into Pakistan and India. Later, the fear of terrorism guided Washington's expedient relationship with Pakistan. Whether the interests of Washington were served in the short-term is debatable, but U.S. interference in South Asia prolonged and intensified the regional conflict. The arrogance of U.S. decision makers did not allow consideration of the priorities and self-interest of India and Pakistan. Consequently, the South Asian regional conflict transformed into a global problem of nuclear proliferation and terrorism. While the results of Washington's obsession with the Cold War are quite apparent in hindsight, the long-term impacts of the "war on terrorism" remain to be seen.

---

73   See arguments made by Daniel Markey, "A False Choice in Pakistan," *Foreign Affairs* 86, no. 4 (2007): 85-102.
74   For an analysis, see McMahon, "United States Cold War Strategy in South Asia," 812-840.
75   C. Christine Fair, *Fighting to the End: The Pakistan Army's Way of War* (New York: Oxford University Press, 2014), 199.

The United States and Pakistan Relations: A Study in Self-Defeat

As an ally against the march of communism and later in the "War on Terrorism," Pakistan has received significant amounts of American aid during the last six decades. Between 1951 and 2011, the United States has pledged approximately $67 billion (in 2011 constant dollars) to Pakistan.[76]

As Figure 1 above shows, aid was never regular, as periods of disengagement from Pakistan led to the reduction or cessation of assistance by the United States. However, in the last twelve years alone, Pakistan has received approximately $28 billion from America, $18 billion of which was directed toward military aid and CSF reimbursements.[77] Unfortunately, U.S. aid has been beset with corruption and questionable gains—consider Pakistan's reliability as an ally against Islamic militants, or as a partner dedicated to stabilizing the political situation in Afghanistan. Despite the significant financial investment that the United States has made in Pakistan, there remains widespread anti-American sentiment among the people of Pakistan.[78] In fact, distrust and suspicion against the United States is not just rife in the Pakistani public, but also in the Pakistan Army. Lieven traces some of this resentment and opposition to the United States' dictates that the Pakistan Army crack down on the Afghan Taliban and its Pakistani sympathizers.[79]

While the Pakistani elite have claimed to be deceived by the Untied States, the deception felt by Pakistan's military was different from that felt by the polity of Pakistan, which has suffered enormously because of the United States' support of the Pakistan Army. American support for General Yahya Khan's military regime alone saw the massacre of over a million East Pakistani Bengalis and the creation of over ten million refugees. While the Pakistani military was killing its citizens in April 1971, Archer Blood, the U.S. consul general in Dacca (the capital of East Pakistan), was sending home accounts of massacres and forced expulsions. Dacca quickly became a ghost town, with three quarters of its population fleeing for their lives. On April 6, Blood explicitly described the Pakistan Army's massacres as a "genocide." The cable was extraordinary: collectively authored by Blood and his staff, for five pages it denounced American policy concerning Pakistan, pointing out its failure to condemn the violent atrocities in East Pakistan and the military's suppression of democracy. It also scathingly criticized American continued support of Pakistan's military regime.[80] One week after Blood's telegram, Nixon and Kissinger met in the Oval Office where Kissinger argued against pressuring

---

76   Center for Global Development, "Aid to Pakistan by the Numbers," 1.
77   Kronstadt and Epstein, "Direct Overt US Aid and Military Reimbursements to Pakistan," 1.
78   Ibid.
79   Anatol Lieven, *Pakistan: A Hard Country* (New York: Public Affairs, 2011), 8, 47.
80   Bass, *The Blood Telegram*, 77-78.

Pakistan since it would result in leftist extremists coming to rule in Bengal, weakening the fight against Soviet communism. America's perceived interests had clearly prevailed.

The people of Pakistan have also paid for the United States' support of the Pakistan Army through the rise of sectarian violence directly connected to Zia's Islamization project, as well as through terrorist violence emanating from the proxies that the Pakistani armed forces have supported for decades. The returns for American investment have been not only questionable for themselves, they have been quite disastrous for everyone involved.

The United States' Cold War preoccupations led not only to both India and Pakistan's continued engagement in their nuclear programs; they also made the region more dangerous, as nuclear deterrence allowed Pakistan to take increasingly risky actions against India, such as the incursion in Kargil in 1999, which brought the two nuclear states on the brink of a full-scale war.[81]

America made no substantial efforts to encourage Pakistan to engage in domestic reforms or move towards civilian rule. Consequently, Islamabad continued with its single-track foreign policy obsession, neglecting the development of its social, political, and physical infrastructure. Additionally, Islamabad also continued with the colonial practice of neglecting the development of its tribal areas and failing to incorporate these areas into its polity. By supporting successive autocratic military regimes in Pakistan, the United States disenfranchised the Pakistani people as civil rule eroded and the military power was further entrenched. As Figure 1 above indicates, since 1958, more U.S. foreign aid has reached Pakistan when it has been under military or military-turned-civilian rulers than when it has been under the rule of representatives from civil society. Compare the military-dictatorship periods to 1970–77 and 1988–99, when Pakistan was under nominal representative governments: Pakistan received more sanctions or threats of sanctions from U.S. administrations during the tenures of elected regimes.[82] Kundi argues that from early on in Pakistan's existence, the United States has promoted military regimes above all democratic alternatives, as military regimes have historically assured their commitment to serving U.S. interests.[83]

---

81 For an overview, see P. R. Chari, Pervaiz I. Cheema, and Stephen P. Cohen, *Four Crises and a Peace Process: American Engagement in South Asia* (Washington, DC: Brookings Institution Press, 2007).
82 For a discussion, see Mansoor A. Kundi, "Politics of American Aid: The Case of Pakistan," *Asian Affairs* 29, no. 2 (2007): 22-39.
83 Ibid., 34.

Since the late 1950s, U.S. administrations have preferred, bolstered, and provided support for military regimes in Pakistan. Unfortunately, aiding the army has undermined democracy in Pakistan. The person most responsible for the radicalization of Pakistan, General Zia, received the largest amount of military and economic aid from the United States, and military rule under Zia spawned some of the most militant groups that the United States is now attempting to suppress and eliminate.[84] In 1980s, democracy in Pakistan was seen as a threat to the general stability afforded by General Zia' military regime. Similarly, later U.S. administrations acquiesced to General Musharraf's argument that democratization could bring incompetent politicians or Muslim radicals to power.[85] After 9/11, the United States continued to bolster Musharraf at the expense of Pakistan's already weak civilian institutions. This further encouraged Pakistan's military to continue its strategy of employing jihadists to further its foreign policy.

Ignoring the internal contradictions of Pakistan while providing it aid, the United States also indirectly assisted with ethnic strife in the country. Pakistan's military regimes have historically exacerbated ethnic conflicts, the worst example of which was West Pakistan's brutal suppression of Bengali linguistic and ethnic agitation, which eventually led to the secession of Bangladesh in 1971.

The United States' current goals in South Asia can be summed up as such: to eliminate or at least reduce threats emanating from the area along the Afghan-Pakistan border, and to transform Pakistan into a stable state that supports U.S. interests in the region. On both accounts, the United States has failed to achieve significant progress. Violent jihadi groups thrive in Pakistan and export terrorism abroad, Pakistan's intelligence agency supports radical Islamists, and Pakistan's people have a very unfavorable impression of the United States.[86]

---

84   Bennett-Jones, Pakistan: *Eye of the Storm*; Hussain, *Frontline Pakistan*; Rashid, *Descent into Chaos*.
85   Cohen, *The Idea of Pakistan*, 305.
86   Pew Research Global Attitudes Project, "U.S. Image in Pakistan Falls No Further Following bin Laden Killing," 2011.

Bloodlines: The Imperial Roots of Terrorism in South Asia

CHAPTER 4

CONCLUSIONS

When powerful empires expand their colonial control over weaker nations rich in resources, they frequently claim civilizational superiority in order to justify their unjust hegemony. The British justified their colonial rule using patronizing moral arguments: that misgoverned and backward societies ruled by despots could be placed on a path of civilizational advancement with the help of British intervention. However positively the British Empire framed its intervention, it cannot be denied that the colonial decisions it made in India resulted in spectacularly violent events, even decades after decolonization. It also initiated a vicious cycle, as current interventions by superior military powers are consequences of prior imperial interventions. Thus, interventions of the past must be dealt with through interventions in the present.

Today's imperial interventions are formulated in terms of security or global wars on terrorism. Explanations given for the causes of violence in the subcontinent rarely move beyond Orientalist superficialities, blaming the perfidiousness of Islam, the radicalization of illiterate and backwards Muslim masses in Afghanistan and Pakistan, and a global Islamic agenda to bring back the caliphate. In reality, the true purveyor of violence in South Asia was British colonialism, which, through its waning days continued to exploit political and regional differences in the Indian subcontinent. South Asia demonstrates that when powerful foreign governments exploit ethnic, cultural, and regional differences for short-term gains, the long-term impacts can be cataclysmic, affecting innumerable members of future generations.

In order to improve revenue extraction and expand their empire in India, the British not only had to rely on force, they also had to impose on their subjects a framework that simplified their colonial administration. When the British introduced the census in India for administrative efficiency, their Orientalist biases imposed a rigid system of pre-defined categories that did not adequately account for the subcontinent's diverse populations. The Indian census created new communities and modified existing communities, constructing political groupings while shaping and manipulating ethnic and social identities. This effectively created modern politicized communities in India. Furthermore, the Empire also officially sanctioned and perpetuated religious nationalism by invidiously creating separate electorates for different religious communities. This action enforced the idea that religion and political representation were inextricably linked.

Despite posing a critical threat to British rule, the 1857 Rebellion ended in victory for the British Empire. The British Empire needed to reestablish its authority in the region. To do so, it ruthlessly retaliated against the "mutineers" and revoked the political and social status of India's Muslim aristocracy. Britain went to extreme lengths to prevent future rebellions and its brutal measures created long-term impacts in the region. When the colonial government in the post-rebellion period transformed its military recruitment strategy and fostered the notion of "martial races" in the subcontinent, seeds were sown that would one day create the conditions for Punjabi and Muslim domination in the Pakistan Army. There is no other possible explanation for creation of the myth of martial races in British India except the colonial power's need to justify its discriminatory recruitment practices. Without glorifying the martial Punjabi Muslims in order to separate them from (and create spite toward) the Orientalist caricature of "effeminate" Hindus and Bengalis, this prejudice would not have entered the British Indian Army and would not have been transferred to its colonial successor armies.

From the 1920s, when it became unfeasible to staff the officer corps using solely British personnel, Indians had to be admitted into the middle and higher ranks of the army. These personnel were recruited from conservative and pro-colonial groups and segregated from the lower-rank native soldiers. These new, Indian officers were indoctrinated by and assimilated into the British officer corps, creating distance between Indian officers and the Indian soldiers. In the process, the officers internalized the British colonial view of their subordinates.

After the British generals departed, the Pakistani military's colonial framework remained intact. British perceptions still marked the ideology of the elitist officer corps. The relatively privileged position of the majority of the officer corps distanced them from Indian nationalistic struggle. Instead, they emulated their colonial superiors, their colonial role models, and their colonial system of governance. The British Indian Army had defended the empire for almost two centuries and helped perpetuate British colonial rule; in the newly created Muslim state, they fought to maintain their privileged position. As the army quickly took over the reins of power and governance in Pakistan, its rule was justified using colonial terms: however, instead of a superior civilization civilizing the savages of the East, it was now the burden of the elite professionals of the army to keep the naïve subjects safe from corrupt politicians and their intrigue.[1]

---

1   Indian Army officers were the product of the same imperial mindset, with the exception that there was no single dominant "martial race" in the Indian Army. Furthermore, the Indian Army remained under the control of the civilian government.

CONCLUSIONS

British efforts to promote caste and tribal sensibilities, which were institutionalized in the British Indian Army, had a direct connection to the demeaning attitude of West Pakistani generals toward East Pakistani citizens. The negative effects of this racist attitude would culminate in the 1971 genocide. Similarly, the consolidation of Pakistan's Islamization project after the secession of Bangladesh is rooted in the Raj's careful discrimination against the Brahmans and Bengali mutineers following 1857. In other words, Pakistan's negative nationalism and its exploitation of Islam for political ends can trace its history back to colonial times.

The colonial need to impose or help impose centralized authority on multi-national states such as Afghanistan and India, as well as its tendency to force its own conception of identities on diverse peoples, has continued to disrupt and destabilize post-colonial societies. The diverse populations of Afghanistan and India probably would have fared better as a conglomeration of autonomously ruled provinces, loosely bound together with historical and cultural connections. When centralized colonial authorities, justified for administrative convenience under an iron-fisted imperial rule, forced a centralized government on these populations, the result was ultimately destructive and unstable. The British, Soviet, and American experience in Afghanistan reveals how forcing imperial puppets on diverse populations can bring ceaseless conflict as groups pushed out of governance rebel against real and perceived oppression. Pashtun lords ruled Afghanistan in the late 19th century with the help of swords and British subsidies; this iniquity did not make continued Pashtun domination acceptable to the sizable nations of Tajik, Hazara, and Uzbeks living within the boundary of what is now called Afghanistan. The material support of imperial powers exacerbated divisions and conflicts in Afghanistan and denied the various nations within Afghanistan the ability to reach some accommodating governance.

South Asia's people are still paying the price for the Afghan frontiers created by imperial Britain, as are the victims of terrorism as far away as New York. The demand for Pashtunistan, instead of being a call for Pashtun autonomy, remained a rhetorical tool for continuing conflict between Afghanistan and Pakistan. The colonially created conflict was simply transferred to the authoritarian regimes of Pakistan and Afghanistan, who still require the conflict to distract their misgoverned populations. Similarly, the Indian elite, instead of considering the Kashmir issue in nationalistic or humanitarian terms, instinctively assessed it in colonial terms. Nehru's government, as well as the Congress leaders (whose pervasive anti-colonial attitude came from the years they had spent in prisons during the nationalist struggle), automatically responded negatively towards Pakistan's demand for Kashmir, construing it as a colonial act. Thus the colonial die was cast also on the India-Pakistan frontier.

Pakistan was an accidental creation, a last minute unintended and begrudging product of British colonialism. When August 1947 approached, its founders had no idea of its true boundaries and no tangible administrative or governance plans. Pakistan came into existence as anti-Hindu and anti-India. The birth of a state from the matrix of negative nationalism (defined by opposition or hatred) was not a propitious beginning. As Maya Tudor describes, "The League demand for Pakistan and the content of Pakistani nationalism was primarily defined negatively (by opposing the procedure of majority-rule with constitutional protections for minorities advocated by Congress) rather than positively, in terms of what specific programs a Pakistan state would embody."[2]

Pakistan continued this negative nationalism by sustaining their narrative of an external Hindu-Indian enemy threat and also by creating internal enemies (demands for provincial autonomies or representation), ensuring that it would be always at war against someone. Pakistan's patrons largely enabled Pakistan's continued oppositional identity. As an underdeveloped country with almost no industrial infrastructure, without external patrons it would have been nigh impossible to wage a ceaseless war against its larger more powerful neighbor. Had the United States not supported Pakistan's military so excessively, the trajectory of history in South Asia would have been quite different. Pakistan's stunted economic and political development is as much a fault of the military and economic aid it received from the United States as it is of the imperial causes of Pakistan's creation.

There is a popular folk story in India and Pakistan about Kashmir. It is said that when the great Mughal Emperor Jahangir (1569-1627) saw the valley of Kashmir, he was so struck with the beauty of the land that he recited a Persian couplet attributed to the poet Amir Khusro (1253-1325):

اگر فردوس بر روی زمین است همین است و همین است و همین است

(If paradise exists on the earth, it is here, it is here, it is here)

The beautiful landscape loved by emperors and commoners alike has been turned into a miserable hell for Kashmiris for the last few decades. As the Kashmiri poet Agha Shahid Ali expressed his feelings about the state of Kashmir, "I am being rowed through Paradise on a river of Hell." Both India and Pakistan are responsible for turning this paradise into hell.

---

2 Maya Tudor, *The Promise of Power: The Origins of Democracy in India and Autocracy in Pakistan* (New York: Cambridge University Press, 2013), 94.

While the two neighbors, congenitally joined by the bonds of history and geography, have staked their claim on Kashmir on ideological grounds, their quest has been a colonial one. India and Pakistan never were interested in the aspiration of Kashmiris. Although India claimed to be the largest democracy in the world, it treated the territory as a virtual colony. Afraid of the true wishes of the Muslims of Kashmir for more autonomy and independence, India has subverted the democratic process in the state, alienating the population. Almost five decades ago, Indian nationalist and prominent Indian opposition leader, Jayaprakash Narayan, told Prime Minister Indira Gandhi, "We profess democracy, but rule by force in Kashmir. We profess secularism, but let Hindu nationalism stampede us into establishing it by repression. Kashmir has distorted India's image in the world as nothing else has done. The problem exists not because Pakistan wants to grab Kashmir, but because there is deep and widespread discontent among the people."[3] Narayan could have expressed this same sentiment in the year 2014 and it would not be any less true.

Britain's imperial decisions were made to perpetuate their empire in the Indian subcontinent; in the process they disrupted India's incredibly diverse society, which has resulted in serious and unexpected long-term outcomes. Events as far back as 1857 (ninety years before Pakistan was created) can be connected to events that occurred in 1947, 1971, and 2001. Without Britain's interference, there might be no political Islam, no radical Pakistan, and no enduring state of conflict in South Asia. The British East India Company and the guardians of the British Raj in India cannot be blamed for failing to foresee the inadvertent outcomes that might arise from tinkering with large, diverse, and interdependent societies. However, by examining South Asia as a model system, one can see the outcomes of imposing self-serving systems on foreign societies.

A thought experiment may help one evaluate the hypothesis that British Empire had a discernible impact on a string of disasters in South Asia, from one instance of genocidal violence and the uprooting of millions in 1947, to another in 1971; from the untold deaths and flight of millions of people in 1980s to a sequence of terrorist actions originating from Pakistan-Afghanistan region. Had there been no British colonial intervention in the Indian subcontinent, the largely ceremonial Mughal authority may or may not have survived the onslaught of its regional competitors. Most likely, various power blocs would have accommodated each other and from it a decentralized structure with a ceremonial central authority might have evolved. Alternatively, the center might have gradually disappeared in favor of autonomous provinces with a loose or even non-existent "India," since

---

3   Sumantra Bose, *Contested Lands: Israel-Palestine, Kashmir, Bosnia, Cyprus, and Sri Lanka* (Cambridge, MA: Harvard University Press, 2010), 175.

the linguistic- and geographically-based nation states that already existed in the subcontinent may have become strengthened over the years. This system would have prevented the future conflicts generated by the impositions of a distant "central" and authoritarian government.

There is no evidence that Hindu-Muslim antagonism at the organic level would have occurred but for British intervention. The old system of syncretism forced by necessity, with Hindu generals employed in a Muslim emperor's army, Hindu moneylenders as financiers of the Mughal Emperor, and regional Muslim governors may well have lasted. The foundation for extreme group antagonism in colonial India was nationalism and competition for power that was not indigenous or evolutionary, but reactive. And it was reactive not just because it was a response to external stimuli, but also because the parameters of the response were dictated by the external. After all, only the imperial center could dispense status and power. Even if Congress and the Muslim League acted solely as subservient clients of the colonial rulers, competition for power was ultimately settled by the imperial power and not through mutual negotiations. The Empire controlled to its final days, how and when different groups competed for their place in the state. Without constant British interventions, made to advance and further their Empire, there would have been no Pakistan, no Hindu-Muslim conflict of the intensity seen in 1940s, no Bangladesh war, no Pashtunistan conflict, and no use of Pakistan-Afghanistan territory to train Islamic militants.

Though this thought experiment is an exercise in fantasy, it is based on historical realities that point to what might have emerged but for consistent imperial short-term necessities. This thought experiment could be replicated in country after country where imperial expediencies imposed artificial boundaries on colonial subjects, blatantly disregarding the milieu within which the native populations interacted. Around the globe, the ways in which colonial powers have historically sought alliances with native collaborators, favoring one group over another in order to perpetuate their own political control, have created hostility between native groups after decolonization and have been at the root of post-colonial violence in many Asian and African states.

The colonial British regime relied on the Muslim League's negative nationalism to counterbalance the positive nationalism of the Indian National Congress. By its very nature, negative nationalism relies on autocratic personalities instead of democracy and an open party system. This ensured that Pakistan's trajectory was headed toward autocratic governance and military control. Pakistan's ideational and foundational security dilemmas also ensured that the military would dominate the government after the nation's creation. In summary, Pakistan's turn towards autocratic rule after its independence has colonial roots.[4]

It is important to recognize that the self-destructive, dangerous behavior of Pakistan is a result of its elite's interests, tracing back to before Pakistan's creation. Rhetorical use of Islam as a unifying banner was closely related with the struggle to create Pakistan. Islam continues to be used as a political slogan as well as a tool for stifling dissent, perpetuating authoritarian behavior, and blaming external enemies of Islam for the structural ills of society. The threats of Hindu India and Afghanistan's claims to Pashtunistan have resulted in Pakistan's sponsorship of Islamist militants and asymmetric warfare. Pakistan's numerous victims of sectarian and religious violence can thank their own generals for the suicide bombings and mass murders that occur with great regularity in Pakistan.

For Pakistan to begin to transform its identity in a positive and fulfilling direction, and become a nation-state that focuses on the welfare of its citizens instead of the welfare of its army, settling the Kashmir conflict would be the first step in that positive direction. Resolving Kashmir's status is not an intractable problem; Pakistan's civilian elite has long since come to understand that Kashmir cannot be won, and seems to desire an honorable exit from the enterprise. It is the institutional interests of the Pakistan Army, India's intransigent hawks, and rogue, non-state jihadi actors that stand to lose from peace. While civilian regimes in Pakistan might attempt to normalize their relationship with India, normalization is not in the military's interest. Many in Pakistan recognize the need to resolve this conflict with India; however, the entrenched interests that benefit from the conflict's continuation are, naturally, averse to resolution.

The Pakistan Army possesses an incredible ability to derail any process towards a peace with India; there are numerous examples of it sabotaging civilian peace efforts with India. Prime Minister Nawaz Sharif's efforts at normalization were scuttled by General Pervez Musharraf's military in 1999 when Musharraf started a covert intrusion that escalated into the Kargil War with India. Kept in the dark, Sharif was humiliated and his peace process was killed. Ironically, a few years later it was Musharraf who, as Pakistan's President, initiated backdoor peace negotiations with India.[5] This time, the spectacular Mumbai terrorist attacks of 2008 carried out by LeT—a group strongly supported by the ISI and Pakistani military—destroyed what both sides believed was an achievable peace deal.

---

4 For a detailed analysis of the reasons why India turned secular democratic and Pakistan became authoritarian, see Tudor, *The Promise of Power*.
5 Coll, "The Back Channel: India and Pakistan's Secret Kashmir Talks."

Since the inception of Pakistan, the Pakistani military has been the most significant and powerful interest group in the nation. As it continues to consolidate power, it reaps the benefits and privileges that come with unchallenged domination. Given that its power is based on fundamental fears of national destruction at the hands of India or the West, the Pakistani military's existence would largely end if the South Asian conflict were to be resolved. Its reason for being would cease to exist. However, the blowback from the military's reliance on Islamist militants to fight its wars in Afghanistan and India results in horrendous terrorist attacks in Pakistan itself. This also might change the attitude of Pakistan's military toward using militant proxies to achieve its nebulous and self-destructive foreign policy goals.

Moral imperatives as well as practical considerations indicate that India would immensely benefit from changing its long-standing status quo policy on Kashmir. To achieve that, India should unilaterally institutionalize autonomy in Kashmir, with a future referendum on whether the regions of Kashmir under India's control would prefer self-rule or to join India or Pakistan. Additionally, India needs to open the Kashmir border to allow movement across the Pakistan-controlled and India-controlled sections. India should also support Pakistan's attempts to get civilian nuclear deals with United States and other nuclear states and offer to enter into a non-proliferation regime. Since both the neighbors possess nuclear weapons, and since Pakistan has been asking for access to civil nuclear technology to meet its acute energy shortage,[6] the goodwill gesture would carry tremendous weight and open up at least a possibility that negotiations for disarmament and nonproliferation in future might be feasible. Practically, India does not have much to lose by supporting a civil nuclear deal for Pakistan or giving full autonomy to Kashmir.

Giving autonomy to Kashmir, having an independent Kashmir on its border, or having Kashmir be a part of Pakistan all are bound to be economically and militarily advantageous. The enormous expense of permanently stationing close to half a million soldiers (collectively more soldiers than what the United States used in Iraq and Afghanistan) for more than two decades is a drain that India can ill afford in perpetuity. By changing its hidebound Kashmir posture, India would also give Pakistan the opportunity to save face in an arena where it has expended all its energies during the last six decades, allowing it an honorable exit. Additionally, unilaterally removing reasons for the Pakistan Army's existence would assist in developing Pakistan's civil polity. The Pakistan Army may not embrace Indian gestures but the political establishment, long hamstrung by the Army, might gain

---

6   "Pakistan Looking Forward to Cooperation in Civil Nuclear Energy: Nawaz," *Express Tribune*, March 24, 2014.

some breathing room so it could begin to challenge the Army's domination. A focus on opening up borders and allowing bilateral trade to flourish would greatly benefit both India and Pakistan. Due to their adversarial relations, movement of people and goods across borders is at present minuscule. The neighbors that constitute South Asia's largest economies currently trade approximately $2.5 billion worth of goods; in terms of percentages, Pakistan accounts for barely 0.5% of India's trade and India accounts for approximately 3% of Pakistan's trade. If relations between the two countries were normalized, it is estimated that bilateral trade could expand to more than twenty times to $50 billion.[7]

A consistent theme in the history of empires has been the ways in which they use Machiavellian strategies to achieve local goals. These techniques are typically shortsighted, focused on immediate benefits, and blind to long-term outcomes. This is not only true in terms of the British Empire; U.S. administrations have consistently engaged in the same shortsighted expediencies with respect to Pakistan and South Asia. In the last decade, Washington has made decisions that are remarkably similar to 18th and 19th century British imperial decisions; for example, it has exploited the differences between ethnic groups for short-term gains in Iraq and South Asia. There is no way of knowing the long-term outcomes of these present expediencies. However, some of the outcomes of manipulating Pakistan since 1954 have become quite apparent in recent years.

Since early on in Pakistan's development, the United States has disrupted Pakistan's civil society by using it as a proxy against the Soviet Union. This aim was accomplished by supporting the Pakistan Army and its dictators at the expense of civilian institutions. Historically, Washington allied primarily with Pakistan's military to achieve Cold War goals and rewarded Pakistan with substantial military and economic assistance in exchange for acting as its proxy. This aid strengthened Pakistan's military at the expense of it civilian institutions while also ensuring the difficulty of any peaceful resolution to the India-Pakistan conflict. Instead of peace, the Pakistani military was encouraged to engage in risky adventurism, the biggest example of which was empowering Islamist militants during the Afghan jihad. The genocidal violence in East Pakistan in 1971 would not have been as painless for Yahya's regime if Pakistan's military regime had not been able to rely on Nixon and Kissinger for full support.[8] Except episodic attempts to prevent wider conflagrations and nuclear war, America has made no significant or sustained efforts to encourage Pakistan to resolve its conflict with India. By

---

7 Mohsin Khan, "India-Pakistan Trade Relations: A New Beginning" *New America Foundation Report* 14 (2013): 2.
8 For detailed documentation and analysis of Nixon and Kissinger's rather disturbing attitude and response towards the massacre of Bengali population, and their tilt towards the Pakistan's dictator at the time, see Bass, *The Blood Telegram*.

consistently supporting autocratic military regimes in Pakistan, the United States has in fact disenfranchised the Pakistani people and contributed to the consistent erosion of civil rule in the state. Thanks to substantial assistance and support by Washington, the military controls the state as its fiefdom, and its domination is directly responsible for Pakistan's radicalization and its consociate terrorism.

Short-term, expedient decisions may provide immediate advantages, but their long-term consequences can be severely disruptive. While British imperialism was at the foundation of South Asia's troubling past and present, beginning in 1950s, the United States began superimposing its own foundation of expediency over those of Britain. The United States' use of Pakistan as a proxy against the Soviet Army in Afghanistan is an instructive example of this tactic at work. Although in the short term the United States was able to roll back the Soviet invasion, the Pakistani-supported insurgency gave rise to radical jihadi groups, a devastating civil war in Afghanistan, Taliban rule, and cultivated the region to become a source of global terrorism. The most ironic aspect of U.S. military aid to the Pakistani military is related to the Pakistani military's financing, support, and training of terrorist groups, some of which have targeted U.S. soldiers in Afghanistan and elsewhere. In effect, the Pakistani-supported militants have used U.S. aid to kill U.S. citizens and to finance terrorist plots. This is a shocking implication of the United States' largesse to Pakistan's military regimes even after the events of 9/11.

Terrorist groups cannot survive and thrive without financing, safe havens, a constant supply of recruits, and reliable sponsors. Without Pakistan's support for the Afghan Taliban and associated terrorist organizations, bin Laden could not have found secure refuge in Afghanistan. After his expulsion from Sudan in 1996, Osama bin Laden was left without a base and in a precarious situation. His own country had revoked his passport and there was no other country willing to host him.[9] It was the Taliban-governed Afghanistan that provided him with a safe haven and an existing terrorist training infrastructure, and all of this was the gift of U.S. financing and the ISI's making. If Pakistan had not enabled Islamist militants in Afghanistan and then plotted ceaselessly to place a friendly regime in Afghanistan, al Qaeda could not have found a safe refuge in Afghanistan.

The Pakistani military stands to lose its privileges if peace is achieved with India, conflicts are resolved with Afghanistan, and the threat of terrorism is reduced in South Asia. But by using financial and military aid to back the Pakistani military instead of Pakistan's civil governments, Washington has ensured perpetual conflict

---

9 Wright, *The Looming Tower*, 195.

in South Asia. On an even darker level, this conflict itself benefits the U.S. military-industrial-business complex (MIB), which requires a string of enemies in order to keep flourishing.

The relationship between the United States and Pakistan has been expedient, exploitative, and strategic, based upon short-term U.S. strategic interests and the utilitarian rentier interests of Pakistan. The strategic component of the relationship needs to be transformed with a long-term view toward global U.S. interests. While this does not mean that short-term goals in the region should be placed on the back burner, there is a need to break from past practices that have relied on short-term expediency at the expense of long-term negative implications. U.S. interests are better served in South Asia not by simply focusing on eliminating al Qaeda and the Taliban, but through judicious policies that take into consideration the historical forces that gave rise to these and similar violent, radical groups.

Recommendations

Using historical data to provide recommendations may appear to be a complex conceptual exercise, however, the lessons that can be learned from it are tangible, reflected in current conflicts of the world, and relevant. To use a common metaphor, it is about treating the root causes of a disease rather than dealing solely with its symptoms. Knowing about the long-term impacts of imperial expediencies will not necessarily force decision makers to make the right decisions. Imperial needs and the Machiavellian methods used to achieve them may not necessarily change by exposing truth to decision-makers. After all, imperial impositions are based on short-term benefits and exploitation.

Sometimes imperial masters and ministers simply do not care about the impact of expediencies. The decisions made by the British Empire in colonial India were meant to divide different communities, regardless of their effects. Similarly, long-term impacts were implicitly disregarded when the United States financed the most fundamentalist Islamic militants during the Afghan jihad.

Exploitation is not given up simply because of moral imperatives or adverse unintended consequences in the distant future. What, then, is the utility of discussing what might lie ahead? The framework within which nation states interact has changed dramatically in the past, especially after the Second World War. The impact of interventions is significant for both the subject as well as the purveyor of imperial expediency. The United States' 1979-1989 intervention in Afghanistan caused deaths and displacement of an untold number of Afghans, devastated the country, set back its infrastructure as well as its polity, spread Islamic militancy (which filtered out to Pakistan, the U.S. proxy), and resulted in terrorist attacks around the world. Linda Bilmes has estimated that the total costs for the Iraq and Afghanistan wars may run as high as $6 trillion.[10] The "Costs of War Project," based at Brown University's Watson Institute for International Studies, estimates that the wars in Afghanistan, Pakistan, and Iraq have directly and indirectly caused the death of over 350,000. The number of civilians killed in Afghanistan alone was estimated to be 220,000, and this study acknowledges that the number of civilians killed has been significantly undercounted. The cost to the United States for both Iraq and Afghanistan/Pakistan is going to be close to $4 trillion, not including future interest costs on borrowing for the wars. The estimate concludes, "The human and economic costs of these wars will continue for decades, some costs not peaking until mid-century."[11] Not even the sole superpower in the world can afford such costs in human and economic terms. Furthermore, prudence demands that even war-related decisions be made judiciously, if not for moral, then for practical, return-on-investment reasons.

A true return of investment assessment is not possible without knowing history and its impact on the region before an intervention is initiated. If interventions are necessary, they must be based on sound analysis, which invariably requires understanding the people, places, and their histories. Before providing military aid to Pakistan in 1954, Washington's decisions should have been guided by an analysis of its rivalry with India and the possibility of an arms race in the region. Similarly, the U.S. mission to drive Soviet forces from Afghanistan did not require militant Islamists and could have been achieved by supporting a unified and moderate opposition.

After 9/11, Washington failed to display any coherent regional policy in South Asia. As a result, even after spending more than half a trillion dollars it is difficult to see that any tangible progress has been made toward eradicating the threat of insurgency. Furthermore, since the seat of the insurgency is localized in Pakistan, reducing U.S. combat forces may reverse the gains that the United States has achieved through its counter-insurgency efforts.

U.S. policies in South Asia will soon require redirection as the United States has removed the majority of its troops from Afghanistan and the reduction in force footprint brings a corresponding change in influence. From a height of approximately 100,000 U.S. troops in Afghanistan in 2011, it is expected that a

---

10   Bilmes, "The Financial Legacy of Iraq and Afghanistan", 1. The total direct costs for Afghan war, FY2001-2013 reach $641.7 billion, based on Anthony H. Cordesman, "The U.S. Cost of the Afghanistan War: FY2002-FY2013. Cost in Military Operating Expenditures and Aid and Prospects for 'Transition,'" *Center for Strategic and International Studies* (2012), 1-13.
11   http://costsofwar.org/

residual force of 9,800 will remain there after 2014.[12] The total authorization of U.S. aid funding, which went from $39.5 billion in 2006 to $98 billion in 2012, dropped to $9.66 billion in 2013.[13] During the fiscal year 2014, Department of Defense aid to Afghanistan will drop to $1.04 billion and economic and governance aid to $1.1 billion. Furthermore, the precipitous drop in both troop levels and aid is likely to erode the United States' leverage and its influence over Kabul and Islamabad. With Pakistan consistently attempting to impose a government of its choice in Afghanistan, unless India, Afghanistan, and Pakistan come to some agreement, the result may be increased violence in the region, the severity of which depending on Pakistan's level of support for insurgents and India's support for the Kabul regime. With Pakistan's support and encouragement, Taliban insurgents will be able to cross the Durand Line without fear, targeting the Kabul government much more boldly and effectively.

Iranian interference would also modulate the evolving violence in the region, and Russia, China, and other neighboring Central Asian states would no doubt also attempt to influence the evolving conflict. However, it is all but certain that if U.S. troops withdraw without some tangible support for Afghanistan, the aftermath of the Soviet withdrawal will be repeated, with serious blood-letting as the Taliban and other groups opposed to the Ashraf Ghani Ahmadzai regime fight it out for influence and territory. It is critical that U.S. residual forces remain and back the Afghan National Security Forces (ANSF) after the declared end of combat in December 2014. A training and supporting role does not require as extensive an investment of manpower and resources as a full scale war, but it will be invaluable in developing the ANSF.

The diplomatic efforts and financial and military aid used to purchase Pakistan's cooperation against Islamist militancy and terrorism would have been better spent instead on mediating a rapprochement between India, Pakistan, and Afghanistan. The post-9/11 buildup of Pakistan's military was invariably going to worsen relations between India and Pakistan, considering their still unresolved conflicts. The United States' attempt to counterbalance China by making India eligible to buy U.S. dual-use nuclear technology (including materials and equipment that could be used to enrich uranium or reprocess plutonium), won by Congressional approval in October 2008, was another poorly thought-out strategy.[14] Once again,

---

12   Karen DeYoung, "Obama to Leave 9,800 Troops in Afghanistan," *Washington Post*, May 27, 2014.
13   Anthony Cordesman, "The Reality Beyond Zero and 10,000: Choosing a Meaningful Option in Afghanistan," *Center for Strategic and International Studies*, February 4, 2014. Accessed March 5, 2014, http://csis.org/publication/reality-beyond-zero-and-10000-choosing-meaningful-option-afghanistan.
14   Jayshee Bajoria and Esther Pan, "The U.S.-India Nuclear Deal," *Council on Foreign Relations*, November 5, 2010.

no thought was given to the impact such a deal would have on Pakistan, where it was viewed as favoritism toward India and raised a good deal of tension. In contrast, the following proposed recommendations have the potential to foster sound decision-making and lower the intensity of conflicts in South Asia:

- Sound U.S. policy requires policymakers to consider how South Asia's colonial history has shaped current conflicts in Afghanistan, India, and Pakistan.
- Washington's focus on "stability"—which since 1958 has been the code word for supporting the military and dictators of Pakistan—must change.
- To make better policy decisions, it is essential to see South Asia as a complex natural system.
- The United States must confront the reality that both al Qaeda and the Afghan Taliban exist because of the state of Pakistan.
- It is imperative that the United States ceases all military aid to Pakistan.
- As military aid to Pakistan comes to an end, economic and humanitarian aid to Pakistan should be coordinated through the civilian authorities alone and they must be held strictly accountable for it.
- There should be a clear and transparent move from supporting the Pakistani military to supporting its civilian government.
- United States should support the control of Pakistan's civilian government over its nuclear assets and policy.
- The United States, without appearing patronizing, should use its influence on India and Pakistan in order to resolve the Kashmir dispute.
- In Afghanistan, Washington needs to encourage negotiations with the Taliban. It also needs to abandon the colonial-minded central government model in Afghanistan, encouraging the people of Afghanistan to move towards a federal system in which power is devolved to its provinces.
- U.S. policy in South Asia must be realistic. It is time to abandon short-term expediencies and accept natural risks, including some inherent volatility as complex systems adapt and move towards freedom. U.S. policy objectives should focus on adaptability and resilience, not immediate stability.
- Washington must be careful not to use India as a counterbalancing power in the region.

Conflicts between Afghanistan, Pakistan, and India have manifested in the terrorism that has spawned across the region. Since the origin of terrorism is tied to local conflicts, a regional solution (instead of external manipulation, which has thus far been the norm) is required to resolve the conflict. The first step toward long-term stability should be settling of the conflicts between Afghanistan, India, and Pakistan.

CONCLUSIONS

In 2007, with Pakistan's people agitating against Musharraf and demanding freedom, the United States chose to shore up its "ally in the war on terror." This has been the United States' pattern of behavior in the region since General Ayub Khan took over in a coup in 1958. The trend of backing "stability" over the chaos of democracy needs to be reversed since it is exactly this quest for stability that has created the matrix from which terrorism in South Asia has evolved. These facts are stark reminders that any further expedient policies in Pakistan would only prove more destabilizing and dangerous in the future.

South Asia has ethnically, linguistically, religiously, politically, and culturally diverse populations; these make up a complex natural system that should be treated as such. It is not a simple linear system where a single expedient intervention results in a single required outcome. Taleb and Blyth relate the 2011 turmoil in Arab states to the support that the United States provided to dictatorships in that region for the sake of stability. Instead of propping up of authoritarian regimes for the sake of stability, "the U.S. government should stop supporting dictatorial regimes for the sake of pseudostability and instead allow political noise to rise to the surface" which would promote robustness in the political system.[15]

There are additional complications: the United States intends to destroy al Qaeda and conclude their missions in Afghanistan, while Pakistan aims to keep their U.S. cash spigot open, and therefore, has an interest in continuing the conflict. Furthermore, Pakistan has strategic interest in supporting the radical groups it intends to use once the United States leaves the region. Due to these feedback loops, the conflict, instead of being resolved, continues. This cycle needs to be broken.

History demonstrates that continuing to support the military at the expense of civilian institutions in Pakistan has been counterproductive in the long run; al Qaeda and the Afghan Taliban exist because of Pakistan. It is always frustrating to deal with a democratic system with its oppositional pulls, political grandstanding, and entrenched bureaucracy, especially when a divergence of interests may not result in desired cooperation or outcomes. In contrast, it is much easier to deal with a single-point decision maker in a dictatorship. In the case of U.S.-Pakistan relations, "coordinating issues of military intelligence and operational and tactical level planning is much simpler when done through a single authoritarian leader than with the warring factions of a dysfunctional parliament."[16] However, enabling Pakistan's dictators has disabled the forces of its democracy. As a direct result of U.S. pressures, Pakistan's civil society has been stunted and regressed.

---

15   Taleb and Blyth, "The Black Swan of Cairo," 34.
16   Malou Innocent, "Pakistan and the Future of U.S. Policy," *Policy Analysis* 36 (2009): 16.

Difficult decisions need to be made—ones that fall outside the comfort zone of U.S. policymakers. Historically, they have relied on simplistic linear cause and effect relationships: stable dictators bring predictability and reliability to the region, keep Islamic fundamentalism and chaos at bay, are easier to deal with, and can be useful in safeguarding American interests. However, past decisions along such lines have led to the United States' direct engagement in Afghanistan. Having expended approximately $640 billion in direct costs so far, decisions that may bring unpredictability now but stability in the long run may be far more preferable.[17]

There are few, if any, possibilities of instability arising out of a chain of command where the elected officials exercise control over nuclear weapons. In fact, the effect is likely to be the opposite. One of the reasons Pakistan has supported terrorism and risky adventurism inside India is because of nuclear blackmail: due to the danger of a nuclear Armageddon, the Pakistan Army expects external pressure to prevent an India from escalating the situation, as in the 1999 Kargil incident.

Besides an absolute control over Pakistan's foreign policy, the Pakistan Army exercises a zealous, absolute, and secretive control over the nation's nuclear weapon assets, program, and nuclear use doctrine. While the elected leaders of Pakistan theoretically control Pakistan's nuclear arsenal by chairing the National Command Authority (responsible for Pakistan's nuclear arsenal and nuclear policy), the army has never allowed civilians to control the nuclear program. Unlike India, Pakistan has refused to adopt a "no first use" policy. The first use posture is used as a coercive deterrent against India's conventional military superiority, allowing the Pakistan Army to use terrorism and asymmetric warfare in Kashmir without the possibility of massive Indian retaliation.

While concerns have been expressed that Pakistan's nuclear weapons might fall in the hands of radical Islamists, the likelihood of such events is remote. Despite its ideological empathy and support for radical Islamists, there is no evidence that the Pakistan Army would relinquish its iron grip on nuclear weapons to jihadists. Furthermore, there are no credible threats that any jihadi group would be capable of taking control of Pakistan's nuclear weapons. The more tangible threats from Pakistan's nuclear weapon program are related to state-sponsored technology transfers and proliferation, as observed in the past nuclear black marketing to Libya, Iran, and North Korea.

---

17   Cordesman, "The U.S. Cost of the Afghanistan War: FY2002-FY2013," 3.

CONCLUSIONS

Pakistan's civilian leadership has shown interest in a rapprochement with India for some time now, but this is not in the interests of the Pakistan Army. Transferring nuclear decision making to civilian governments is more likely to reduce Pakistan Army's adventurism and control over Pakistan's polity, thus reducing its power and influence.

The most salient recommendation for stabilizing South Asia would be for the United States, without appearing patronizing, to use its influence on India and Pakistan in order to resolve the Kashmir dispute. This one step would significantly reduce Pakistan's means of raising jihadi proxies, and the civilian government in Pakistan appears to genuinely desire peace-building measures with India. However, without the Pakistan Army's sanction, no rapprochement is possible, and again, it is not in the Pakistan Army's interest to see the conflict end, as its existence and privileges depend upon the conflict between Pakistan and India. Thus it is imperative that the United States ceases all military aid to Pakistan. The perks of the Pakistani military come not only from its stranglehold on the state, but also through Washington's financing.

As military aid to Pakistan comes to an end, economic and humanitarian aid to Pakistan should be coordinated through the civilian authorities alone and they must be strictly accountable for it. A lack of transparency and accountability for U.S. funds has strengthened the Pakistani military and engendered corruption. While this step would provoke loud protests from the army, it is essential to drain the resources of radical proxies in order to achieve stability and peace in South Asia. There is no evidence that economic aid to Pakistan has been substantially used to benefit infrastructure development or to support civilian institutions. Without good governance and accountability, the aid has not only encouraged corruption, but has weakened the civil institutions that would be crucial to changing Pakistan's trajectory.

There should be a clear and transparent move from supporting the Pakistani military to supporting its civilian government. No contacts should be made with Pakistani military without civilian oversight and the civilian government's approval. This step would require a clean and difficult break from historical tradition and would cause consternation and possibly retaliation from the Pakistan Army, which is long used to the largesse and special treatment it has enjoyed for decades. However, instability induced by this step would be worth it in exchange for the long-term stability that might emerge from a strengthened civil polity in which the military does not function as the state and instead remains in the service of the civilian administration. In 2008, Musharraf's autocratic regime was brought down by a galvanized Pakistani civil society and the U.S. administration continued to support him even as the citizens of Pakistan fought for democracy. This hidebound approach of relying on Pakistani generals must be rejected if there is to be long-term stability and peace in the region.

It does not help the U.S. government's credibility to ignore Pakistan's ongoing support for terrorism, nuclear proliferation, and its military's vice-like grip on state and society. All of this is currently allowed in exchange for only partial support of U.S. objectives in South Asia and is conducted while broader U.S. objectives are simultaneously undermined. For the sake of American credibility as well as undermining the use of terrorism as a tool of the state, Pakistan should be declared a state that has supported and supports terrorist groups. While this might temporarily strengthen the Pakistani military, the United States' unbalanced emphasis on short-term benefits has led to the current toxic situation in the first place. Arguments have been made that Pakistan might stop supporting U.S. counterterrorism measures. The fact is that inducements have not worked with Pakistan. Rather, some have made the argument that the United States' recent success with Pakistan was brought about by using the proverbial "stick"—an ultimatum given to Pakistan in September 2001 that caused it to abandon the Taliban, its surrogate in Afghanistan. While the move to abandon the Taliban regime after 9/11 was a tactical choice planned as a temporary move by Pakistan, the threat of force did make Pakistan give up not only on its proxy but also the "strategic depth" it had been seeking in Afghanistan for decades. In light of the U.S. troop reduction starting in 2014, it is less critical now that the United States maintain a supply line to troops through Pakistan. Realpolitik aside, what is more important is to ensure that South Asia's historical conflicts do not continue to destabilize or endanger the region and pose terrorist threats to the rest of the world as well.

The top-down approach of installing a malleable regime in Afghanistan has to be abandoned in favor of a decentralized governing system in which autonomous adjunctive provinces collaborate in a loosely held federal structure. This step alone would help deal with a major source of conflict in Afghanistan.

U.S. policy in South Asia must be realistic, taking into account that economic and military inducement cannot make Washington's clients abandon their existential beliefs. Removing terrorist safe havens, supporting stability in South Asia, and reducing future nuclear confrontations requires abandoning short-term expediencies and accepting natural risks. In time, the complex system of the subcontinent would stabilize, even though short-term volatility might be the immediate outcome. The goal of a sound foreign policy should be adaptability and resilience. The United States' fixation with immediate stability has proven to bring with it undesirable long-term outcomes.

It is critical that Washington not use India as a hedge against China or as a counterbalancing power in the region. It would only invite more arms races in an already volatile and underdeveloped region that can ill afford more military spending. It would also guarantee that the Indo-Pakistan conflict would continue. In the 1950s, the United States exploited Pakistan's insecurities for its own Cold War interests, perpetuating the conflict between India and Pakistan and even adding to its toxicity. Instead of aiming at short-term benefits, U.S. policies must consider South Asia's history as it pertains to its ongoing conflicts. Striking at the roots of terrorism does not require financing and encouraging Pakistan's generals. It requires Washington to distance itself from prior habits of expediency and realpolitik in South Asia, and its benefits will be far-reaching for all.

Bloodlines: The Imperial Roots of Terrorism in South Asia

APPENDIX

REGIONAL MAPS

India in 350 A.D.

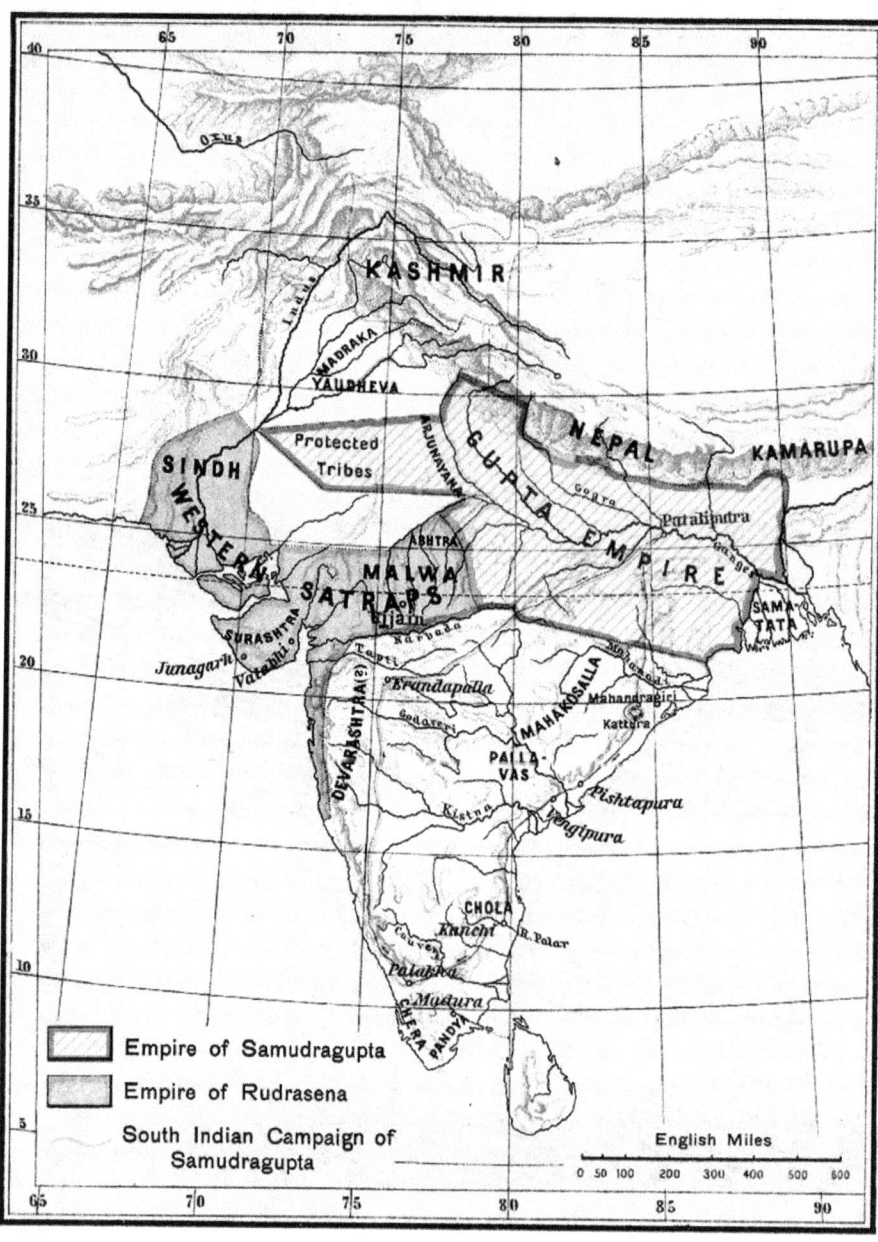

Source: Joppen, Charles [SJ.] (1907), A Historical Atlas of India for the use of High-Schools, Colleges, and Private Students, London, New York, Bombay, and Calcutta: Longman Green and Co.

APPENDIX

India in 1022.

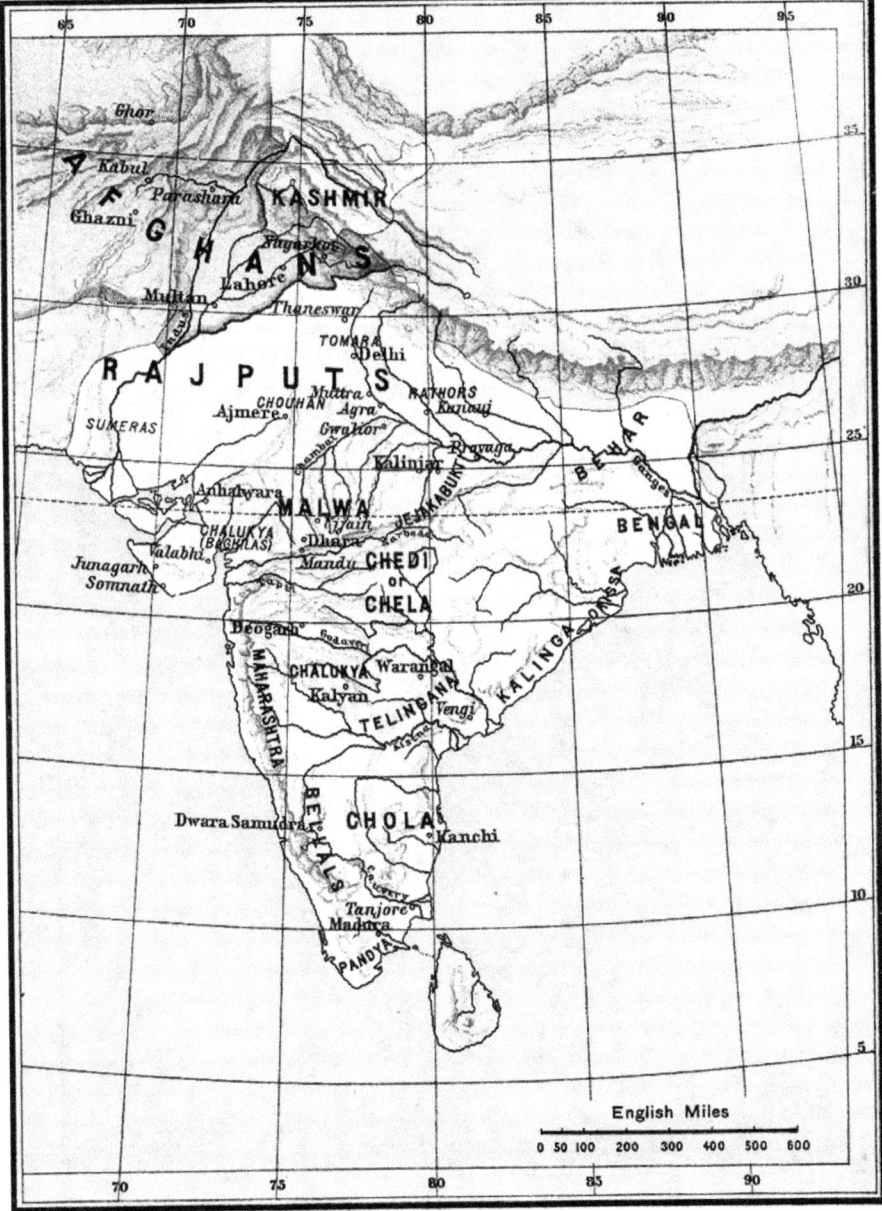

Source: Joppen, Charles [SJ.] (1907), A Historical Atlas of India for the use of High-Schools, Colleges, and Private Students, London, New York, Bombay, and Calcutta: Longman Green and Co.

India in 1795.

Source: Joppen, Charles [SJ.] (1907), A Historical Atlas of India for the use of High-Schools, Colleges, and Private Students, London, New York, Bombay, and Calcutta: Longman Green and Co.

APPENDIX

Kashmir Region

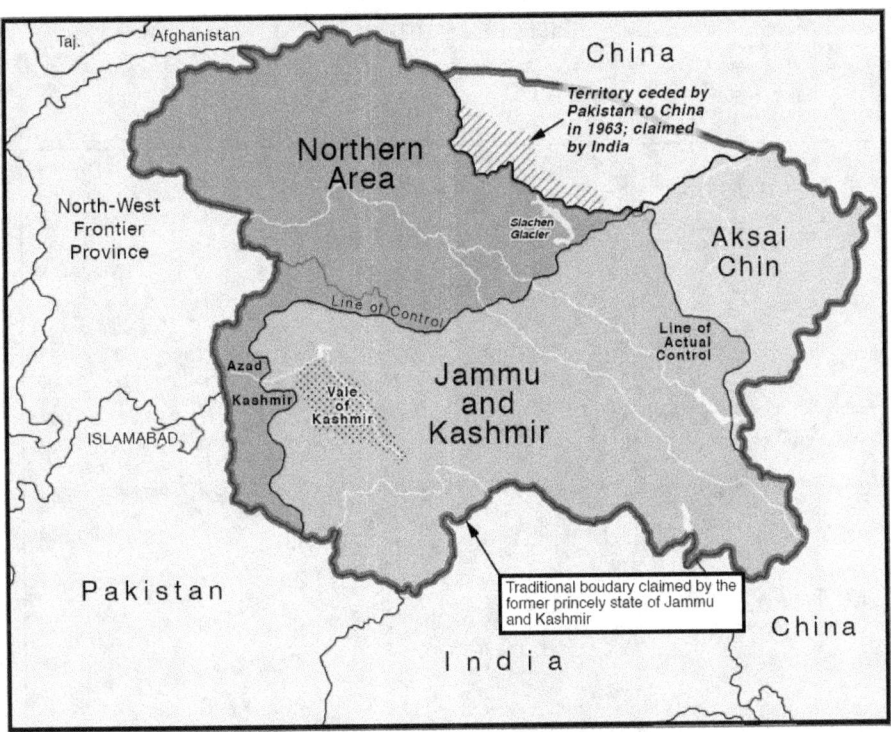

BEFORE PARTITION

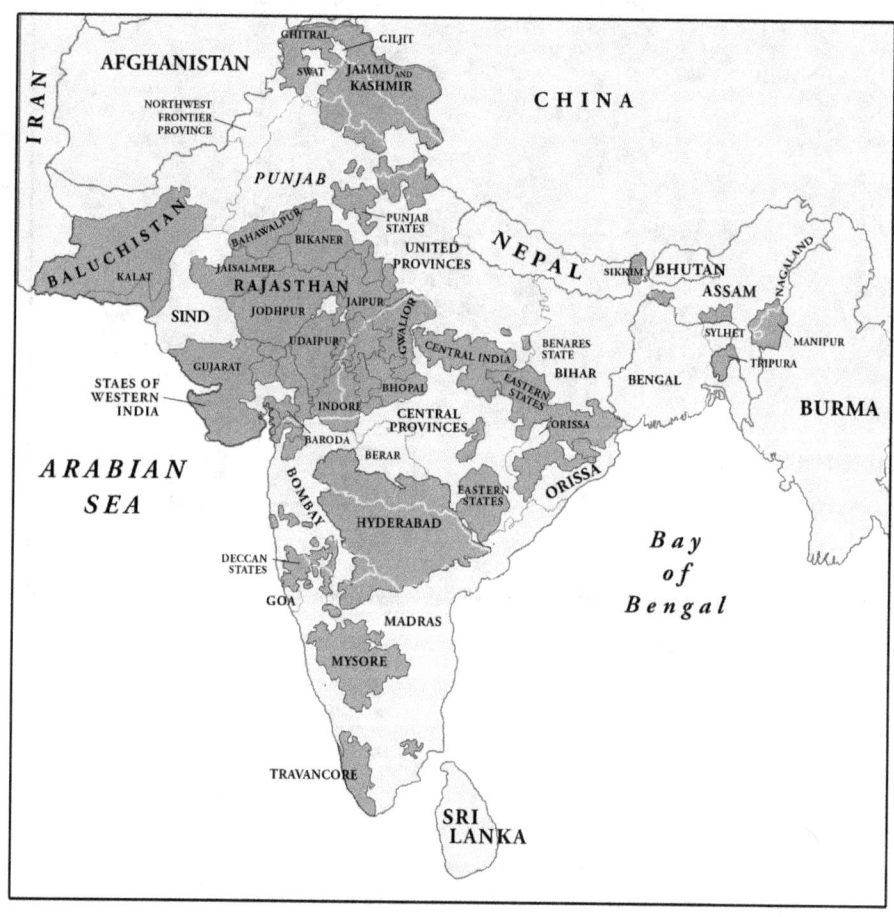

APPENDIX

AFTER PARTITION

BLOODLINES: THE IMPERIAL ROOTS OF TERRORISM IN SOUTH ASIA

Abbas, Hassan. *Pakistan's Drift into Extremism: Allah, the Army, and America's War on Terror*. Armonk: M. E. Sharpe, 2005.

Ahmad, Eqbal, and David Barsamian. *Eqbal Ahmad, Confronting Empire: Interviews with David Barsamian*; Foreword by Edward W. Said. Cambridge, MA: South End Press, 2000.

Ahmed, Ishtiaq. "The 1947 Partition of India: A Paradigm for Pathological Politics in India and Pakistan." *Asian Ethnicity 3*, no. 1 (2002): 9-28.

------. "Splitting India." *Friday Times*. Pakistan, September 20-26, 2013. Accessed September 30, 2013. http://www.thefridaytimes.com/beta3/tft/article.php?issue=20130920&page=22.

------. *The Punjab: Bloodied, Partitioned and Cleansed; Unraveling the 1947 Tragedy Through Secret British Reports and First Person Accounts*. 2nd ed. New Delhi: Rupa, 2011.

Akbar, Mobashar J. *Tinderbox: The Past and Future of Pakistan*. New Delhi: Harper Collins India, 2011.

Alavi, Hamza. "Bangladesh and the Crises of Pakistan." *Socialist Register 8*, no. 8 (1971): 289-317.

Ali, Tariq. *The Clash of Fundamentalisms: Crusades, Jihads and Modernity*. London: Verso, 2002.

------. *The Duel: Pakistan on the Flight Path of American Power*. New York: Scribner, 2008.

Amin, Tahir. "Afghan Resistance: Past, Present, and Future." *Asian Survey* 24, no. 4 (1984): 373-399.

Anderson, Perry. "Gandhi Center Stage." *London Review of Books* 34, no. 13 (2012): 3-11. Accessed August 9, 2012. http://www.lrb.co.uk/v34/n13/perry-anderson/gandhi-centre-stage

Appadurai, Arjun. "Number in the Colonial Imagination," in *Orientalism and the Postcolonial Predicament: Perspectives on South Asia*, edited by C. A. Breckenridge, and P. V. D. Veer, 314-339. Philadelphia: University of Pennsylvania Press, 1993.

Armajani, Jon. *Modern Islamist Movements: History, Religion, and Politics.* Chichester, West Sussex: Wiley-Blackwell, 2011.

Baber, Zaheer. "Race, Religion and Riots The Racialization of Communal Identity and Conflict in India." *Sociology* 38, no.4 (2004): 701-708.

Bagchi, Amiya Kumar. "The Other Side of Foreign Investment by Imperial Powers: Transfer of Surplus from Colonies." *Economic and Political Weekly* 37, no. 23 (2002): 2229-2238.

------. *Perilous Passage: Mankind and the Global Ascendancy of Capital.* Lanham: Rowman and Littlefield Publishers, 2008.

Bajoria, Jayshree. "The ISI and Terrorism: Behind the Accusations". *Center on Foreign Relations*, May 4, 2011. Accessed July 8, 2011. http://www.cfr.org/pakistan/isi-terrorism-behind-accusations/p11644.

Bajoria, Jayshee, and Esther Pan. "The U.S.-India Nuclear Deal." *Center for Foreign Relations.* November 5, 2010. Accessed September 21, 2014. http://www.cfr.org/india/us-india-nuclear-deal/p9663.

Balz, Dan, Bob Woodward, and Jeff Himmelman. "Afghan Campaign's Blueprint Emerges." *Washington Post*, January 29, 2002. Accessed October 9, 2011, http://www.washingtonpost.com/wp-dyn/content/article/2006/07/18/AR2006071800687_5.html.

Barfield, Thomas. *Afghanistan: A Cultural and Political History.* Princeton Studies in Muslim Politics. Princeton: Princeton University Press, 2012.

------. *The Durand Line: History, Consequences, and Future.* Istanbul: American Institute of Afghanistan Studies and The Hollings Center for International Dialogue, 2007.

Bass, Gary J. *The Blood Telegram: Nixon, Kissinger, and a Forgotten Genocide.* New York: Knopf, 2013.

Bayly, Christopher A. *Indian Society and the Making of the British Empire.* The New Cambridge History of India. 2nd ed. Cambridge, UK: Cambridge University Press, 1988.

------. "The Pre-history of 'Communalism'? Religious Conflict in India." *Modern Asian Studies* 9, no. 2 (1985): 177-203.

BIBLIOGRAPHY

Bayly, Christopher A., and Tim Harper. *Forgotten Armies: The Fall of British Asia, 1941-1945*. Cambridge, MA: Belknap Press of Harvard University Press, 2005.

Bayly, Susan. *Caste, Society and Politics in India from the Eighteenth Century to the Modern Age*. The New Cambridge History of India. New York: Cambridge University Press, 2001.

Belasco, Amy. "The Cost of Iraq, Afghanistan, and Other Global War on Terror Operations Since 9/11." Congressional Research Service. March 29, 2011. Accessed October 1, 2011. http://fas.org/sgp/crs/natsec/RL33110.pdf.

Bennett-Jones, Owen. *Pakistan: Eye of the Storm*. 3rd ed. New Haven: Yale University Press, 2009.

Bhatia, Michael V., and Mark Sedra. *Afghanistan, Arms and Conflict: Armed Groups, Disarmament and Security in a Post-War Society*. Contemporary Security Studies. Abingdon, Oxon: Routledge, 2008.

Bhattacharya, F. "East Bengal," in *A History of Pakistan and its Creation*, edited by C. Jafferlot, 39-60. London: Anthem Press, 2002.

Bilmes, Linda J. "The Financial Legacy of Iraq and Afghanistan: How Wartime Spending Decisions Will Constrain Future National Security Budgets." *Harvard Kennedy School Faculty Research Working Paper Series*, RWP13-006, 1-22. 2013.

Blom, Amelie. "Pakistan: Coercion and Capital in an 'Insecurity State.'" *Paris Papers* 1 (2011): 1-64.

Bose, Sumantra. *Contested Lands: Israel-Palestine, Kashmir, Bosnia, Cyprus, and Sri Lanka*. Cambridge, MA: Harvard University Press, 2010.

------. *Kashmir: Roots of Conflict, Paths to Peace*. Cambridge, MA: Harvard University Press, 2003.

Bourke-White, Margaret. *Halfway to Freedom: A Report on the New India in the Words and Photographs of Margaret Bourke-White*. New York: Simon and Schuster, 1949.

Braithwaite, Rodric. *Afgantsy: The Russians in Afghanistan, 1979-89*. London: Profile Books, 2011.

Brantlinger, Patrick. *Rule of Darkness: British Literature and Imperialism, 1830-1914*. Ithaca: Cornell University Press, 1990.

Brass, Paul R. "The Partition of India and Retributive Genocide in the Punjab, 1946-47: Means, Methods, and Purposes." *Journal of Genocide Research* (2003).

Brendon, Piers. *The Decline and Fall of the British Empire, 1781-1997*. New York: Alfred A. Knopf, 2008.

Breuilly, John. *Nationalism and the State*. 2nd ed. Chicago: University of Chicago Press, 1994.

Bryant, G. J. "Indigenous Mercenaries in the Service of European Imperialists: The Case of the Sepoys in the Early British Indian Army, 1750-1800." *War in History* 7 (2000): 2-28.

Burke, Jason. *Al-Qaeda: Casting a Shadow of Terror*. London: I. B. Tauris, 2003.

Butalia, Uravashi. *The Other Side of Silence: Voices from the Partition of India*. Durham: Duke University Press Books, 2000.

Byman, Daniel. *Deadly Connections: States that Sponsor Terrorism*. New York: Cambridge University Press, 2005.

Carpenter, Ted G. "The Unintended Consequences of Afghanistan." *World Policy Journal* 11, no. 1 (1994): 76-87.

Carroll, James. *Constantine's Sword: The Church and the Jews: A History*. Boston: Houghton Mifflin, 2001.

Carter, Lionel. *Punjab Politics 1 January 1944-3 March 1947: Last Years of the Ministries, Governors Fortnightly Reports and Other Key Documents*. New Delhi: Manohar, 2006.

Center For Global Development. "Aid to Pakistan by the Numbers." Accessed September 21, 2014. http://www.cgdev.org/page/aid-pakistan-numbers.

Chadbourne, Melissa. "U.S. Policy Toward Afghanistan and Pakistan: Implications for the U.S. and Its Allies." *Johns Hopkins School of Advanced International Studies*. Spring (2009), 1-2.

Chari, P. R., Pervaiz I. Cheema, and Stephen P. Cohen. *Four Crises and a Peace Process: American Engagement in South Asia*. Washington: Brookings Institute Press, 2007.

Chatterjee, Amal. *Representations of India, 1740-1840: The Creation of India in the Colonial Imagination.* New York: St. Martin's Press, 1998.

Chester, Lucy P. "Boundary Commissions as Tools to Safeguard British Interests at the End of Empire." *Journal of Historical Geography* 34, no. 3 (2008): 494-515.

------. "Drawing the Indo-Pakistani Boundary During the 1947 Partition of South Asia." *Yale University*, 2002.

------. "The Mapping of Empire: French and British Cartographies of India in the Late-Eighteenth Century." *Portuguese Studies* 16 (2000).

------. "Parting of the Ways." *History Today* 50, no. 3 (2000): 40-43.

Clarke, Ryan. "Lashkar-I-Taiba: The Fallacy of Subservient Proxies and the Future of Islamist Terrorism in India." *The Letort Papers.* Strategic Studies Institute, 2010.

Cohen, Stephen P. *The Idea of Pakistan.* 2nd ed. Washington: Brookings Institution Press, 2004.

Cohn, Bernard S. "The British in Benaras". *Comparative Studies in Society and History* 4: 2 (Published online, 2009).

------. "The Census, Social Structure and Objectification in South Asia," in *An Anthropologist among the Historians and Other Essays*, XX-XX. Delhi: Oxford University Press, 1987.

Coll, Steve. "The Back Channel: India and Pakistan's Secret Kashmir Talks." *New Yorker* 38 (2009). Accessed August 9, 2010, http://www.newyorker.com/magazine/2009/03/02/the-back-channel.

------. *Ghost Wars: The Secret History of the CIA, Afghanistan, and Bin Laden, from the Soviet Invasion to September 10, 2001.* New York: Penguin Books, 2004.

Cooley, John. *Unholy Wars: Afghanistan, America and International Terrorism.* 2nd ed. London: Pluto Press, 2002.

Copley, Antony. *Religions in Conflict: Ideology, Cultural Contact and Conversion in Late Colonial India.* New Delhi: Oxford University Press, 2011.

Cordesman, Anthony. "The Reality Beyond Zero and 10,000: Choosing a Meaningful Option in Afghanistan." *Center for Strategic and International Studies (CSIS)*. February 4, 2014. Accessed March 5, 2014. http://csis.org/publication/reality-beyond-zero-and-10000-choosing-meaningful-option-afghanistan.

------. "The U.S. Cost of the Afghanistan War: FY2002-FY2013. Cost in Military Operating Expenditures and Aid and Prospects for 'Transition.'" *Center for Strategic and International Studies (CSIS)* Report. 2012.

Cordovez, Diego, and Selig S. Harrison. *Out of Afghanistan: The Inside Story of the Soviet Withdrawal*. New York: Oxford University Press, 1995.

Cragin, R. Kim. "Early History of Al-Qa'ida." *The Historical Journal* 51, no.4 (2008): 1047-1067.

Cruickshank, Paul. *The Militant Pipeline Between the Afghanistan-Pakistan Border Region and the West*. Counterterrorism Strategy Initiative Policy Paper, 2010.

Daechsel, Markus. "Military Islamisation in Pakistan and the Spectre of Colonial Perceptions." *Contemporary Southeast Asia* 6, no. 2 (1997): 141-160.

Dalrymple, William. *The Last Mughal: The Fall of a Dynasty, Delhi, 1857*. London: Bloomsbury, 2007.

------. *White Mughals: Love and Betrayal in Eighteenth-century India*. New York: Penguin, 2004.

DeYoung, Karen. "Obama to Leave 9,800 Troops in Afghanistan," *Washington Post*, May 27, 2014. Accessed June 5, 2014.

Dirks, Nicholas B. *The Scandal of Empire India and the Creation of Imperial Britain*. Cambridge, MA: Belknap Press of Harvard University Press, 2006.

Dorronsoro, G. *Revolution Unending: Afghanistan, 1979 to the Present*. CERI Series in Comparative Politics and International Studies. London: C. Hurst, 2005.

Dutta, Sunil. "Bin Laden, Pakistan and the End of Terrorism." *Los Angeles Daily News*, May 7, 2011.

------ "Clash of Identities: the Reason for India-Pakistan Conflict?" *Pakistan Daily Times*, May, 21, 2012.

------. "Viewpoints: End to Afghan War Must Involve India, Pakistan." *Sacramento Bee*, July 20, 2010.

Eaton, Richard M. *A Social History of the Deccan, 1300-1761: Eight Indian Lives*. The New Cambridge History of India. Cambridge: Cambridge University Press, 2008.

Editorial, "Obama's Troubled Handling of Afghanistan." *Washington Post*, March 13, 2012. Accessed September 29, 2013. http://www.washingtonpost.com/opinions/obamas-troubled-handling-of-afghanistan/2012/03/13/gIQAYN6NAS_story.html.

Edwards, David B. *Before Taliban: Genealogies of the Afghan Jihad*. Berkeley and Los Angeles: University of California Press, 2001.

Emadi, Hafisullah. "Durand Line and Afghan-Pak Relations." *Economic and Political Weekly* 25, no. 28 (1990): 1515-1516.

Evans, Alexander. "The Kashmir Insurgency: As Bad as It Gets." *Small Wars and Insurgencies* 11, no. 1 (2000): 69-81.

Ewans, Martin. *Conflict in Afghanistan: Studies in Asymmetric Warfare*. Abingdon, Oxon: Routledge, 2005.

Fair, C. Christine. *Fighting to the End: The Pakistan Army's Way of War*. New York: Oxford University Press, 2014.

------. "Lashkar-e-Tayiba and the Pakistani State." *Survival* 53, no. 4 (2011): 29-52.

------. "The Militant Challenge in Pakistan." *Asia Policy* 11 (2011): 105-137.

------. "Militants in the Conflicts: Myths, Realities, and Impacts," in *Asymmetric Warfare in South Asia: The Causes and Consequences of the Kargil Conflict*, 233. New York: Cambridge University Press, 2009.

------. "Pakistan's Partial War on Terror: The Deadly Results of Cooperation with Terrorists." *Wall Street Journal*, October 9, 2009. Accessed October 20, 2011. http://online.wsj.com/articles/SB10001424052748704107204574470004052709162.

------. "Ten Fictions that Pakistani Defense Officials Love to Peddle. War on the Rocks, Analysis. 2014. Accessed March 14, 2014, http://warontherocks.com/2014/01/ten-fictions-that-pakistani-defense-officials-love-to-peddle/.

------. "Time for Sober Realism Renegotiating U.S. Relations with Pakistan." *Washington Quarterly* 32, no. 2 (2009): 149-172.

Fayyaz, Shabana. "Towards a Durable Peace in Waziristan." *Pakistan Security Research Unit (PSRU)*. Brief Number 10, 2007.

Fisk, Robert. "Was He Betrayed? Of Course. Pakistan Knew bin Laden's Hiding Place All Along." *The Independent*, 2011. Accessed May 4, 2011. http://www.independent.co.uk/opinion/commentators/fisk/robert-fisk-was-he-betrayed-of-course-pakistan-knew-bin-ladens-hiding-place-all-along-2278028.html.

Freitag, S. B. *Collective Action and Community: Public Arenas and the Emergence of Communalism in North India*. Berkeley and Los Angeles: University of California Press, 1990.

Fremont-Barnes, Gregory. *The Indian Mutiny 1857-58*. Essential Histories. Oxford: Osprey Publishing, 2007.

"Frontier Crimes Regulation Amended: Political Activities Allowed in FATA." *Daily Times*, August 13, 2011.

Gall, Carlotta. "Former Pakistani Officer Embodies a Policy Puzzle." *New York Times,* 2010. Accessed October 12, 2013. http://www.nytimes.com/2010/03/04/world/asia/04imam.html?_r=0;.

------. *The Wrong Enemy: America in Afghanistan, 2001-2014*. Boston: Houghton Mifflin Harcourt, 2014.

Gandhi, Indira. *India: Speeches and Reminiscences*. Hodder, Stoughton, 1975.

Ganguly, Sumit. *Conflict Unending: India-Pakistan Tensions Since 1947*. New York: Columbia University Press, 2001.

------. "Pakistan's Slide Into Misery: Exploring a Half-Century of Misrule." *Foreign Affairs* 81, no. 6 (2002): 1068-1095.

Ganguly, Sumit, and Nicholas Howenstein. "India Pakistan Rivalry in Afghanistan." *Journal of International Affairs* 63, no. 1 (2009): 127-40.

Ganguly, Sumit, and S. Paul Kapur. "The Sorcerer's Apprentice: Islamist Militancy in South Asia." *Washington Quarterly* 33, no. 1 (2010): 47-59.

Gartenstein-Ross, Daveed, and Tara Vassefi. "The Forgotten History of Afghanistan-Pakistan Relations." *Yale Journal of International Affairs* 7, no. 1 (2012): 38-45.

Gerges, Fawaz A. *The Far Enemy: Why Jihad Went Global.* 2nd ed. New York: Cambridge University Press, 2009.

------. *The Rise and Fall of Al-Qaeda.* New York: Oxford University Press, 2011.

Ghufran, Nasreen. "Pashtun Ethnonationalism and the Taliban Insurgency in the North West Frontier Province of Pakistan." *Asian Survey* 49, no. 6 (2009): 1092-1114.

Girardet, Edward. *Killing the Cranes: A Reporter's Journey Through Three Decades of War in Afghanistan.* White River Junction, VT: Chelsea Green, 2011.

Government of India, Ministry of Home Affairs, Office of the Registrar General and Census Commission. "Distribution of Population by Religion", 2001, Table 21. Accessed March 6, 2012. http://censusindia.gov.in/(S(4o3ma155tb55nv55ppd1dn55))/Census_And_You/religion.aspx.

Green, W. A., and J. Deasy. "Unifying Themes in the History of British India, 1757-1857: An Historiographical Analysis." *Albion: A Quarterly Journal Concerned with British Studies* 17, no. 1 (1985): 15-45.

Gress, Michael A., and Lester W. Grau. *The Soviet-Afghan War: How a Superpower Fought and Lost.* Lawrence: University Press of Kansas, 2002.

Griffin, Michael. *Reaping the Whirlwind: The Taliban Movement in Afghanistan.* London: Pluto Press, 2000.

Guardian Data Blog, "Development Data: Sixty Years of US Aid to Pakistan: Get the Data," July 11, 2011. Accessed March 15, 2014. http://www.theguardian.com/global-development/poverty-matters/2011/jul/11/us-aid-to-pakistan#start-of-comments.

Habib, Irfan. "Colonization of the Indian Economy, 1757-1900." *Social Scientist* 3, no. 8 (1975): 23-53.

------. "The Coming of 1857." *Social Scientist* 26, vol. 1/4 (1998): 6-15.

Haqqānī, Husain. *Pakistan: Between Mosque and Military.* Washington, D.C.: Carnegie Endowment for International Peace, 2005.

------. "The Role of Islam in Pakistan's Future." *Washington Quarterly* 28, no.1 (2004): 83-96.

Hasan, Khurshid. "Pakistan-Afghanistan Relations." *Asian Survey* 2, no. 7 (1962): 14-24.

Hasan, Mushirul. *India Partitioned: The Other Face of Freedom.* New York: Roli Books, 1997.

------. "The Muslim Mass Contact Campaign: An Attempt at Political Mobilisation." *Economic & Political Weekly* 21, no. 52 (1986): 2273-2277.

Hasan, S. "India and Pakistan: Common Identity and Conflict." *Refugee Survey Quarterly* 24, no. 4 (2005): 74-80.

Hegghammer, Thomas. "Abdallah Azzam and Palestine." *Welt des Islams* 53, no. 3-4 (2013): 353-387.

Hersh, Seymour M. "The Getaway: Questions Surround a Secret Pakistani Airlift." *New Yorker*, 2002.

Howenstein, Nicholas. "The Jihadi Terrain in Pakistan: An Introduction to the Sunni Jihadi Groups in Pakistan and Kashmir." Pakistan Security Research Unit (PSRU). Research Report 1 (2008): 28-31. Accessed Nov 19, 2014. http://costsofwar.org/.

Hume, R. A. "The Indian National Congress." *The Journal of Race Development* 1, no. 3 (1911): 367-371.

Hussain, T. "U.S.-Pakistan Engagement. The War on Terrorism and Beyond". *United States Institute of Peace Special Report* 145 (2005:, 1-15.

Hussain, Zahid. *Frontline Pakistan: The Path to Catastrophe and the Killing of Benazir Bhutto.* New Delhi, Delhi: Penguin Books India, 2008.

Ibrahim, Azeem. "U.S. Aid to Pakistan: U.S. Taxpayers Have Funded Pakistani Corruption." Belfer Center Discussion Paper, International Security Program. Harvard Kennedy School, 2009-06, 44, 2009. Accessed March 14, 2014. http://belfercenter.ksg.harvard.edu/files/Final_DP_2009_06_08092009.pdf.

BIBLIOGRAPHY

Indurthy, R. "Kashmir Between India and Pakistan: An Intractable Conflict, 1947 to Present" *The Beyond Intractability Project,* The Conflict Information Consortium, University of Colorado. (2003) Accessed February 2, 2012. http://www1.appstate.edu/~stefanov/Kashmir%20 Between%20India%20and%20Pakistan.pdf.

Innocent, Malou. "Pakistan and the Future of U. S. Policy." *Policy Analysis* 36 (2009): 1-25.

International Crisis Group. "Pakistan's Tribal Areas: Appeasing the Militants." *ICG Asia Report,* Report No. 125 (2006).

Iqtidar, Humeira. "Collateral Damage from the Afghanistan Wars: Jamaat-ud-Dawa and Lashkar-e-Tayaba Militancy." *Middle East Report* 251 (2009): 28-31.

Isby, D. *Afghanistan: Graveyard of Empires: A New History of the Borderland.* Rev. ed. New York: Pegasus, 2011.

Jabeen, Mussarat, Amir Chandio, and Zarina Qasim. "Language Controversy: Impacts on National Politics and Secession of East Pakistan." South Asian Studies 25, no. 1 (2010): 99-124.

Jafferlot, Christophe. "Islamic Identity and Ethnic Tension," in *A History of Pakistan and Its Origins,* edited by Christophe Jafferlot, 9-48. London: Anthem Press, 2002.

Jahan, Raunaq. "Genocide in Bangladesh," in *Century of Genocide: Eyewitness Accounts and Critical Views,* edited by S. Totten, W. S. Parsons, and I. W. C. Charny, 291-316. New York: Garland, 1997.

Jalal, Ayesha. "Conjuring Pakistan: History as Official Imagining." *International Journal of Middle East Studies* 27, no. 1 (1995): 73-89.

------. "South Asia" in *Encyclopaedia of Nationalism,* edited by A. Motyl, 1529. San Diego: Academic Press, 2000.

------. *The State of Martial Rule: The Origins of Pakistan's Political Economy of Defence.* Cambridge: Cambridge University Press, 1990.

Jamal, Arif. "Former Pakistan Army Chief Reveals Intelligence Bureau Harbored bin Laden in Abbotabad." *Terrorism Monitor. Jamestown Foundation* 9, no. 47 (2011).

------. *Shadow War: The Untold Story of Jihad in Kashmir.* Brooklyn: Melville Publishing House, 2009.

Johnson, Thomas H., and M. Chris Mason. "No Sign Until the Burst of Fire: Understanding the Pakistan-Afghanistan Frontier." *International Security* 32, no. 4 (2008): 41-77.

Jones, Seth G. "Pakistan's Dangerous Game." *Survival* 49, no.1 (2007): 15-49;

------. "The Terrorist Threat from Pakistan." *Survival* 4 (Fall 2011): 1-25.

Jones, Sir William. *The Letters of Sir William Jones.* Edited by Garland Cannon. Oxford: Clarendon Press, 1970.

Kakar, M. Hassan. *A Political And Diplomatic History of Afghanistan, 1863-190.* Brill's Inner Asian Library. Leiden: Brill Academic Publishers, 2006.

Kaplan, Robert D. "South Asia's Geography of Conflict." *Center for a New American Security Paper* (2010): 1-18.

Kapur, Ashok. *India-Pakistan Conflict An Enduring Rivalry,* edited by T. V. Paul. New York: Cambridge University Press, 2005.

Kapur, S. Paul. "The Kashmir Conflict: Past, Present, and Future," in *The Routledge Book of Asian Security Studies*, edited by Sumit Ganguly, Andrew Scobel, and Joseph Liow, 103-114. London: Routledge, 2010.

Kapur, S. Paul, and Sumit Ganguly. "The Jihad Paradox: Pakistan and Islamist Militancy in South Asia." *International Security* 37, no. 1 (2012): 111-141.

Kauman, Chaim D. "When All Else Fails: Ethnic Population Transfers and Partitions in the Twentieth Century." *International Security* 23, no. 2 (1998): 120-156.

Kaushik, Surendra N. *Contesting Identities in Pakistan: Region, Religion and the Nation-State.* Jaipur: Pointer Publishers, 2005.

Kfir, Isaac. "Pakistan and the Challenge of Islamist Terror: Where to Next." *Middle East Review of International Affairs* 12, no. 3 (2008): 1-19.

Khan, I. "Contending Identities Of Pakistan And The Issue Of Democratic Governance." *Peace and Democracy in South Asia* 2, no. 1 and 2 (2006).

Khan, M. Ayub. *Friends Not Masters, a Political Autobiography*. New York: Oxford University Press, 1967.

Khan, Mohsin. "India-Pakistan Trade Relations: A New Beginning." *New America Foundation Report* 14 (2013): 2.

Koelbl, Susanne. "Spiegel interview with Pervez Musharraf: 'Pakistan is always seen as the rogue.'" *Der Spiegel*, October 4, 2010. Accessed March 12, 2014. http://www.spiegel.de/international/world/spiegel-interview-with-pervez-musharraf-pakistan-is-always-seen-as-the-rogue-a-721110.html.

Kronstadt, K. Alan. "Pakistan-U.S. Relations: A Summary." *CRS Report for Congress*, R481832, May 16, 2011.

Kronstadt, K. Alan, and Bruce Vaughn. "Terrorism in South Asia." *CRS Report for Congress*, RL32259, December 13, 2004.

Kronstadt, K. Alan, and Susan B. Epstein. "Direct Overt US Aid and Military Reimbursements to Pakistan, FY2002-FY2015," *Congressional Research Service*, 1. 2014. Accessed April 16, 2014. fas.org/sgp/crs/row/pakaid.pdf.

Kruijtzer, Gijs. *Xenophobia in Seventeenth-Century India*. LUP Dissertaties. Leiden University Press, 2009.

Kumar, Dharma, and Meghnad Desai. *The Cambridge Economic History of India: Volume 2, c.1751-c.1970*. Cambridge, UK: Cambridge University Press, 1983.

Kundi, Mansoor A. "Politics of American Aid: The Case of Pakistan." *Asian Affairs* 29, no. 2 (2007): 22-39.

Kux, Dennis. *The United States and Pakistan, 1947-2000: Disenchanted Allies*. Washington, D.C.: Woodrow Wilson Center Press, 2001.

Lamb, Alastair. *Incomplete Partition: The Genesis of the Kashmir Dispute, 1947-1948*. New York: Oxford University Press, 2002.

Lange, Matthew, and Andrew Dawson. "Dividing and Ruling the World? A Statistical Test of the Effects of Colonialism on Postcolonial Civil Violence." *Social Forces* 88, no. 2 (2009): 785-817.

Larson, Gerald J. *India's Agony Over Religion*. SUNY Series in Religious Studies. Albany: State University of New York Press, 1995.

Lavoy, Peter R. *Asymmetric Warfare in South Asia: The Causes and Consequences of the Kargil Conflict*. New York: Cambridge University Press, 2009.

Lieberman, Samuel S. "Afghanistan: Population and Development in the Land of Insolence." *Population and Development Review* 6, no. 2 (1980): 271-298.

Lieven, Anatol. *Pakistan: A Hard Country.* New York: Public Affairs, 2011.

Macaulay, Thomas Babington. "Minute recorded in the General Department by Thomas Babington Macaulay, law member of the governor-general's council, dated 2 February 1835," in *The Great Indian Education Debate: Documents Relating to the Orientalist-Anglicist Controversy, 1781-1843*, edited by Lynn Zastoupil and Martin Moir, 165-66. Abindon, Oxon: Routledge, 2013.

Mahadevan, Prem. "The Paradoxes of Ethnographic Intelligence: A Case Study of British India." *Faultlines* 20 (2011) Accessed October 12, 2012. http://www.satp.org/satporgtp/publication/faultlines/volume20/Article1.htm.

Mahdavy, Hossein. "Patterns and Problems of Economic Development in Rentier States: The Case of Iran," in *Studies in the Economic History of the Middle-East: From the Rise of Islam to the Present Day*, edited by M.A. Cook. Oxford: Oxford University Press, 1970.

Maley, William. *The Afghanistan Wars*. 2nd ed. New York: Palgrave Macmillan, 2002.

Mamdani, Mahmood. *Good Muslim, Bad Muslim: America, the Cold War, and the Roots of Terror*. New York: Pantheon, 2004.

Markey, Daniel. "A False Choice in Pakistan." *Foreign Affairs* 86, no. 4 (2007): 85-102.

Marshall, Peter James. *Bengal, The British Bridgehead: Eastern India, 1740-1828*. 2nd ed. Cambridge, UK: Cambridge University Press, 2006.

Mascarenhas, Anthony. *The Rape of Bangla Desh*. New Delhi: Vikas Publications, 1971.

Mcleod, Duncan. "India and Pakistan: Friends, Rivals Or Enemies?" *Pakistan Security Research Unit (PSRU)*. Brief Number 45 (2008): 1-19.

McMahon, Robert J. *The Cold War on the Periphery: The United States, India, and Pakistan.* New York: Columbia University Press, 1994.

------. "United States Cold War Strategy in South Asia: Making a Military Commitment to Pakistan, 1947-1954." *The Journal of American History* 75, no. 3 (1988): 812-840.

Metcalf, Thomas R. *Ideologies of the Raj.* The New Cambridge History of India. Volume 3, pt 4. Cambridge: Cambridge University Press, 1997.

Meyer, Karl E. "The Invention of Pakistan: How the British Raj Sundered." *World Policy Journal* 20, no. 1 (2003): 77-92.

Misdaq, Nabi. *Afghanistan: Political Frailty and External Interference.* Routledge Studies in Middle Eastern History. Abingdon, Oxon: Routledge, 2006.

Moon, Penderel. *Divide and Quit.* Great Britain: Chatto and Windus, 1963.

Morris-Jones, W. H. "Thirty-Six Years Later: The Mixed Legacies of Mountbatten's Transfer of Power." *International Affairs* 59, no. 4 (1983): 621-628.

Mosley, Leonard O. *The Last Days of the British Raj.* Jaico, 1971.

Mozaffari, M. "What is Islamism? History and Definition of a Concept." *Totalitarian Movements and Political Religions* 8, no. 1 (2007): 17-33.

Mukerjee, Madhusree. "Wreath for an Imperial Famine." *Huffington Post Online*, 2013. Accessed October 3, 2013. http://www.huffingtonpost.com/madhusree-mukerjee/wreath-for-an-imperial-famine_b_3690185.html.

Mukerjee, Madhusree. *Churchill's Secret War: The British Empire and the Ravaging of India During World War II.* New York: Basic Books, 2011.

Mukherjee, Aditya. "Empire: How Colonial India Made Modern Britain." *Economic and Political Weekly* 45, no. 50 (2010): 74.

Mukherjee, Rudrangshu. *Spectre of Violence: The 1857 Kanpur Massacres.* New Delhi: Vikas, 1998.

Nandal, Randeep S. "State Data Refutes Claim of 1 Lakh Killed in Kashmir." *Times of India*, 2011. Accessed October 9, 2013. http://timesofindia.indiatimes.com/india/State-data-refutes-claim-of-1-lakh-killed-in-Kashmir/articleshow/8918214.cms.

Nandy, Ashis. *Intimate Enemy: Loss and Recovery of Self Under Colonialism*. Delhi: Oxford University Press, 1983.

Nasr, Vali. "National Identities and the India-Pakistan Conflict," in *India-Pakistan Conflict: An Enduring Rivalry*, edited by T. V. Paul, 179. New York: Cambridge University Press, 2005.

Nawaz, S. *Crossed Swords: Pakistan, Its Army, and the Wars Within*. Karachi: Oxford University Press, 2008.

Nelson, Dean. "Pakistani President Asif Zardari Admits Creating Terrorist Groups." *Daily Telegraph*, July 8, 2009. Accessed March 12, 2014. http://www.telegraph.co.uk/news/worldnews/asia/pakistan/5779916/Pakistani-president-Asif-Zardari-admits-creating-terrorist-groups.html.

Obama, Barack. "President Obama Speaks on U.S. Counterterrorism Strategy at the National Defense University." Washington, D.C.: White House Press Release, May 23, 2013. http://www.whitehouse.gov/the-press-office/2013/05/23/remarks-president-national-defense-university.

Oldenburg, Philip. "'A Place Insufficiently Imagined': Language, Belief, and the Pakistan Crisis of 1971." *The Journal of Asian Studies* 44, no. 4 (1985): 711-733.

Page, David. *Prelude to Partition: The Indian Muslims and the Imperial System of Control*. New Delhi: Oxford University Press India, 1999.

"Pakistan Looking Forward to Cooperation in Civil Nuclear Energy: Nawaz," *Express Tribune*, March 24, 2014.

Pandey, Gyanendra. *The Construction of Communalism in Colonial North India*. 2nd ed. New Delhi: Oxford University Press, 2006.

------. "Remembering Partition: Violence, Nationalism and History in India." *Social Scientist* 32, no. 1/2 (2004): 77-80.

Panigrahi, Devendra. *India's Partition: The Story of Imperialism in Retreat*. London: Routledge, 2004.

Parsons, Christi, and David Cloud. "U.S. to Reduce Troop Level in Afghanistan to 9,800 by Year's End," *Los Angeles Times*, May 28, 2014. Accessed May 29, 2014. http://www.latimes.com/world/afghanistan-pakistan/la-fg-obama-troops-afghanistan-20140528-story.html#page=1.

Paul, Thaza V. "Causes of the India-Pakistan Enduring Rivalry," in *The India-Pakistan Conflict: An Enduring Rivalry*, edited by T. V. Paul, New York: Cambridge University Press, 2005. 3-24.

Pennington, B. *Was Hinduism Invented? Britons, Indians, and the Colonial Construction of Religion*. New York: Oxford University Press, 2004.

Perkovich, George. "Stop Enabling Pakistan's Dangerous Dysfunction." *Carnegie Endowment for International Peace Policy Outlook*. 2011. Accessed October 10, 2011, http://carnegieendowment.org/2011/09/06/stop-enabling-pakistan-s-dangerous-dysfunction/8klt.http://carnegieendowment.org/2011/09/06/stop-enabling-pakistan-s-dangerous-dysfunction/8klt.

Pew Research Global Attitudes Project. "U.S. Image in Pakistan Falls No Further Following bin Laden Killing." 2011. Accessed January 17, 2012. http://www.pewglobal.org/2011/06/21/u-s-image-in-pakistan-falls-no-further-following-bin-laden-killing/.

Racine, Jean-Luc. "Living with India: Relations Between Pakistan and India," in *A History of Pakistan and Its Origins*, edited by C. Jafferlot, London: Anthem Press, 2002. 112-133.

------. "Pakistan in the Game of the Great Powers," in *A History of Pakistan and Its Origins*, edited by C. Jafferlot. Anthem Press, 2002.

Rahman, S. "Bangladesh: Political Culture and Heritage," in *Government and Politics in South Asia: Sixth Edition*, edited by Y. K. Malik, M. Lawoti, S. Rahman, et. al., 235-250. Boulder: Westview Press, 2008.

Rahman, Tariq. "Madrasas: the Potential for Violence in Pakistan," in *Madrasas in South Asia: Teaching Terror?* Edited by J. Malik, 61-84. Routledge Contemporary South Asia. London: Routledge, 2007.

Ramusack, Barbara N. *The Indian Princes and Their States*. The New Cambridge History of India, Volume 3, Part 6. Cambridge: Cambridge University Press, 2004.

Rasanayagam, Angelo. *Afghanistan: A Modern History: Monarchy, Despotism or Democracy? The Problem of Governance in the Muslim Tradition*. Rev. ed. U.K.: I.B. Tauris, 2005.

Rashid, Ahmed. *Descent into Chaos: The U.S. and the Disaster in Pakistan, Afghanistan, and Central Asia*. New York: Penguin Books, 2009.

------. *Pakistan on the Brink: The Future of America, Pakistan, and Afghanistan.* New York: Viking Adult, 2012.

------. *Taliban: Militant Islam, Oil And Fundamentalism In Central Asia.* 5th ed. New Haven: Yale University Press, 2000.

Rawat, Ramesh. "Perception of 1857." *Social Scientist* 35, no. 11/12 (2007): 15-28.

Ray, Anil B. "Communal Attitudes to British Policy: The Case of the Partition of Bengal 1905." *Social Scientist* 6, no. 5 (1977): 34-46.

Raychaudhuri, Tapan, and Irfan Habib. *The Cambridge Economic History of India. Volume 2, c.1200-c.1750.* Cambridge, UK: Cambridge University Press, 1983.

Read, Anthony, and David Fisher. *The Proudest Day: India's Long Road to Independence.* New York: W. W. Norton, 1998.

Report of the Commissioners Appointed to Inquire into the Organisation of the Indian Army with Minutes of Evidence and Appendix (1859). Report of the Peel Commission. Punjab Committee recommendations quoted in 'Precis of Replies to Questions Having Reference to the Native Infantry of the Bengal Army' by Lieutenant Colonel H.M. Durand, 4 September 1848, in Appendix 71, p 540, in the Report of the Commissioners Appointed to Inquire into the Organization of the Indian Army; together with Minutes of Evidence and Appendix in PP, Cmd. 2515, 1859, Session 1, Vol. 5.

Richards, John F. *The Mughal Empire.* New Cambridge History of India. Cambridge: Cambridge University Press, 1996.

Riedel, Bruce O. *Deadly Embrace: Pakistan, America, and the Future of the Global Jihad.* Washington, D.C.: Brookings Institution Press, 2012.

------. "Pakistan and Terror: The Eye of the Storm." *Annals of the American Academy of Political and Social Science* 618: 31-45.

Rizvi, Hasan-Aaskari. *Military, State and Society in Pakistan.* Houndmills: Palgrave Macmillan, 2000.

Robb, Peter. *A History of India.* Houndmills: Palgrave Macmillan, 2002.

Robins, Nick. *The Corporation That Changed the World How the East India Company Shaped the Modern Multinational.* 2nd ed. London: Pluto Press, 2012.

Robinson, Francis. "The British Empire and Muslim Identity in South Asia." *Transactions of the Royal Historical Society (Sixth Series)* 8 (1998): 271-289.

Roy, Kaushik. "Military Loyalty in the Colonial Context: A Case Study of the Indian Army During World War II." *Journal of Military History* 73 (2009): 497-529.

Roy, O. "Islam and Foreign Policy: Central Asia and the Arab-Persian World," in *A History of Pakistan and its Origins*, edited by C. Jafferlot, 134-148. London: Anthem Press, 2002.

Rubin, Alissa. "Retiring Envoy to Afghanistan Exhorts U.S. to Heed Its Past." *New York Times*, July 28, 2012. Accessed July 29, 2012. https://www.nytimes.com/2012/07/29/world/asia/ambassador-crocker-sees-fraught-foreign-landscape-ahead.html?pagewanted=all&_r=0.

Rubin, Barnett R., and Abubakar Siddique. *Resolving the Pakistan-Afghanistan Stalemate.* United States Institute of Peace, Special Report, 2006.

Rummel, Rudolph J. *Statistics of Democide: Genocide and Mass Murder Since 1900.* LIT Verlag Münster, 1998. Accessed March 3, 2013. http://www.hawaii.edu/powerkills/SOD.CHAP8.HTM.

Said, Edward W. *Orientalism.* New York: Vintage Books, 1979.

Saikal, Amin. *Modern Afghanistan: A History of Struggle and Survival.* London: IB Tauris, 2004.

Sarila, N. S. *The Shadow of the Great Game: The Untold Story of India's Partition.* New York: Carroll, Graff Publishers, 2005.

Schaffer, T. C., and Schaffer, H. B., *How Pakistan Negotiates with the United States: Riding the Roller Coaster,* Cross-Cultural Negotiation Books. Washington: United States Institute of Peace, 2011.

Schmidt, John R. *The Unraveling: Pakistan in the Age of Jihad.* New York: Farrar, Straus and Giroux, 2011.

Schofield, V. *Afghan Frontier.* London: Tauris Parke Paperbacks, 2004.

Schofield, V. *Kashmir in Conflict: India, Pakistan and the Unending War.* London: Tauris Parke Paperbacks, 2010.

Shafique, Atif, "The Case for Constructivism in Analyzing the India-Pakistan Conflict," *E-International Relations,* September 7, 2011. Accessed October 11, 2012, http://www.e-ir.info/?p=13716.

Shah, Aqil. "Pakistan's Quest for Security," in *The Routledge Handbook of Asian Security Studies,* edited by S. Ganguly, A. Scobell, and J. Liow. Routledge Handbooks. London: Routledge, 2010.

Shahrani, Nazif M. "War, Factionalism, and the State in Afghanistan." *American Anthropologist New Series* 104, no. 3 (2002): 715-722.

Shahzad, Syed S. *Inside Al-Qaeda and the Taliban: Beyond Bin Laden and 9/11.* London: Pluto Press, 2011.

Shaikh, Farzana. *Making Sense of Pakistan.* New York: Columbia University Press, 2009.

Sharpe, Jenny. "The Unspeakable Limits of Rape: Colonial Violence and Counter-Insurgency." *Genders* 10 (1991): 25-46.

Siddiqa, Ayesha. "Pakistan's Counterterrorism Strategy: Separating Friends from Enemies." *Washington Quarterly* 34, no. 1 (2011): 149-162.

Siddiqi, Shibil. "Afghanistan-Pakistan Relations: History and Geopolitics in a Regional and International Context: Implications for Canadian Foreign Policy." *Walter and Duncan Gordon Foundation* (2009): 1-55.

Sisson and Rose. *War and Secession: Pakistan, India, and the Creation of Bangladesh.* Berkeley: University of California Press, 1991.

Smith, David O. "Facing Up to the Trust Deficit: The Key to an Enhanced U.S.–Pakistan Defense Relationship." *Strategic Insights* VI, no.4 (2007).

Soherwordi, Syed H. S. "'Punjabisation' in the British Indian Army 1857–1947 and the Advent of Military Rule in Pakistan." *Edinburgh Papers in South Asian Studies* 24 (2010).

Spilsbury, Julian. *The Indian Mutiny.* Great Britain: Widenfeld & Nicolson, 2007.

Staniland, Paul. "Caught in the Muddle: America's Pakistan Strategy." *Washington Quarterly* 34, no. 1 (2011): 133-48.

Stockholm International Peace Research Institute, SIPRI Military Expenditure Database, http://milexdata.sirpi.org.

Streets, Heather. "The Rebellion of 1857: Origins, Consequences, and Themes." *Teaching South Asia: An Internet Journal of Pedagogy* I, no. 1, (Winter 2001) http://www.sdstate.edu/projectsouthasia/Resources/upload/The-Rebellion-of-1857-Streets.pdf.

Strindberg, Anders, and Mats Wärn. *Islamism: Religion, Radicalization, and Resistance.* Cambridge, UK: Polity, 2011.

Subramanian, Samanth. "The Long View: the Partition Before Partition." *New York Times*, October 3, 2011. Accessed November 12, 2012, http://india.blogs.nytimes.com/2011/10/03/the-long-view-the-partition-before-partition/?_r=0.

Swami, Praveen. "Kashmir: Fewer Troops, More Peace." *The Hindu*, 2014. Accessed March 4, 2014,. http://www.thehindu.com/todays-paper/tp-opinion/kashmir-fewer-troops-more-peace/article5598893.ece?css=print.

------. *India, Pakistan and the Secret Jihad: The Covert War in Kashmir, 1947-2004* Asian Security Studies. Abingdon, Oxon: Routledge, 2007

Talbot, Ian. *India and Pakistan: Inventing the Nation.* London: Arnold, 2000.

------. *Pakistan: A Modern History.* 2nd ed. Houndmills: Palgrave Macmillan, 2009.

------. "Religion and Violence: the Historical Context for Conflict in Pakistan," in *Religion and Violence in South Asia: Theory and Practice,* edited by J. R. Hinnells and R. King, 147-163. New York: Routledge, 2007.

Talbot, Ian, and Gurharpal Singh. *The Partition of India.* New Approaches to Asian History. Cambridge, UK: Cambridge University Press, 2009.

Talbot, P. "The Subcontinent: Menage a Trois." *Foreign Affairs* 50, no. 4 (1972): 698-710.

Taleb, Nassim Nicholas. *The Black Swan: The Impact of the Highly Improbable.* 2nd ed. New York: Random House, 2010.

Taleb, Nicholas Nassim, and Mark Blyth. "The Black Swan of Cairo: How Suppressing Volatility Makes the World Less Predictable and More Dangerous." *Foreign Affairs* 90, no. 3 (2011): 33-39.

Tankel, Stephen. "Domestic Barriers to Dismantling the Militant Infrastructure in Pakistan." *United States Institute of Peace Report* 89 (2013): 59.

Tellis, Ashley J. "Pakistan and the War on Terror: Conflicted Goals, Compromised Performance." *Carnegie Endowment for International Peace* (2008): 1-57.

Thapar, Romila. "Imagined Religious Communities? Ancient History and the Modern Search for a Hindu Identity." *Modern Asian Studies* 23, vol. 2 (1989): 209-231.

------. "Tyranny of Labels." *Social Scientist* 24, vol. 9/10 (1996): 3-23.

The Guardian, Development Data: Datablog, "Sixty Years of US Aid to Pakistan: Get the Data." (July 11, 2011). http://www.theguardian.com/global-development/poverty-matters/2011/jul/11/us-aid-to-pakistan#start-of-comments.

The White House. "White Paper of the Interagency Policy Group's Report on U.S. Policy Toward Afghanistan and Pakistan." Lanham: Federal Information & News Dispatch, Inc., 2009, 1. Accessed January 17, 2012. http://www.whitehouse.gov/assets/documents/Afghanistan-Pakistan_White_Paper.pdf.

------. "National Strategy for Counterterrorism." White House Press Releases, Fact Sheets and Briefings, June 28, 2011, 3. Accessed January 17, 2012. http://www.whitehouse.gov/sites/default/files/counterterrorism_strategy.pdf.

Thornton, Thomas P. "Pakistan: Fifty Years of Insecurity," in *India and Pakistan: The First Fifty Years*, edited by S. S. Harrison, P. H. Kreisberg, and D. Kux, 171. Cambridge: Cambridge University Press, 1999.

Tomsen, Peter. *The Wars of Afghanistan: Messianic Terrorism, Tribal Conflicts, and the Failures of Great Powers*. New York: Public Affairs, 2011.

Tudor, Maya J. *The Promise of Power: The Origins of Democracy in India and Autocracy in Pakistan*. New Delhi: Cambridge University Press, 2013.

------. *Twin Births, Divergent Democracies: the Social and Institutional Origins of Regime Outcomes in India and Pakistan, 1920-1958*. Princeton: Princeton University, 2010.

U.S. Embassy Fact Sheet. *U.S. Assistance to Pakistan to Promote Security*. 2014. Accessed July 15, 2014. Islamabad.usaembassy.gov/fact-sheets.html.

U.S. Policy toward Afghanistan and Pakistan. 2009.

United States Department of State, Bureau of South and Central Asian Affairs. "U.S. Relations with Pakistan." *U.S. Department of State Fact Sheet*, 2013. Accessed March 14, 2014. http://www.state.gov/r/pa/ei/bgn/3453.htm.

Usher, Graham. "The Afghan Triangle: Kashmir, India, Pakistan Graham Usher." *Middle East Report* #251, vol. 39 (Summer 2009).

Veer, Peter V. D. *Religious Nationalism: Hindus and Muslims in India*. Berkeley: University of California Press, 1994.

Vira, Varun, and Anthony H. Cordesman. "Pakistan: Violence vs. Stability: A National Net Assessment." *Center for Strategic and International Studies Burke Reports*, June 7, 2011. Accessed January 2012. http://csis.org/files/publication/110607_Stabilizing_Pakistan.pdf.

Weinbaum, Marvin G., and Jonathan B. Harder. "Pakistan's Afghan Policies and Their Consequences." *Contemporary South Asia* 16, no. 1 (2008): 25-38.

Wolpert, Stanley A. *India and Pakistan: Continued Conflict or Cooperation?* Berkeley and Los Angeles: University of California Press, 2010.

------. *A New History of India*. 6th ed. New York: Oxford University Press, 2009.

------. *Roots of Confrontation in South Asia: Afghanistan, Pakistan, India and the Superpowers*. New York: Oxford University Press, 1982.

Wright, Lawrence. "The Double Game: The Unintended Consequences of American Funding in Pakistan." *New Yorker* 87, no.13 (May 16, 2011): 91-95. Accessed July 8, 2011. http://www.newyorker.com/magazine/2011/05/16/the-double-game.

------. *The Looming Tower: Al-Qaeda and the Road to 9/11*. New York: Vintage, 2007.

Yong, Tai Tan. *The Garrison State: Military, Government and Society in Colonial Punjab, 1849-1947* (Sage Series in Modern Indian History). Thousand Oaks: SAGE Publications, 2005.

Yong, Tai Tan. and Gyanesh Kudaisya. *The Aftermath of Partition in South Asia.* Routledge Studies in the Modern History of Asia. New York: Routledge, 2002.

Yousan, Mohammed, and Mark Adkin. *Afghanistan: The Bear Trap; The Defeat of a Superpower.* Havertown, PA: Casemate, 2001.

BIBLIOGRAPHY

BLOODLINES: THE IMPERIAL ROOTS OF TERRORISM IN SOUTH ASIA

INDEX

A

Abbotabad *127, 131-133*
Abdali, Ahmad Shah *3*
Afghanistan-Pakistan border *XII, XVII, XVIII, XIX, XXII, 21*
Afghan national Jirga, Pakistan's opposition to *93*
Afghan refugees *95, 96, 108, 136*
Afghan resistance, Afghan-Soviet war *XI*
Afghan Taliban *XIX, 124, 132, 154, 168, 172, 173*
Agha Shahid Ali *162*
Ahmad, Eqbal *XX*
Ahmad, Mahmoud *121, 122, 125, 126*
Akbar Khan, General *68*
Akbar, Mughal Emperor *37*
Al Qaeda *111, 119*
Al-Azhar University *87, 105*
Al-Farouq mosque, Brooklyn *117*
Al-Gamaa al-Islamiyya *105*
Al-Islambouli, Mohammed Shawky *106*
Ali, Agha Shahid *162*
Ali, Rahmat *53*
Amery, Leopold *48*
Amin, Hafizullah *87, 88*
Amin, Tahir *86*
Amir, Sultan, aka Colonel Imam *125*
Anderson, Perry *6*
Appadurai, Arjun *30*

Arab Spring *XV*
Armajani, Jon *112*
Armitage, Richard *121*
Asymmetric Warfare *XV, XX, 23, 70-72, 75, 84, 128, 145, 151, 165, 174*
Atef, Mohammed *118*
Attash, Khalid-al *127*
Auchinleck, Sir Claude, Field Marshal *62*
Aurangzeb, Emperor *3*
Awami League Party *81, 82*
Awami National Party of Afghanistan (ANP) *22*
Azhar, Masood *120*
Azzam, Abdullah *74, 105-107, 116, 118*
  fatwa, Defense of Muslim Lands *106*
  fund-raising in the United States *107*

B

Babrakzai, Umar *93*
Badabar *144*
Baluchistan *24, 26, 64, 70, 91, 94, 126*
Bangladesh *XVI, 8, 17, 70, 71, 79, 81-83, 156, 161, 164*
Bangladesh, declaration of Independence *81*
Barelvi *53, 100*
Bari, Maulana Abdul *72*
Battle of Plassey *2, 5, 7*
Bayly, Christopher *35, 48*
Bayly, Susan *36*
Bengal *2, 5, 8, 10-12, 15-17, 30, 44, 48, 56-60, 70, 78, 80,*
83, 155
Bengal Army *8, 10-12, 15, 16, 30*
Bengal, division of, 1905 *44*
Bengal famine *48*
Bengali refugees *149-150*
Bhatia, Michael *107*
Bhutto, Benazir *110, 114, 117*
Bhutto, Zulfikar Ali *23, 68, 81, 88, 98, 114*
Bilmes, Linda *170*
Black Swan events *XV*
Blood, Archer *154*
Blyth, Marc *XV*
Bogra, Mohammed Ali *142*
Bombay Army *10*
Bourke-White, Margaret *61, 137, 144*
Bowles, Chester *147*
Brass, Paul *XIX, 60-61*
Brigadier Dyer *40*
British East India Company *1, 2, 5, 6, 10, 36, 163*
British Empire *XII, XX, XXIII, 2, 8, 15, 18, 20, 38, 40, 43, 45, 51, 52, 56, 142, 159, 160, 163, 167, 169*
British Indian Army, also Imperial Army *9-11, 15-19, 30, 46, 52, 62, 67, 160, 161*
British Raj, also Raj *2, 6, 10, 20, 29, 42-44, 84, 163*
Brodrick, Sir John *44*
Burke, Jason *98, 116*

Bush, George Herbert Walker *114*
Butt, Ziauddin *133*

C

Canning, Charles John *1*
Carpenter, Ted *95*
Carroll, James *XX*
Carter, aid to Pakistan *100*
Carter, Jimmy *100, 151*
Census. *See* Decinnial Census
Central Treaty Organization (CENTO) *146*
Chester, Lucy *56*
China *XI, XII, XIII, 8, 119, 147, 148, 149, 151, 153, 171, 177*
China, British Opium trade *8*
Church, Frank *149*
Churchill, Winston *47*
Coalition Support Funds (CSF) *133-135, 154*
Cohen, Stephen *79, 146*
Cohn, Bernard *31, 38*
Cold War *XI, XIII, XVII, 115, 139-141, 145, 152-155, 167, 177*
Coll, Steve *104*
Colonial India
  partition of. *See* Partition
Communal *43, 61*
Communal Award *43*
Congress, Indian National Congress *XX, 27, 38-48, 51-59, 63, 66, 102, 115, 132, 141, 149, 161, 162, 164*
Copley, Antony *36*
Cornwallis, Charles Lord *7*

Costs of War Project *170*
Cragin, Kim *106*
Crocker, Ryan *XIII*

D

Dacca *82, 154*
Daeschel, Markus *99*
Daoud. *See* Khan, Mohammad Daoud
Dawson, Andrew *XX*
Decinnial Census *30, 31, 32, 159*
Declaration of War Against the Americans Occupying the Land of the Two Holy Places *111*
Delhi Sultanate *2*
Deobandi *89, 99, 100, 117, 125*
Deoband Islamic movement *53*
Directorate for Inter-Service Intelligence (ISI) *25, 72, 74, 88, 89, 92, 94-97, 102-114, 119, 120, 121, 124, 125, 128, 132, 133, 135, 165, 168*
Direct Overt U.S. Aid Appropriations and Military Reimbursements to Pakistan *136*
Divide-and-Rule *XX, 44*
Dostum, Abdul Rashid *108*
Dow, Alexander *6*
Dulles, John Foster *142, 146*
Durand Line *XXII, 17-26, 51, 72, 84, 86, 89, 101, 103, 107, 116, 126, 127, 171*

Durand, Sir Mortimer *20*
Durrani Pashtun *96*

E

East Bengal *44, 80*
East Pakistan *XVI, 8, 56, 70, 71, 78-83, 149, 150, 154, 167*
Eaton, Richard *27*
Edwards, David *94*
Eisenhower administration *142, 144, 146*
Emperor Akbar *37*
Emperor Babar *28*
Engineer Machmud *110*

F

Fair, Christine *76, 131*
Faisalabad *126, 127*
Federally Administered Tribal Areas, (FATA) *17, 21, 24-26, 64, 125, 126, 127*
Frontier Crimes Regulations (FCR) *24*
Fulbright, William *147*

G

Gailani, Syed Ahmad *90*
Gall, Carlotta *125*
Gandhi, Indira *150, 163*
Gandhi, Mohandas Karamchand; Mahatma *40*
Gerges, Fawaz *106*
Ghilzai Pashtun *92*
Girardet, Edward *XI-XII*
Glancy, Bertrand, Governor of Punjab *54*
Global war on terrorism (GWOT) *131*. *See also* war on terrorism

INDEX

Gorbachev, Mikhail *107, 114*
Goss, Peter *121*
Gottschalk, Peter *37*
Great Game *18, 142*
Griffin, Michael *95*
Group of Seven (IUAM-7) *89*
Group of Three (IUAM-3) *89*
Gul, Hamid *114, 115*
Gupta Empire *2*

H

Haq, Abdul *88*
Haqqānī, Husain *XVIII, XXII*
Haqqani, Jalaluddin *107, 125*
Haqqani Network *XIX, 125*
Harakat-e-Inqilab-e-Islami (The Islamic Revolutionary Movement, IRMA) *90*
Harakat-ul-Mujahideen *XVIII, 74, 120*
Harder, Jonathan *104*
Harkat-ul-Ansar *74, 124*
Harkat-ul-Mujahideen (HM) *25, 124*
Harrison, Selig *24, 110*
Hazara tribes *20*
Hegghammer, Thomas *106*
Hekmatyar, Gulbuddin *87-89, 107*
Henderson, Loy *141*
Hildreth, Horace *143*
Hindu identity *XIX, 14*
Hindu-Muslim
  adversarial relations *29*
  symbiosis *36*
Hindu religion *28*
Hizb-i-Islami (HI) *89-90, 95-96*
Hizb-i-Wahdat *92*
Hizb-ul-Mujahideen *25, 73, 74*
Homeland Security *XIV, XV, XVIII, XXIII*
Hope, Victor, 2nd Marquess of Linlitgow *8, 45*
Hume, Allan Octavian *38*

I

Ibrahim, Azeem *134*
Idangai *34*
India Independence Act *55*
Indian Airlines Flight 814, hijacking of *120*
Indian census. *See* Census
Indian Council Act, 1909 *42*
Indian Islam, syncretism *37*
Indian subcontinent *XII, XVI, XX, XXIII, 1, 2, 4, 18, 20-22, 27-31, 33, 34, 37, 48, 51, 60, 68, 159, 163*
India-Pakistan war, 1971 *78*
International Islamic University, Islamabad *105*
Iqbal, Zafar *74*
Iran *XI, XII, XIII, 21, 23, 35, 48, 88, 92, 93, 101, 136, 137, 174*
Islamabad *75, 96, 105, 108, 110, 112, 126, 151, 155*
Islamic Emirate of Afghanistan *109, 127*
Islamic fundamentalism *XV, 96, 145*
Islamic rhetoric *55, 78, 84, 113*
  employment by Pakistan in Kashmir *78*
Islamic sloganeering *53*
1946 elections *53*
Islamist, definition *23*
Ittehad-e-Islami *97, 110*
Ittehad-i-Islami Mujahideen-i-Afghanistan (Islamic Unity of Afghan Mujahideen, IUAM) *89*
Ittihad-i-Islami party (The Islamic Union for the Liberation of Afghanistan, or IUA) *90*

J

Jafar, Mir *5*
Jaish-e-Mohammad *25, 73, 75, 120, 124*
Jalalabad *110, 114, 115*
Jallianwala Bagh massacre *40*
Jamaat-e-Islami *25, 55, 72, 74, 86, 87, 124, 128*
Jamaat-ud-Dawa (JuD), and Lashkar-e-Taiba (LeT) *74*
Jamiat al-ulama-i-Hind *53*
Jamiat-i-Islami (JIA) *89, 95*
Jamiat-I Ulema-I Islam *74*
Jamiyat al-Ulama *55*
Jammu and Kashmir legislative assembly, bombing *120*
Jammu and Kashmir Liberation Front, JKLF *72*
Janjalani, Abdurajak Abu Bakr *117*

Jebh-e-Nijat-i-Milli (The Afghanistan National Liberation Front, ANLF) 90
Jihad 73, 106, 107, 117, 118, 124
Jinnah, Muhammad Ali 45
jirga 22, 93, 94
Jones, Sir William 7

K

Kabul, and Mujahideen 108-110
Kabul University 86-87
Kakul Military Academy 132
Kamal, Mina Keshwar 95
Kandahar 19, 109-111, 119, 120, 125
Karachi 76, 103, 126, 127, 148
Kargil 75-77, 123, 155, 165, 174
Karmal, Babrak 87, 88, 89, 101
Khaldan training camp 117
Khalis, Muhammad Yunus 88
Khalq 87-88
Khan Abdul Ghaffar Khan, Frontier Gandhi 43
Khan, Ayub, General 79-81, 142, 143, 173
Khan, Ismail 89
Khan, Mohammed Daoud 23
Khan, Sayyid Ahmad, also spelled Syed 52
Khan, Yahya 81, 148, 154
Khomeini, Ayatollah Ruhollah 101
Khost 119
Khyber Pakhtunkhwa 20

King Abdul Aziz University, Jeddah 105
Kissinger, Henry, trip to China 148
Krakowski, Elie 94
Kunar Province 74
Kundi, Mansoor 155
Kunduz 90, 126
Kushan Empire 2, 28

L

Lahore Resolution 46, 53
Lange, Matthew XX
Lashkar-e-Taiba, LeT XVIII, 25, 73-75
Lawrence, John 1
Lieven, Anatol 154
Lindemann, Frederick 48
Line of Control, Kashmir 74, 76, 77
Linlithgow, Viceroy 46, 47 and Jinnah 23, 45, 46, 48, 52, 54, 57, 137-141
Lord Curzon 44
Lord Minto 41
Lord Salisbury 10
Loya Jirga 22

M

Maccaulay, Thomas 39
Madani, Husain Ahmad 53
Madras Army 10
Madrasas 53, 99-100, 105, 109
and Zia 99-100, 105
Mahaz-e-Milli Islami (the National Islamic Front of Afghanistan, NIFA) 90
Majrooh, Sayd Bahauddin Majrooh 95
Maktab al-Khidamat (Service Bureau, MAK) 106, 117
Maley, William 93
Malik, Mohammad Yasin 73
Markaz al-Dawa wal-Irshad, MDI 74
Martial Races 17, 30, 68, 80, 160
Mascarenhas, Anthony 82
Massoud, Ahmad Shah 88, 89, 108, 119
Maududi, Abul ala Maulana 53
Maulana Azad 43
Maulvi Sanzoor 110
Maurya Empire 2
McMahon, Robert 136, 140-145, 153
Meerut 12
Mehmaan mujahideen 75
Metcalf, Thomas 42
Mian Iftikharuddin 43
Minute on Indian Education 39, 79
Mohajirs 78
Mohammad, Khalid Shaikh 118, 127
Mohammedi, Maulana Mohammad Nabi 90
Morley-Minto Reforms 42
Mountbatten, Lord, Viceroy 56, 60, 65
Mughal Empire 2-5, 12-15, 28, 30
Mughal rule, and Hindu Kings 1-6, 12, 28-30, 36, 37, 57, 162-164
Muhammad, Din 88
Mujaddidi, Sighbatullah 90, 109
Mujahed, Falz Haq 110
Mujahideen XVIII, 25, 73, 74, 89, 103, 108, 109, 120

Mukti Bahini 83
Mullah Omar, Amir al-Mo'mineen, "Commander of the faithful" 90, 111, 125
Mumbai terrorist attacks, 2008 165
Musharraf, Pervez XIX, 77, 165
Muslim Brotherhood 23, 86, 87, 105, 107
Muslim communal identity 38
Muslim electorate, separate electorate 41
Muslim identity 35, 78
Muslim mass contact plan 55
Muslim nationalism 63
Muslim Youth, Afghanistan 87

N

Najibullah, Mohammad 108
Naqshbandi 90, 92
Narayan, Jayaprakash 163
Nasr, Vali 63, 64
National Defense University XXII
National Security Decision Directive "US Policy, Programs, and Strategy in Afghanistan" 104
NATO XI, XII, 132, 144
  Chicago Summit Declaration XI
Nazimuddin, Khwaja 142
Nehru, Jawahar Lal 55, 140-143, 147, 161
Niazi, Ghulam M. 86
Nixon, Richard 83, 135, 143, 148-150, 154,

167
  and Bengali genocide 149
  tilt toward Pakistan 150
Nizam of Hyderabad 29
Noon, Malik Feroz Khan 141
Northern Alliance 119, 122, 126
Northern Light Infantry, Pakistan 75
North Waziristan 125

O

Oakley, Robert 114
Obama administration XIII, XXI
Ojiri Camp 103
Oldenburg, Philip 81
Omar, Mullah Mohammad 109
Operation Enduring Freedom 123
Operation Gibraltar 71
Operation Grand Slam 71
Operation Infinite Reach 119
Operation Searchlight 82
Orientalism XIV
Osama bin Laden XVI, 87, 98, 105, 106, 110, 111, 118-120, 122, 125-127, 132, 168
  and ISI 25, 72, 74, 88, 89, 92, 94-97, 102-105, 107-114, 119-121, 124, 125, 128, 132, 133, 135, 165, 168
  and the Taliban XI, XIII, XVI, XVII, XVIII, XXII, XXIV, 2, 17, 21, 23, 25, 26, 85, 90, 94, 108, 109, 110-113, 118-127,

131, 137, 148, 151, 168, 169, 171, 172, 176
Sudan 118, 119, 168

P

Page, David 42
Pakistan
  alliance with the United States 122, 123, 137
  and al-Qaeda 121, 124
  and American aid 72, 112, 115, 137, 138, 140, 154
  and Bengalis 17, 44, 48, 64, 79-82, 154, 160
  and Kashmir XVII, XVIII, XIX, XX, XXII, 21, 25, 26, 43, 61, 63, 65-83, 84, 104, 105, 112, 113, 116-124, 127, 131, 132, 137, 143, 145, 147, 148, 151, 152, 161-166, 172, 174, 175
  and mujahideen 74-76, 90, 97, 102-115, 125
  and Taliban XI, XIII, XVI, XVII, XVIII, XIX, XXII, XXIV, 2, 17, 18, 21, 23, 25, 26, 85, 90, 94, 108-113, 118-127, 131, 132, 137, 148, 151, 154, 168-173, 176
  and terrorism XIII, XIV, XV, XVI, XVII, XVIII, XIX, XX, XXI, XXIII, XXIV, 8, 18, 23, 25, 27, 38, 61, 65, 71, 72, 89, 117, 121, 123,

128, 131, 133, 136,
  145, 152, 153, 156,
  159, 161, 168,
  171-177
and United States *XI,
  XII, XIII, XIV, XV,
  XVI, XVII, XVIII,
  XIX, XXI, XXIII,
  XXIV,* 17, 18, 21,
  23, 26, 69, 74, 76,
  84, 89, 92-94, 98,
  100-104, 107, 112-
  156, 162, 166-177
and war on terrorism
  XIII, 123, 153
a rentier state 137
as insecurity state 84
Islamization 93, 98-101,
  105, 152, 155, 161
Mutual Defense Agreement with the
  United States 146
nuclear program 100-
  102, 115, 123, 152,
  174
use of Islam 23, 49, 54,
  78, 79, 165
Pakistan Army *XXII,* 68,
  71, 72, 76, 79-82,
  98, 99, 110, 113,
  114, 123, 127, 133,
  135, 138, 142-146,
  149, 152, 154, 155,
  160, 165-167, 174,
  175
Pakistani Frontier Corps
  119
Pakistani identity 63
Pakistan People's Party 81,
  114
Paktia 74, 90, 93
Pandey, Gyanendra 34
Parcham 87, 88
Pashtunistan 22-24, 86,
  87, 95, 96, 116,
  145, 161, 164, 165

Pashtun, Pathan 79, 81,
  82
Pearl, Daniel 120
Peel Commission 15
People's Democratic Party
  of Afghanistan
  (PDPA) 87
Perkovich, George 131
Perle, Richard 94
Peshawar 19, 20, 88-98,
  103, 105-111, 114,
  117, 144, 149
  Agreement 109
  Seven 89
Plan Bojinka 118
Poonch uprising 66
Powell, Colin 121
President Clinton 76, 119
Pressler Amendment 115
Punjab
  Boundary Force 60
  Committee 15
  Frontier Force 13

Q

Qadir, Abdul 88
Qaid-i-Azam. *See* Jinnah
Quetta 103, 117, 126
Quit India movement 47,
  48, 53
Qutb, Syed 87, 105

R

Rabbani, Burhanuddin
  86, 88-89, 109
Radcliffe Commission 57
Radcliffe, Cyril 58
Radicalization, definition
  23
Rahman, Amir Abdur 20
Rahman, Sheikh Abdel
  Omar 105
Rahman, Sheikh Mujibur
  81
Raj, British Raj 2, 6, 10,
  20, 29, 42, 43, 84,
  163. *See also* Raj
Rashid, Ahmad 105, 111,
  118
Rawalpindi 74, 127
Reagan administration
  aid to Pakistan 97, 102,
  113, 115, 152
Reagan, Ronald 113
Rehman, General Akhtar
  Abdur 72
Revolutionary Association
  of the Women of
  Afghanistan 95
Riedel, Bruce 111, 119
Riots, between Hindus and
  Muslims 34, 35
Ritter, Donald 97
Rizvi, Hasan-Askari 98
Robins, Nick 5
Rowlatt Act 40
Roy, Olivier 99
Rummel, Rudolph 82

S

Saeed, Hafiz Muhammad
  74
Saikal, Amin 109
Saladin 73
Salahuddin, Syed 73
Saudi Arabia 88-90, 93,
  97, 100, 103-106,
  110, 118
Sayyafabad 98
Sayyaf, Abdul Rasul 86,
  90
Sazman-i Azadibakhsh-i
  Mardomi Afghanistan (The
  Organization for
  the Liberation of
  the Afghan People,
  SAMA) 95
Schmidt, John 98, 104
Sedra, Mark 107

Sepoys *10-12*
September 11, 2001, 9/11 *XI, XVI, 121*
Shahi, Agha *103*
Shah, Ijaz *133*
Shah, Mohammad Zahir, King, Afghanistan *23*
Shah, Nadir *3*
Shah of Iran *101*
Shah, Yusuf *73*
Sharif, Nawaz *76, 110, 114, 133, 165*
Sheikh, Abdullah *43, 66, 95*
Sheikh, Ahmed Omar Saeed, aka Sheikh Omar or Omar Sheikh *120*
Shia *35, 37, 90, 92, 100*
Shibh, Ramzi bin al *127*
Sikhs *15-17, 20, 23, 33, 34, 43, 52, 59, 61, 62, 68*
Singh, Hari, Maharaja, Kashmir's ruler *66, 67, 69*
Singh, Jaswant *120*
Sipah-e-Sahaba Pakistan (SSP) *100*
Sipahi. *See* sepoy
Siraj-ud-Daula, Nawab *2, 5*
South Asia, U.S. strategic goals *XXIV*
Southeast Asia Treaty Organization (SEATO) *146*
Sudan *118, 119, 168*
Sufi *35, 90, 92*
Sunni *28, 35, 89, 91, 92, 99, 100, 105, 109*
Sura-yi-enqelab *93*
Swami, Praveen *69*
syncretism *35, 37*
Syncretism, between Islam and Indian society *37*

T

Talbot, Ian *30*
Taleb, Nassim Nicholas *XV*
Taliban *XI, XIII, XVI, XVII, XVIII, XIX, XXII, XXIV, 2, 17-26, 85, 90, 94, 108-113, 118-127, 131-132, 137, 148, 151, 154, 168-173, 176*
and Pakistan *126*
Taloqan *119*
Taraki, Nur Mhuammad *87, 88*
Tawana, Saeed M. Musa *86*
Tehrik-e-Nifaz-e-Fiqh-e-Jafria (TNJF) *100*
Tenet, George *122*
Terrorism *XV, 98, 123, 154*
and South Asia *131, 142, 167*
as state policy *XX*
The North West Frontier Province (NWFP) *20, 22, 24, 43, 64, 70, 104, 126*
Tipu Sultan *7*
Tomsen, Peter *114*
Truman administration *140-141*
Tudor, Maya *162*

U

Umma *67*
United Nations Security Council Resolution 1267 *119*
United Provinces *43, 57,* *78*
United States
aid to Pakistan *XXI, 101, 102, 112, 133, 144, 147-149, 170, 172, 175*
and al Qaeda *XVI, XXIV, 18, 26, 112, 113, 121, 125-127*
and the Taliban *XVI, 118-119, 121, 126, 169*
Embassy bombings *119*
intervention in South Asia *XII, XXI*
strategic goals in South Asia *XXIV*
The National Strategy for Counterterrorism, 2001 *XXI*
United States and Pakistan military assistance *113, 115, 123, 134-135, 143, 147, 149, 150*
University of Da'wa and Jihad, Pabbi, Sayaffabad *117-118*
Urdu, language riots *29, 64, 70, 78, 79*

V

Valangai *34*
Van der Veer, Peter *33*
Victor Hope, Marquess of Linlithgow, Viceroy *8, 45*

W

Weinbaum, Marvin *104*
West Pakistan *78-83, 149, 150, 156*
White Paper of the Interagency Policy Group's Report on U.S. Policy toward

Afghanistan and
  Pakistan *XXI*, *133*
Wilson, Charles *143*
World Trade Center bombing *118*
Wright, Lawrence *135*

Y

Yousaf, Mohammad Brigadier General *97*, *103*
Yousef, Ramzi Ahmed *117*

Z

Zadran *93*
Zakat Ordinance *100*
Zardari, Asaf Ali *XIX*
Zargar, Mushtaq *120*
Zawahiri, Ayman al *105*, *106*, *118*
Zia
  and the United States *XVII, XXI, XXIV, 21, 136, 141, 148, 149*
  Islamization *93, 98-101, 105, 152, 155, 161*
Zia ul Haq, General, Zia *XXIV, 24*
Zubaydah, Abu *127*

Index

BLOODLINES: THE IMPERIAL ROOTS OF TERRORISM IN SOUTH ASIA

ABOUT THE AUTHOR

Sunil Dutta, Ph.D., is a police officer in the Los Angeles Police Department and an adjunct professor of Security Studies at Colorado Technical University.

Sunil was born and raised in a refugee family in India. An outspoken advocate of criminal justice reform, his forward-looking views on policing and history of the Indian subcontinent have appeared in the Washington Post, Chicago Tribune, Los Angeles Times, Christian Science Monitor, Pakistan Times, Newsweek, The Nation, and elsewhere.

He is a scholar of Urdu poetry and translated the renowned poet Mirza Ghalib's poetry with Robert Bly, *The Lightning Should Have Fallen on Ghalib*. Dutta is also a student and promoter of Dhrupad, an ancient musical art of India, and has produced several Dhrupad recordings.

He lives in Los Angeles.

BLOODLINES: THE IMPERIAL ROOTS OF TERRORISM IN SOUTH ASIA

NOTES

NOTES

NOTES

NOTES

NOTES

NOTES

NOTES

NOTES

Notes

NOTES

www.ingramcontent.com/pod-product-compliance
Lightning Source LLC
Chambersburg PA
CBHW070758230426
43665CB00017B/2411